in southern waters

Ian Marchant is from Newhaven in Sussex.
He spent the 1980s working in bookmakers'
shops and singing in obscure pop groups.
He spent the 1990s dealing in second-hand
records and books, and stripping in obscure
northern comedy clubs. He lives in a caravan
which is currently parked in Lancaster.

in southern waters

Ian Marchant

VICTOR GOLLANCZ
LONDON

The right of Ian Marchant to be identified
as author of this work has been asserted
by him in accordance with the
Copyright, Designs and Patents Act, 1988

First published in Great Britain in 1999 by Victor Gollancz
An imprint of Orion Books Ltd,
Orion House,
5 Upper St Martin's Lane,
London WC2H 9EA

A CIP catalogue record for this book
is available from the British Library

ISBN 0 575 06764 0

The characters in this book are entirely fictitious and
bear no relation to any real person, alive or dead, except
Trapper. And Mad Rikki.

Thanks to Sarah Fiske for The Owner's handwriting.

Typeset at The Spartan Press Ltd,
Lymington, Hants
Printed and bound in Great Britain by
Guernsey Press Co. Ltd, Guernsey, C.I.

To Jean and Ralph Foxwell

Contents

The Bloomsbury Group

Almost inevitably, the first person Caroline Woolfit met on moving into the tall old house in Bloomsbury Place was the Eel, his pizzle, shrunken and blue with age, peeping from the gap in the front of his pyjamas. Caroline had beside her in the hall a rucksack, a suitcase, two boxes of books, a hi-fi, a rubber plant and her mother, who was puffing heavily from the exertion of carrying the boxes into the once elegant house, a climb of perhaps eight railinged steps. The Eel had a large head, bald on top and untidily fringed with greasy grey strands, smoker's skin, saurian eyes, a terrible cough and a half-empty bottle of red wine in his left hand.

'D'ye s-see that armchair?' he stammered, gesturing with his bottle towards an overstuffed chair of incalculable antiquity along the hallway.

'Yes,' said Caroline.

'That,' said the Eel imperiously, 'is part of a series of armchairs, one on each landing, put there for me, for my use, by my friends, on account of m-my emphysema. I don't care what else you do in this house, but have the courtesy to keep your fat county arse off of my chairs.'

'I . . . I'm moving into the top flat,' said Caroline. 'I doubt I'll be sitting in the hall.'

'You might put bags on them, or something.'

'I won't use them at all. Really.'

'Please don't. The last hi-fi girl used to rest bags on them all the time on her way up. Damned nuisance, wet bag marks on the cushions.'

'I can appreciate that.'

'Ruins the upholstery. Leaves a musty smell.'

'What do you mean, the last hi-fi girl?'

'The last one like you. The last girl that Blossom had to share the flat. You're the latest in a long line of girls who own hi-fis. He never bothered to get one.' The Eel started to cough, deep and wet, and he sank purple-faced into his chair. Caroline's mother hurried forward.

'Are you all right?' she said.

'Whoheh-heh who-hoo-hark who whoerwhohahheh who is this foul old harpy?' croaked the Eel.

'She's my mother, actually,' said Caroline. 'And she's not a harpy. She's a GP from Haywards Heath, and she's trying to help you.'

'Don't worry, dear,' said Caroline's mother, as she tried to get her hands on the heaving ruins of the Eel's chest. 'I get used to insults from old men. Try and catch your breath.'

'You-hoo-hoohaa-*hah* a harpy. And you're fat,' said the Eel. His coughing subsided a little. 'D'ye want some hehehelp getting the hi-fi and the rest of this clobber up the stairs?' he continued.

Caroline nodded.

'I'm not surprised, the size of her, she won't be much use. Well, if you ring the intercom thing, top button, Blossom or one of his lads will stagger down and give you a hand with the hi-fi. If nothing else.' The Eel rose with some difficulty from the depths of the chair and opened the door of the ground floor flat; Caroline caught a glimpse of herself in a large gilt-framed mirror just inside, not at all fat-arsed but rather slim and dressed in brown combat fatigues and a shiny nylon charity-shop anorak zipped up to her chin, her blue hair pulled back from her high forehead.

'Well, a good day to you both,' said the Eel, stepping over the threshold. 'If ever you feel like going for a drink, or something of the sort, do give me a knock.' He closed the door behind him, and then, obviously struck by an after-thought, opened it again, and poked his head out.

'Although you, madam,' he said, indicating Caroline's mother, 'might be well advised to lay off the booze for a while. Very well advised indeed.' The door closed again, and he was gone.

'I thought you said that there were nice people living here?' said Dr Woolfit to her daughter's back as she turned to press the intercom.

'I'm only sharing the top flat. The man who showed me round . . . Mr Blossom?'

Zzp, crackled the intercom.

'It's Caroline Woolfit. I've got quite a bit of stuff . . .'

Wzzztummnn, said the intercom.

'Would you? That would be very kind,' said Caroline. She turned to her mother. 'There. I told you they were nice. Mr Blossom was, anyhow. I didn't meet any of the others.'

'Others? How many?'

'Two others. I told you, it's a huge flat.'

'And are they *all* men?'

'Yes,' said Caroline thoughtfully. 'And now I come to think of it, I can't remember seeing a stereo when Mr Blossom showed me round. And he did seem very interested in mine . . .'

Footsteps sounded on the staircase: Caroline and her mother looked upwards.

Caroline's mother was, as her daughter had indicated to the drunken old wretch in the hallway, a GP, and she liked to think of herself as a liberal-minded woman, one who over the years had proved herself welcoming and tolerant of Caroline's friends. As uniform restrictions had been lifted when Caroline entered the sixth form, she watched, without undue alarm, as her daughter had transformed herself into a techno-traveller, and spent all her pocket money on piercings, and she had smiled when Caroline had brought home a series of boyfriends, each with a slightly more startling hairdo than the one before, but all with a shared sense that if they didn't eat meat, peace would somehow vanquish war. Caroline's mother was pleased that her daughter had chosen to study at Sussex University, just twenty miles down the road from home, though she was anxious at her daughter's involvement throughout her first year with Carl, a boorish white Rastafarian, whom Dr Woolfit had felt herself unable to like, despite her best efforts. Her misgivings were confirmed in the middle of September, when Caroline, who was spending the summer inter-railing with Carl, had phoned in floods of tears from Prague with the news that her lover had dumped her for a German backpacker and run off with all their money, leaving her stranded.

Dr Woolfit and her husband had wired Caroline money to the British Embassy in order for her to fly home, and she had spent a week mooning about in Haywards Heath before her mother had persuaded her that there was a crisis to be faced. Clearly, it would no longer be possible for Caroline to move into the flat she had arranged to share with Carl and his friends. So where was Caroline to live for her second year? The doctor turned for guidance to the flatshare section in the classified pages of the *Argus*, and had seen the flat in Bloomsbury Place:

Large Attic Room In Spacious Flat. Must Be Vegetarian, Non-Smoker. Suit Female Stereo Enthusiast. £35 p.w.

Caroline had been persuaded into Brighton to see the place, and had returned looking happy for the first time since her ignominious return from Czech Republic.

Bloomsbury Place was one of the many faded Regency streets in Kemptown leading inland from Marine Parade. Most of the other houses had been ruthlessly converted into bedsits, but not number 23. It had been converted, with some taste, into four flats: basement, ground floor, first floor and top. This last, occupying the top two floors of the old house, was the one that Caroline had been to view. It was a beautiful flat, a little flyblown perhaps and in need of a lick of paint, but it had a large and cheerful kitchen, a high-ceilinged, high-windowed living room full of old but comfortable armchairs and sofas, a proper bathroom with vitreous enamelled fittings, and four bedrooms, two on the same level as the rest of the accommodation and two high under the eaves at the top of a spiral staircase which led from the small entrance hall. The room that was to be Caroline's was one of the latter; long and thin, with the roof beams visible, and lit in the bright early-autumn sunshine by three skylights. Mr Blossom (had she heard that right? Blossom?), who had shown Caroline round, was very charming and very kind, and concerned to hear of her plight; he had made her tea and expressed himself delighted that she was a vegetarian. She found herself opening up, and she told him about Carl – Mr Blossom had made the appropriate sympathetic noises, and had asked her some discreet questions about her hi-fi. Caroline loved the flat, and Mr Blossom seemed keen for her to take on the room, and so she did. All this Caroline had told her mother. She had also told the doctor that Mr Blossom was quite good-looking in a ravaged kind of way; was in his late thirties, had a shock of upstanding black hair much like Dylan's, circa 1965, and was probably single. Dr Woolfit had spent 1965 wishing she was a Joan Baez to someone's Bob: and now she dreamed for her nineteen-year-old daughter, school still clinging about her, that Caroline's new flatmate might be romantic and Dylanesque and clean and orderly and sexy and funny and safe and gay.

Now, standing at the bottom of the stairs, Dr Woolfit saw that three men were descending to meet them, the first, from Caroline's description, clearly Mr Blossom. Dr Woolfit saw the Dylan thing, even found him attractive, somehow. Yes, a tall Dylan, or a fat John Cooper Clarke. Shame that he was wearing nothing but a pair of slippers and an ancient and filthy Gannex mackintosh. Shame about the smoking.

Behind Blossom was a weedy little red-haired man in his mid-thirties perhaps, who seemed to take seriously the injunction that those with red hair, even straggling, thinning red hair, should wear green. He wore a torn green T-shirt with the legend 'Trapper is a Wanker' on the front, a green unzipped cardigan, a pair of old green crimplene golfing slacks that stopped some six inches proud of the ankle and a pair of green flip-flops. His freckly face was contorted into an insinuating smirk which showed that he had lovely green teeth too. In her mind Caroline's mother christened him the Creep.

The last of the three was difficult for Dr Woolfit to assess. He wore a clean white Fair Isle sweater, a pair of blue denim jeans, and deck shoes. His hair was blond, and short, and his skin showed signs of a healthy outdoor existence. She had no particular problem with the black patch over his left eye, from under which a white scar extended to the collar of his jersey; she was, after all, a doctor, and she had done some work at the McKindo Burns Unit in East Grinstead. No, the problem was with his bearing, with his attitude, with the way he carried himself. It said, 'I'm a superior being. Don't bother talking to me. You bore me.' But it also said, 'Hello! How are

6

you? Would you like a cup of something?' Dr Woolfit liked that.

'Ah ha!' said Blossom. 'Miss Woolfit!'

'Caroline, please.'

'And you must call me Blossom. Not Mister, not ever. And this must be your sister . . .'

'My mother, actually.'

'*Really?* Really? Well, I'm sceptical, but very pleased to meet you nonetheless.' He took the doctor's hand and shook it firmly. 'And *this* must be,' he continued, 'your stereo. Look, Cats,' he said to the Creep, 'it's a Kenwood.'

'Not bad,' said the Creep, now revealed as Cats. 'Not bad at all.'

Before Caroline could protest, Cats had grabbed the stereo and scuttled up the stairs, clutching it to his breast. Blossom picked up the rubber plant, as the most obviously light item in Caroline's baggage train, and the piratical blond picked up the suitcase and the rucksack, leaving Caroline and her mother to bring up the rear, each with a box of books. The stairs were many, with each successive flight steeper than the last; just as the Eel had asserted, there was an old armchair on each of the landings. As they passed the door of the first floor flat, Caroline thought that she could hear shouting coming from within, but inside the top flat, when they eventually arrived, there was peace. Of Blossom, Cats and the hi-fi there was no sign, though the rubber plant was dumped in the hall. The blond carried the bags up the spiral staircase to Caroline's room and Caroline and her mother followed with some difficulty, finding the boxes of books hard to manoeuvre up the narrow stairs. Caroline's mother liked the room, and felt that her daughter could do some work there, but Caroline herself was feeling anxious.

'Where's my hi-fi?' she asked.

'Front room,' said the blond over his shoulder as he disappeared down the stairs.

'What?' said Caroline, following him down. He was right. In the front room, Cats was already involved in setting it up, while Blossom hopped about ineffectually, flapping a CD.

'Come on, Cats,' he said.

'I thought of setting the stereo up in my room,' said Caroline.

'Oh my dear,' said Blossom, looking at her with some anxiety. 'I thought I had made myself clear. It's a house rule, the only one, really. No hi-fis in the bedrooms. David here,' he said, indicating the blond who stood staring distractedly from the window, from which, if one craned one's neck, the sea could be seen, 'likes a good night's sleep. We find it much better to install all sound equipment here in the front room. Much more convivial.'

'But there is no sound equipment in here,' protested Caroline feebly.

'There is now,' said Cats. 'Here, pass me that CD.' Blossom handed over the disc; Cats put it on, and the room was filled with the sounds of the Beach Boys. Blossom sighed and sank into one of the sofas; Caroline, placed temporarily on the back foot, turned away to find her mother standing beside her in the hall.

'I'll show you down,' said Caroline.

At the front door, Dr Woolfit kissed her daughter and said, 'Are you sure you're going to be all right? If you need anything, you know we're only half an hour up the road . . .'

'I know. I'll be fine. Don't worry.' Caroline returned alone to the flat, and began to sort out her room. 'Surf's Up' sounded clearly through the floor.

Later in the afternoon, her boxes and bags unpacked, her rubber plant installed in the void she had earmarked for her

8

stereo, Caroline stood on a chair and poked her head from the skylight to view her new home.

There is a line which you could draw inland from the Marina, and on one side it might say 'Queer Zone starts here', and on the other it might say 'Here be Queer-bashers'; and on one side of this invisible line live fragrant patrons of ethnicity, their apartments tastefully decorated with arte-facts chosen from across the face of the undeveloped world, pop music from Mali on the ghetto blaster and Nicaraguan coffee brewing in the cafetière, while on the other side someone has spraypainted 'Pakis Out' on the wall of the burnt-out pub next to the bus garage. It is the line which divides the areas where the social workers live from the areas where their clients live, which divides agents from patients. From her lofty eyrie, Caroline was relieved to see that she was some way the good side of this line; to her right, as she faced the sea, she could see the pier, still busy in the bright autumn sunshine, and away to where disreputable Brighton merged into respectable Hove; to her left, she could see that the Marina was at least a comfortable half mile away. Tired now, her survey complete, she lay down on her bed, tried to ignore the muffled bass thump from her stereo through the floor and fell into an uneasy sleep, haunted by vivid dreams . . .

. . . she ran into the kitchen, and collected a plate of buns and a large jug of home-made lemonade from Cookie, and then she trotted down the garden path to the shed that was the HQ of their secret society. She opened the door, and Toby, her cocker spaniel, barked with joy to see her. All the others were already there. 'Come in, Caro,' ejaculated Tubby, the society's chief and a master of disguise, 'and be quick about it. We're holding a very important meeting about what we're going to do with the rest of the holidays.' 'Oh Tubby,' said Leonard, Caro's elder brother, his eyes shining with excitement, 'can't we solve a mystery like

we did in the Easter hols?' 'Well, young Larry,' said Tubby, 'it rather depends on what turns up. Mysteries aren't two a penny, you know, or they wouldn't be mysterious!' Betty, Tubby's clever sister, laughed. 'Oh why doesn't anything ever happen around here?' sighed Caroline. Just then, there came a rapping at the door, and Toby started to bark furiously. Through the window, Caroline could see that it was PC Gumble, the local bobby – the strange thing was that he had his truncheon unsheathed, and he looked suspiciously like Uncle Graham . . .

. . . Caroline awoke, dry-mouthed, and wondered what her dream meant. That she had a mystery to solve? That she still quite fancied Uncle Graham? Better not start thinking about that again. Better go down to the kitchen and make herself a cup of tea, and then begin to come to terms with her new flatmates.

Caroline looked into the front room as she passed. It was full of people and smoke and noise, much of it from her stereo.

'Would anyone like a cup of tea?'

'Ah, Caroline,' said Blossom. 'Come in and be introduced.'

'I will in a minute. But I'm dying for a drink. Would anyone like a cup of tea?'

'Yes please,' said everybody, except the character with the eye-patch who Blossom had referred to as David, who stood silent, looking from the window towards the sea. Caroline counted heads.

'That's five teas,' she said.

'Six, including you,' said Blossom.

'Can I be a nuisance and ask for coffee?' said the only other woman in the room, a tall and elegant creature with expensive hair and a Roman nose who was wearing a washed-out 'Keanu Reeves – Young, Dumb, and Full of Come' T-shirt and who sat in an armchair with her long legs, sheathed in a pair of knitted oatmeal leggings, stretched out languidly in front of her. To Caroline's ear, she seemed to speak with a slight Australian accent.

'Of course,' said Caroline. 'That's five teas and one coffee.'

'Actually,' said Cats, 'can I have coffee too?'

David looked up from his position in the window.

'If it's coffee you're doing, I'll have one as well,' he said.

'And me,' said Blossom.

'A-me,' said the enormously fat bald man who sprawled over the totality of the largest of the sofas. 'Nershugar, ta.'

'I'll have tea, if I may,' said the small, bespectacled, African-looking gentleman who sat at the table by the window with the *Financial Times* spread open in front of him. 'But can I have lemon rather than milk? And two sugars.'

'Oh, I'm sorry, but I haven't any lemon. And now I've lost count.'

'Oh, there's some juice in the fridge. Come on, I'll give you a hand,' said Blossom. He steered Caroline through into the kitchen and insisted that she sit at the table as he made the drinks.

'You must have thought me terribly rude earlier but, you see, I'd just bought "Surf's Up" in anticipation of your arrival and I couldn't wait to hear it.'

'Is that the only reason you had me in the flat? Because of my stereo?'

'Of course,' said Blossom, looking slightly offended. 'I don't know you from Eve. You don't know me from Adam. I liked the sound of your stereo, you liked the look of the flat. A perfect arrangement. Very glad you're here now, of course. Looking forward to getting to know you. I'm sorry if you feel conned.'

'Well, I do a bit. You seemed so interested in everything I had to say. When I told you about Carl . . .'

'Carl? Who the fuck is Carl?'

'My ex, the one who dumped me in Prague. I told you all about it when I came round the other day.'

'Sometimes it's good to talk about our personal problems to total strangers. This does not mean that the total stranger lighted upon for these confessions has to listen to a single word you are saying. You must tell me again one day, and I promise I'll listen this time.'

'You heard about the vegetarianism, though. You agreed with me.'

'I thought you were being ironic, in view of the ad. It wasn't until you'd gone that I saw the *Argus* for myself. They'd misprinted; it should have said, "Must be Smoker, Non-Vegetarian". Sorry.'

He put the drinks on to a tray and carried it through into the front room. 'Come on. Come and meet everybody.' Blossom set the tray on the table and handed round the mugs.

'I'll introduce you. Everybody, this is Miss Caroline Kenwood . . .'

'Woolfit.'

'Yes, of course, Woolfit. Kenwood is the stereo, of course, I'm sorry. Miss Woolfit, who insists that we are to call her Caroline, has just moved into the flat.'

Caroline began to dread that Blossom would conduct a round of arch formal introductions. She was right.

'This is Dr Frances McCade-Holland,' he said, forcing Caroline to shake hands with the tall Australian-sounding woman. 'She lives in the flat downstairs with her husband, Paul, and their two adorable children. She is a lecturer at the university.'

'What do you teach?' asked Caroline.

'Cult Studs.'

'Ah.'

'Moving on,' said Blossom, 'this elephantine figure on the

sofa is called, oddly enough, Porky. Porky used to live here. He's in catering.'

'Oit?' said Porky.

'We don't like him much, but he's rich, so we let him in.' Porky raised two fingers, very slightly.

'Now, I know you've met these two reprobates before, but I don't think you've been properly introduced. This is Cats-meat . . .'

'Call me Cats,' said the Creep.

'Cats plays the bass guitar in a local band, Wurmsbreth. Perhaps you've heard of them?'

'No, I'm sorry, I haven't.'

Cats nodded happily, as though delighted by his obscurity.

'Oh, you should see them. They're very good. They have a drumkit and some special amps which explode. Cats does all the pyrotechnics himself. Don't you?'

Cats smiled modestly into his coffee, and nodded again.

'Now this,' continued Blossom, drawing Caroline over to the window, 'is Sailor Dave.' The big blond turned from the window and looked at Caroline. 'Sailor Dave travels the world! Don't you, Sailor? David? Don't you?' Sailor Dave grunted and stared at Caroline, held her in his gaze. She felt compelled to speak.

'Do you have a boat?'

'Yes,' said Sailor Dave, and he turned away, to look again at the sea.

'That's nice,' said Caroline.

'Right. Good. Good. Well, and this, last but not least,' said Blossom, indicating the lemon-tea drinker, 'is Jeremiah. He's a political exile. Or something, aren't you?' Jeremiah raised an elegant manicured hand.

'How do you do?' he said with high-finish vowels.

'I'm very well thank you,' said Caroline, resisting a strange urge to curtsey. 'How are you?'

13

Jeremiah raised his finger to his lips and winked.

'So,' said Blossom. 'Now you've met everybody . . . er . . . is there anything you'd like to put on the stereo?'

Caroline felt a little annoyed at this, so far as Blossom was concerned, generous and welcoming gesture, but she swallowed her rising bile and declined. She thought she would like to play her Wu-Tang Clan album, very loud, in order to discomfort these complacent and introspective people; in particular the blond sailor.

'Well, would anybody like to hear our new tape?' asked Cats hopefully.

'Thank you, Cats,' said Jeremiah. 'But I think I speak for all of us when I say no.'

Cats looked hurt, and Caroline felt very much the new kid on the block. An awkward silence descended; Frances, an inveterate giver of good seminar, was the first to speak.

'So, Caroline. What is it that you do?'

'I'm a student. At the university.'

Frances seemed a little irritated by this; Caroline was later to discover that she saw students as, at best, a necessary evil.

'And what do you study?'

'Physics.'

Frances brightened. 'Really? That's very good. More women should be involved in yah de yah de yah de yah de . . .'

Caroline felt her attention wandering, as it always did when she found herself the victim of yet another self-righteous talk on the subject of women in science. She smiled, and wondered why Blossom never got dressed, and whether Jeremiah was really a political refugee and where Sailor Dave had got that scar, and why he stared from the window, and why he was so evasive about his boat . . .

'. . . yah di yah di yah di yah the dogs?'

'I'm sorry?' said Caroline, the word 'dogs' alerting her to the fact that she needed to pay attention again. She liked

14

dogs, and already missed Boxer, her English springer, back in Haywards Heath.

'I said, would you like to come to the dogs? Tonight?'

'I'm sorry?'

'The dogs! Dog racing! My husband's dog is running, and we're all going to Hove dogs. Would you like to come?'

Caroline felt the already diminished reservoir of her patience leaking out through her forced smile. Whatever else might happen today, she was not going dog racing. For one thing, she thought, it's inhuman.

'No, thank you very much. I really should be unpacking and settling in.'

'Pish,' said Porky.

'Now there speaks the authentic voice of Regency Brighton,' said Frances. 'Pish. This is the first town in the world that was purpose built for sin; your first night here, and you're proposing to stay in and shelve your books? I think not. Oh, you must come. Everybody else is coming.'

'You must,' said Blossom.

'You must. Yes, yes, you must,' said Cats.

'Too right. Issalarf,' said Porky. Jeremiah looked up from his *FT* and nodded. Only Sailor Dave seemed unmoved.

'The whole house is coming, everybody from all the other flats,' said Blossom. 'I meant to say something myself. Look, I think you should . . . I think some of the others from downstairs might think it a little rude if you didn't, your first night . . .'

Caroline was only fifteen months out of a grammar school where no threat is more effective than being thought rude. She felt her resolve crumbling.

'Oh well, if *everybody* is coming . . .'

Sailor Dave turned to her. 'Don't come if you don't want,' he said. 'Who gives a fuck what anyone else is doing?'

Everybody looked shocked.

'I'm sorry, Caroline,' said Blossom. 'The good sailor is half Belgian, and he is occasionally lacking in understanding of what it really means to be English. Of course she cares, and don't be so fucking . . . Nietzschean!'

Sailor Dave turned back to the view.

'When you say *everyone* in the house is coming, does that include the disgusting old man in the ground floor flat?' This seemed to amuse everybody except Jeremiah, who looked at her sternly.

'Was he coughing a lot?' asked Blossom.

'Was his willy hanging out?' asked Frances.

Caroline nodded.

'Then let me tell you, young lady,' said Jeremiah, though to judge from his appearance he could not have been more than five years Caroline's senior, 'that you have had the . . . the honour to meet Edgar Edwin Luff, Légion d'honneur, MC, DSO and bar, Honorary Colonel in the French Resistance, SOE, Foreign Office, the Delhi Embassy and the greatest living authority on . . . certain . . . political situations in the Indian Ocean. This . . . this great man is known and . . . yes, loved by all of us here . . . and it is an . . . an honour . . . an honour to have known this . . . this . . .'

'Honourable man?' said Blossom.

'Yes, honourable. Yes.'

'He can be vile when he's pissed though. The kids are a bit scared of him,' said Frances.

'True,' said Blossom. 'And his knob will flop out of his pyjamas. Still, he'll be properly dressed tonight.'

'We call him the Eel,' said Cats.

'We all chipped in for his armchairs, so he can get up here,' said Frances.

'It's not his flat, anyway,' said Cats. 'He's only the lodger.'

'Oh?' said Caroline.

'Yes,' said Blossom. 'Bill and Dolly live there really. They let him the spare room. You'll meet them tonight, they're very nice. You must come.'

'Then there's Geoffrey and Jemima in the basement . . .' said Frances, making ready to leave.

'Be nice to Geoff,' said Blossom. 'It's his house. I'm only sub-letting to you.'

'Right. OK,' said Caroline.

Frances stood in the doorway. 'And then there's my lot downstairs . . . I must go,' she said. 'How about a quick look at your room? I'd like to see it.'

'I haven't done much to it yet,' said Caroline.

'Oh come on. Let's have a peep. Then I can get home and cook tea, and you can get ready for tonight.'

Caroline gave way again, and led Frances up the spiral staircase.

'Yes,' said Frances loudly, stepping over the threshold. 'Oh yes, this *is* a nice room . . .' She closed the door behind her and stood with her back to it, so that Caroline could not escape. 'Listen,' she said in an urgent undertone. 'Look, I hope you don't mind, but I thought I'd better say a quick word about the lads . . . and the . . . other men in the house. Don't worry about the old Eel downstairs; he gets a bit funny in the afternoon sometimes, but he's a sweetheart really, and has a fund of bizarre stories.'

'What about the people in this flat?'

'The lads are OK. Blossom is a betting-shop intellectual; you'll see him in what he thinks of as his true element tonight. Sailor Dave . . .' She paused.

'Yes?'

'Sailor Dave is . . . I like him, but will he let go? Will he relax? You can trust him though. He's a roadie; he's away a lot. Cats . . . Cats is a love, but he does have some rather peculiar habits. I think I should tell you that the last hi-fi girl moved out—'

'I don't like being called the hi-fi girl.'

'Sorry. It was me once. That's how I met them all. Anyway, she moved out because she thought that Catsmeat had been wanking off into her knickers . . .'

'*What?!*'

'Yes, I'm afraid so. He sneaks up in the day when everyone is out, and . . . er . . . relaxes the gentleman's way. I'm sorry, but there it is.'

'Fucking hell! Thanks a lot!'

'Don't worry. He only does it over dirty knickers you'd be putting in the machine anyway. He's a laugh.'

'Oh yes, a right laugh, the filthy bastard.'

'He does it in mine, too. If I'm out, and he's down seeing Paul, he goes in the bathroom, gets my pants and loses his mess. It's healthy. It's a release for him. He's only expressing his sexuality.'

'You don't mind?'

'Not much. But listen, he's not the real problem . . .'

'My God! What *is* the real problem, then?'

'It's my husband, Paul.' Frances reached into her bag, pulled out a cigarette, and lit it. 'I'm not saying you shouldn't shag him or anything.' Caroline sat down on her bed and held her head in her hands. 'Shag him if you like, though I suppose I prefer not to know . . .'

'I wouldn't dream . . . I mean, what do you think?' said Caroline, looking up.

'You haven't met him yet. He can be very persuasive. No, all I'm saying is, don't, for fuck's sake, have any kind of affair. Don't fall for him.' Frances's voice had dropped to a whisper.

'I . . . I . . .' Caroline was dumbstruck.

'He's a fucker, honey bear, take it from me. Don't trust him. Be especially on your guard if he tells you that he loves you.'

'My God! This is . . . I mean, does he do it often?'

18

'Oh Christ, yes. Sometimes he even believes it for a bit, and goes off with them. He just gets cuntstruck. He always comes crawling back. He loves the kids.'

'And you have him back?'

'Up to now.'

'Why?'

'It's a career move. In Cult Studs it helps to have a vivid home life. Gives you perspective, kudos, too. Being gay yourself is best, of course, followed by being married to a gay man, preferably HIV, with being married to a total cunt at No. 3. That's me. Single parenthood is coming up fast. I might try that for a bit. Not till I've finished my research, though.'

'Which is?'

'I'm doing attitudes towards women in the work of Stan Lee . . .'

Caroline nodded. She was much better read than people always assume scientists are, but she had not heard of Stan Lee. She guessed he was a famous American writer or something, and she had no intention of revealing her ignorance; partly from embarrassment, partly out of politeness, and partly because she didn't care, and wanted to hear more about Frances's private life.

'. . . and Paul is one of only a tiny handful of people in this country with a complete set of "Silver Surfers". And he's all right really. The kids love him, and he's got a huge knob . . .' Frances arched her eyebrows.

Caroline did not think she could take much more. Anyway, what had size to do with anything?

'So, watch him. Now, listen, the first race is at 7.37, so the taxis will be here at about seven. Bring twenty quid, and tart yourself up a bit.'

'I'm a student! I haven't got twenty quid to spare!'

'Bollocks. See you later.' Frances opened the door and clattered down the spiral stairs.

Caroline sat for a while on the edge of her bed, and determined that she would *not* go to the dogs at all but phone her mother, who would come and take her home, and she would go into the uni every day on the train and just not have any fun, and she shed a few tears, until there was a knock at the door and Blossom appeared, dressed now in a revolting suit with a loud brown check, bearing a tray on which there was a mug of milky coffee and two slices of cheese on toast topped with Worcestershire sauce. He left them next to her, and she was so touched that she cheered up as she ate her modest tea, forgetting even to point out that vegetarians don't eat Worcestershire sauce. She felt a great deal better afterwards – she went for a wash, changed into her best ankle-length skirt and her techno fleece, dug twenty quid out of the two hundred that Dad had given her the night before, and went back downstairs, feeling that going to the dogs was probably what the doctor ordered for homesickness. It would be, if nothing else, a new experience.

As seven approached, she began to relax. She shared a little spliff pipe (no tobacco for Caroline) with her flatmates; she found that this made Blossom talk even more, while Cats giggled, and even Sailor Dave opened up a bit. The intercom announced the taxis. There were three of them; she shared a cab with Frances and the two old ladies from the downstairs flats, Dolly and Jemima, who were very kind, and said that they liked Caroline's blue hair. On arrival at the dog track, Caroline had her first glimpse of Geoffrey, the landlord and Jemima's brother, who to Caroline's eye looked very fierce, very brown and a very fit eighty or so, and Bill, Dolly's husband, a distinguished but friendly-looking gentleman in his seventies. The Eel, walking with the aid of a stick, was now very respectable in an old but expensively cut suit. He waved affably at her, and shouted, 'Settled in all right?' She also saw Paul Holland.

'All right, doll?' he said.

He was about thirty-two, five ten, dressed in black, with funny crooked teeth and hair that stuck up, like a punk haircut that had been abandoned by its previous owners, and was now being eroded by male pattern baldness. She didn't really see the attraction, and felt safe. Mind you, he did have quite a nice bum. She was told that his dog, Wuzco Thunderflash, was running in the third race, and that it couldn't lose. She'd never been to the dogs before; she accepted the drink that Frances offered her, and watched the first race from the comfort of the bar. She found it quite exciting, and for the second she allowed Cats to show her how to put on a £1 place bet with the Tote, accepted another drink, this time from old Bill Ashbrook, and jumped with excitement as her dog came second. She collected her £1.92 winnings, and decided, with Paul Holland's guidance, to put it all on his dog, on the nose. She also accepted a drink from him, and found that he was quite nice, really, whatever his wife thought of him. There was a saucy twinkle in his eye, but Caroline still felt he was not her type. Now Sailor Dave . . . he was kinky, Caroline was sure.

The dog lost, and Holland was a little downcast, so she bought him a drink, and another for herself. Now the races and the bets and the drinks and all the people from the house seemed to whirl past; by the eighth race she was frankly pissed, and a tenner down on the night. She stood by the rail with Frances and Blossom and looked at her racecard.

'I don't seem to be doing very well,' she said. 'But I am having a nice time.'

'Good,' said Blossom distractedly, looking at a mass of information held on a clipboard in his hand.

'What's that?'

'Oh Christ, don't encourage him, for fuck's sake,' said Frances, and wandered off to retrieve her husband from the kennel girls.

'This, my dear, is a lifetime's study of the dogs, distilled into a few pages of concentrated goodness.'

'What are you trying to do?'

'To play with the bookies' money.'

'I don't follow.'

'The bookies' money. We always try to play with the bookies' money.'

'I don't understand.'

'The bookies' money! Look, we start the season with a few bets, carefully crafted over the winter, using our own stake money. We win – we are in front. We put our stake money, and our expenses, and a little something for our trouble back into our pocket; what remains is the bookies' money, and it is with this money that we bet, because we can now afford to bet, to a limited extent, intuitively, creatively, passionately even. I shall not, however, be placing a bet this evening.'

'Why not?' Caroline took Blossom's arm, and stage-whispered at him, 'It's not crooked, is it?'

'An age-old question. It's not so much that, anyway, as the odds not being right.'

'You've lost me.'

'Shit odds – you might lose, and we never lose. We must always come out even. This is only possible on certain horse races; over a year, I look to double my stake. This is what I live off.'

'You're a professional gambler!' said Caroline, a little loudly for Blossom's taste.

'Shh . . . no, of course not. I'm a writer.'

'A writer? How exciting! What do you write?'

'History. At least, I will, when I've finished my research.'

'What are you researching?'

'The whaling trade in South Georgia. Well, that's how it started. It's kind of evolved into a general history of Antarctic exploration. The book is to be called *In Southern Waters*. It will make my name and my fortune. But until then, I need an income, and mine comes from betting on the Flat.'

'If you only bet on the Flat, why do you come to the dogs?'

'For fun. Look.' He showed Caroline his figures, and launched into an explanation of his fool-proof system for picking winners at the dogs, but Caroline was far too drunk to take it in.

'Yes, OK, but who is going to win this next race?'

'Watch.' He handed Caroline the clipboard, and walked across to one of the bookmakers on the rail.

'Trap Four,' said Holland.

'Six to four,' said the bookie.

'A ton.'

'Six to four for a ton. Trap Four.'

The bookie turned to the clerk who popped the money that Blossom handed over into a large black bag. He scribbled in a ledger, and whispered to the bookie.

'Eleven to eight the jolly!' shouted the bookie as he chalked up the new price. Blossom took his clipboard from Caroline.

'You just had a bet,' she said.

'I did not!' said Blossom with some force.

'You did! I saw you! That was what all the numbers were. You betting.'

'Oh, that? That was just a flutter.'

'How much did you flutter?'

'A hundred quid.'

'Bloody hell.'

'What? It's just to have an interest in the race. Not anything like a real bet. What you have done?'

'Trap Two. I liked the name.'

'No chance,' said Blossom.

The Tannoy sparked into life.

'The hare's running.' The shutters at the Tote windows came banging down, and Caroline stood with Blossom, and they shouted home their selections. Caroline won; the Tote dividend was such that she came out a little ahead on the evening. Blossom made a note on his clipboard, and smiled triumphantly.

'There!' he said. 'A few more adjustments, and the system will be perfect.' Caroline had not been this drunk since Prague, and she laughed properly for the first time since her return. Frances and Paul found her, still smiling minutes later.

'Someone's cheered up,' said Frances.

'Me,' said Caroline. 'Where's Blossom?'

'He's in the enclosure. Look.' The Tannoy confirmed this.

'To present the winning owner with the trophy and the cheque for £43, here is Hove's own Mr Computer, Robertson Blossom!' Caroline started laughing again.

'Is his first name really Robertson?'

'Certainly,' said Paul Holland.

'How come he gets to present the prizes?'

'They love him here,' said Frances. 'No one has ever lost, in relative terms, so much money at a dogtrack by such convoluted means in the whole history of the NGRA.*

Caroline was still smiling as they led her out to the taxi twenty minutes later.

Afterwards, when the younger, giddier part of the company, including the Hollands and Porky, who'd come round to try and ponce some blow, were back in the flat, Caroline reflected that she hadn't enjoyed herself so much for a long time. She had listened and laughed as her new friends swapped their stories, and, as Frances filled her with coffee

* National Greyhound Racing Association. It is not big or clever to lose lots of money at the dogs, so don't try.

and Paul filled her with dope, she found her own tongue, and she sat on the sofa next to Sailor Dave and told him about Prague, and Carl, and how she had been dumped. He might not be a great talker, the One-Eyed Sailor, she thought, but by Christ, he's a good listener. He seemed happy enough, as he had had a winning evening himself. Caroline talked and talked; she didn't notice that everybody else had taken themselves off to their beds. Sailor Dave sat beside her, his legs out in front of him, his head tilted back, his eyes on the ceiling. Every so often, he said, 'Uh.' This was all the encouragement Caroline needed to continue.

'. . . and I can see *now* that I was just projecting everything on to him, including some kinda liberal guilt-trip thing. I mean, come on, a white Rastafarian? What's that, for fuck's sake? I should have known, I was so stupid. I mean, I didn't even laugh when he told me he accepted the divinity of Haile Selassie. "Bob Marley never died," he used to say. "He's in the room. Can't you feel Him?" Well, love, no, I felt like saying, but I never did . . .'

'Would you like to see my boat?' said Sailor Dave suddenly.

'Now?'

'Yes.'

'Yes please.'

'Follow me.' Sailor Dave rose from his sofa, led the way into the hall, up the spiral staircase and into his bedroom. He did not turn on the light. Caroline followed him. His room was bare, except for a tin trunk in one corner and a hammock slung in another. He bent down and picked something up; by the light from the open door, Caroline could see that it was an oar. As Caroline followed Sailor Dave into the room, her eyes adjusted to the semi-darkness, and she could see that in a third corner a ladder led up to a trapdoor, which Sailor Dave now poked open with the oar. He climbed the ladder, and Caroline followed. She climbed out behind Dave on to the flat roof of the house. If you wished, you could climb over low walls and over the roofs of all the houses in Bloomsbury Place until you reached the parapet of the end house. The moonlight made shadows of the chimneys; Caroline thought of *Mary Poppins* and half-expected Dick Van Dyke to come out from behind one of the stacks. The light was good enough that Caroline could see Sailor Dave standing next to a beautiful, sixteen-foot, clinker-built fishing dinghy, there on the roof beside the open hatch.

'It's . . . lovely!' said Caroline breathlessly.

'Thanks,' said Sailor Dave.

'How did it get up here?'

Sailor Dave smiled. 'I built it,' he said. 'I built it up here . . . there was nowhere else, but . . . but . . .' His grin was getting bigger and bigger. 'I . . . I never worked out . . . how to get it down!!' He was laughing now, and Caroline found it infectious and caught it, one of those shared bouts of hysteria, with each person's laughter fuelling the other's, as sometimes happens when we are young, or happy, or in love. Sailor Dave and Caroline rolled on the flat roof in the moonlight, and laughed till they wept. Then they stopped and looked at each other, and then Caroline touched Dave's lip with her forefinger.

Sailor Dave sat up and said, 'Would you like to come aboard?'

'What?'

'Would you like to come aboard?'

That was not what Caroline had been thinking, but she said, 'That would be wonderful. Thank you.' He climbed over the transom and offered Caroline his hand, which she took as she stepped gently aboard, and as she sat down. Sailor Dave sat with his legs stretched under the thwart.

'She is beautiful.'

'I think so.'

'What's she called?'

'*Lookfar.*' Dave lay back, and looked up at the stars. Caroline slipped into the bottom of the boat and lay beside him, under the thwarts, and looked up too. She liked him being there. Perhaps he was just shy. There was no rush. Why had Frances warned her about Holland, sweet though he was, when David was so nice?

'Thank you. Thank you for this,' said Caroline, touching his arm.

'Any time,' he said, moving away slightly. 'Where would you like to sail to?'

'Somewhere, some time. You choose.'

'*Surf's Up,*' said Sailor Dave. 'Hold on.'

'Not now though. It's just right here.'

The Sailor did not reply, and Caroline put her hands behind her head and watched a shooting star arc across the clear sky.

'Dave? Did you see that?'

She turned to him again, but Dave had sailed away on a lager sea; his breathing regular and loud, his eye closed. Trust a man to fail to live up to romantic expectation, she thought. Caroline watched the sky for a minute until she felt cold. Then she scrambled out of the boat, careful not to disturb the Sailor, and climbed down the ladder, watching her step, to spend her first night in her new room in the flat at the top of the old house in Bloomsbury Place.

Helping the Handicapped

Frances Holland was nervous. Things had been going so well! She had a great job, a smashing flat, two gorgeous and intelligent children and a husband of such monumental fecklessness, such Olympian uselessness that she felt confident she would be able to continue to write the devastating anti-male prose for which she was so justly famous throughout the world of Gender Studies for the rest of her working life. Would she have written her ball-breaking piece on 'Nose-picking and *A Question of Sport*' for *Popular Culture and Sex* if she had *not* been married to Paul Holland for the last five years? No. And what of her forthcoming piece for the *Modern Review*, 'On The Skids: Calvin Klein vs. the Klingon Empire'? Could she really have written that if she had been spared sleeping in the same room as his underpants for all this time? Of course not. She was not just any old feminist, sister; she was a professional, she had letters after her name, she'd published books, and she knew that she owed it all to him.

When they met, what, ten years or so ago, she'd been a small-time model in a ra-ra skirt, distributing free sachets of Cup-a-Soup in supermarkets, a plaything for men, and she had neither known nor cared. And then he had come along, and the veil was lifted from her eyes, and she saw men for what they were: lily-livered, work-shy, conniving sneaks who think with their pricks, who smell and fart and care only about football and big tits. He helped her, more than anything else, to understand just why it was that she needed to complete her degree, then her Master's, and then her Ph.D. in Women's Studies. Ten years together, five years of marriage, two lovely children and still he had never blotted his copybook with one thoughtful act; not for one moment had he ever demonstrated that he cared, except when he wanted something. He was perfect, flawless. And the secret of their highly successful relationship was predicated on the fact, she felt almost superstitiously, that she and Paul and the kids lived in Brighton, and her dull, nice, kind parents lived in Christchurch, NZ. As a lecturer in popular culture, no one outside the bridge of the Starship *Enterprise* knew better than she how vital it was that matter and anti-matter must under no circumstances come into contact. And here was a letter from her mother, insisting on just that.

Frances had been able to stage-manage everything brilliantly. Once a year, every year since coming to Britain, Frances had gone home to NZ for a month. Since the kids had been born, she had always taken them to see their grandparents, which she felt should be more than enough to keep her folks away. But no. Her parents were coming to England, for three months, November, December and January, which meant that they would insist upon meeting their son-in-law for the first time, which meant that they would see the truth, and they wouldn't like the truth at all. Because when she first told her parents that she was pregnant, she had to think of something to say about the father of her child. To appease her heartbroken daddy, she had had to think of something that he would like. She remembered the rush of blood to the head when her parents had first asked, 'And what does this Paul do?' – the feeling of hopelessness,

the realization that saying 'He's a professional benefit clai-
mant' would just make things worse. And he had to be a
professional *something*. Her father was the most successful
orthopaedic surgeon on the South Island; he was impressed
by nothing except law, medicine and the Church. And . . .
and . . . and . . . Golf!

And Frances would not have been able to claim that Paul
was a solicitor, or a doctor, or a vicar, for fuck's sake, without
dissolving into hysterical laughter. So Frances said, 'Golf.
He's a professional golfer.' And ever since, her father had had
a good feeling about his son-in-law, knowing that anyone
who played a lot of golf must be one hell of a nice fellow, and
he had asked all kinds of technical questions about handi-
caps and the European Tour which Frances had done her best
to fend off. But this – this was Doomsday, unavoidable and
inevitable. Unless . . . Frances picked up the phone, and
dialled upstairs. Blossom answered.

'Are you at home?'

'To you, honey, always.'

'I'm coming up. Get the stinger on.'

When Blossom opened the door to Frances, he was wearing
his 'Support Limited Scientific Whaling' T-shirt, a sure sign
that he had been working on *In Southern Waters*. But he
welcomed her in with a smile and a song.

'What is that song?'

' "Matchstalk Men and Matchstalk Cats and Dogs". Sorry.
It was just on the radio.'

'Unplug the radio, *put on the stinger*, make me a *nice* cup of
coffee, sit down, shut up, and listen.'

Blossom went whistling into the kitchen, while Frances
paced about the front room, sucking her fag and twiddling
the hair at the back of her neck.

'What do you know about golf?' said Frances when
Blossom reappeared.

'Ah! So that's it, is it? That's how come so mysterious, is it? Golf, is it now?'

'Fuck off. What do you know about golf, you dopey cunt?'

'As Confucius said, to know that we know what we know, and that we don't know what we don't know, that is the root of all wisdom. On this basis, I can lay claim to *satori*, in that I don't know anything about golf, and what's more, I know that I don't know very very well indeed.'

Frances put her hands over her ears and groaned.

'I don't even want to know; I mean, why only one glove? And why leave it dangling from your back pocket? I don't know, and I don't care.'

Frances moaned, and started to rock very gently back and forth.

'But,' continued Blossom, 'if you are so desperate to talk about golf, Cats is your man, or had you forgotten?'

'Cats! Oh God, yes! Cats! I'd forgotten! Cats! Yes, he used to be a professional, didn't he?'

'An apprentice, at any rate.'

'Oh God, yes. Didn't he get the sack for going through the lady members' lockers?'

'To be specific, he was dismissed when he was caught having a wank into a pair of kinky knee-length boots left by one of the younger ladies in the changing room.'

'Poor old Cats.'

'He still goes out on the East Brighton. He's pretty hot. Why do you think he always wears those horrid trousers?'

'Cats. The answer to a maiden's prayer.'

'Who'd've thought it?'

'Where is he?'

'At the workshop. He always comes home for lunch. He likes to see *Neighbours* at the first sitting; claims that Sailor Dave always spoils the five thirty-five showing by taking the piss out of Harold Bishop, just because he's Cats's favourite.'

'I must see him.'

'I've never heard anyone say that about Cats. I must avoid him at all costs, yes, but I must see him is a first. Well, you'd better wait for an hour, which will give you time to tell me what the fucking ada you need to talk about golf to Cats for.'

'I need his help.'

'He won't do it. Whatever it is, he won't do it. He's a TV repair man; he always thinks people want him to repair things. So now, even if someone asks him to pass the sugar, he always says No, in case they drop the bowl and ask him to repair it.'

'I need him to teach Paul to play golf.'

'Haaaaaaaaaaaaaaaaaa! Aaaaaaaaaaaaaaaaaaaaaaaah! That's very good!!'

'No, really. You must help.' And she told him why.

'I'll help,' said Blossom at the conclusion of Frances's narrative. 'But it won't be easy.'

'How will we start?' asked Frances.

'With soft cop/hard cop, that's how. We've got just under an hour to rehearse. Now listen . . .'

Cats came home at one, as advertised, and ate some pilchards on toast in front of the TV.

'You've been growing a moustache, Cats,' said Frances.

Cats nodded happily, his green eyes twinkling with pleasure.

'It suits you. It makes you look distinguished. Just . . .'

'What?'

'The pilchard. It gets stuck in it.'

'Sorry.' Cats looked sad, and Frances felt guilty.

'It does look very good though. Just remember to comb it, that's all.'

'OK.' Cats smiled again.

'It looks like a twelve-year-old's minge got stuck on your face,' said Blossom.

'Fuck off,' said Frances. 'It looks great.'

'Thanks, Fran,' said Cats.

Don't call me Fran, thought Frances. But she kept on smiling. 'Listen, Cats, there's something I've got to ask you . . . are you still any . . . I mean, do you still play golf? At all?'

'Of course. I pay green fees. I'm not a member of a club or anything.'

'Well, except the Chaingang,' said Blossom.

'I am not!'

'You were chucked out for being a pervert then.'

'I was not!'

'Chucked out of a perverts' club for being a pervert.'

'It's not true!'

'Of course it's not true, Cats, I know that. The thing is, Cats, I really need your help.'

'Well . . . I don't really, you know, like to repair things for friends, Fran. It might come between us. If you've got some clubs you want doing up or something, you should take them to a shop.'

'The only thing he'll help you do is make your clothes look as if they've had slugs crawling all over them. Unless you pay him seven quid an hour.'

'That's not fair!' said Frances. 'Cats is always very careful.'

'Thank you,' said Cats, modestly.

'And anyway, Cats, I don't want you to repair anything. I want you to teach Paul how to play golf.'

'He'll never do it,' said Blossom. 'He couldn't. He's lost it. He never had it.'

'I fucking did! I did! I had it!'

'You never had it.'

'I did!! I've still got it!!!'

'You can't do it!'

'I could! I could!'

'Do it then,' said Blossom.

'Please, Cats,' said Frances. 'For me. And I'll pay you. Five pounds an hour.'

'I will then,' said Cats triumphantly. 'I will.'

Frances leaned across and kissed him. 'I knew you would,' she said. 'Only . . .'

'Oh, I know, you want me to repair your video first.'

'No. The only thing is, you've got to turn him into a world-class player. In three weeks.'

Cats looked thoughtful. 'I can try,' he said. 'I can only try.'

So it was that the next day Cats and Paul Holland found themselves standing on the first tee on the pitch 'n' putt course at Rottingdean, each carrying a seven iron and a putter hired from the little hut under the shadow of the derelict windmill. Frances had little difficulty in persuading her husband that he needed to become very good at golf very quickly; she found persuasion much easier since the Bobbitt case. He knew that if he could not pull off this golf gig, things might get well heavy, but he was not unduly worried; I mean, all you got to do is hit this pill with this stick, right? He had made sure that he had a couple of pipes before coming out on to the links; that should help his hand/eye co-ordination, no question.

'OK,' said Cats. 'We're starting here 'cos no one minds if you're crap.'

'Yeah? Well maybe I won't be crap. Maybe I'll be brilliant.'

'If all goes well, you'll be brilliant in a couple of weeks. Well, not brilliant. Passable. Better than you are now. Today, we're just going to deal with first principles. We'll go out on a real course tomorrow.'

'Yeah, don't worry about that, man. I've played PGA golf on the kids' PlayStation. It can't be too different.'

'Are you any good?'

'No, man, I'm shit. But I expect I'll be better when it's real.'

'So you know what you have to do?'

'Course I do. Whack this fucker at the flag.'

'Well, that's it, I suppose. It's not as easy as it looks, though.'

'Watch me.'

Cats had prepared himself for every eventuality, except the one that occurred: Holland took up a perfect stance, instinctively held the club in a Ben Hogan grip, executed a swing of textbook perfection, and hit the ball on to the little green. It bounced twice and rolled into the hole.

'That's that,' said Holland. 'Shall we go down the White Horse?'

'Er . . . um . . .'

'What about them?' Frances, in order to help Holland remember his children's names, had christened them Erica and Umberto, Er and Um to everyone in Bloomsbury Place.

'No, nothing,' said Cats. 'I mean, er, um, I think we'd better finish the round first, or Frances will kill us.'

'Oh all right, man. It's quite fun anyway. Easier than the fuckin' PlayStation.'

Cats took his shot, and holed out in three; he took the trouble to pencil in the scores, though he felt he could not face the humiliation if everything carried on like this. Which, of course, it did not.

For example, Holland never recaptured his instinctive grip; hole after hole, Cats patiently attempted to reconstruct what it was that Holland had done so right untutored, but it had gone, never to return. His perfect swing degenerated into a vicious slash, which, on the rare occasions when it connected with the ball, sent it off on exciting, wild and unpredictable journeys. At the fourth tee, Holland sliced the ball on to the A259 in the path of an oncoming No. 27 bus; on his ninth shot at the tenth hole he hooked it over the boundary fence and on to the head of a war-blinded pensioner walking in the grounds of St Dunstan's. His putting was better, in that it was less psychopathic than his fairway work; it put Cats in mind of a silent comedian, Chaplin perhaps, endlessly hitting a ball to and fro as the sun goes down, changing from side to side, always taking the identical shot to no effect whatsoever.

But at last Holland holed out at the 18th and Cats totted up the scores: he had got round in 68, while Holland had taken 203.

'You won, then?'

'Yes.'

'Don't I get anything for a hole-in-one?'

'Yes. You get to buy me a drink.'

'Fuck right off, man! You buy *me* a drink, yeah?'

'No. It's a tradition. If you get a hole-in-one, you have to buy a drink for everyone in the clubhouse. But I'll settle for a pint in the White Horse.'

'This,' said Holland reflectively, 'is going to be much harder than I thought.'

After Cats's gloomy report to Frances that evening, it was decided that the pair should stay on the pitch 'n' putt working on the basics of grip, swing and aim, and there they stayed every day for four days, until at last Holland broke through the magic 200 barrier; Cats, realizing that the moment could be postponed no longer, announced that the next day they would go out on a full-sized course. He refused, however, to take Holland out on to the East Brighton, where he still had hopes of being accepted as a member one day – so it was that Cats and Holland, in full golfing regalia, sat on the No. 12 and made their way to the even more downmarket Peacehaven course.

Frances had taken Holland shopping, and had chosen a tasteful turquoise and tartan outfit for her husband to wear: turquoise polo shirt, turquoise Pringle sweater and a pair of tartan trousers, whose predominant colour was turquoise. She also bought him a glove, which dangled proudly from his back pocket, and a pair of turquoise golfing shoes with turquoise fringes to keep the rain from his turquoise socks.

'What clan has a turquoise tartan, man?' Holland had asked.

'The MacPooves. Now shut up,' Frances had replied. On the subject of clubs, Frances had held firm. The second-hand set with trolley and bag that Cats had recommended was a grand, and she had refused to bite, insisting that Cats would lend or at least hire whatever was necessary for the duration. So it was Cats's old golf bag that the two lugged from the bus and across to the clubhouse at the Peacehaven course. Green fees duly paid, Cats and Holland awaited their turn at the first tee, Cats trying to fill Holland's head with desperately needed advice.

The first hole at Peacehaven is a par 3. The tee and the green are separated by a shallow valley, through which flows a small stream. The tee is higher than the green; the idea is that your shot from the tee, using, perhaps, a four iron, should carry the stream and deposit you safely on the green for a couple of easy putts. Generations of rabbit golfers, on achieving this modest goal, had been cheered and encouraged by the hole. Holland did not seem even to want to join this noble company. The fifth time Holland hit his ball into the stream, Cats sighed. The seventh time, he rolled his eyes to heaven. The twelfth time, he sat down on the concrete block which denoted the back of the tee. Before the seventeenth ball into the stream, Cats asked Holland to pause, to allow a foursome of WRVS ladies through, and after the twenty-third he called a halt to the proceedings. They went for a drink at the bar, left Cats's bag in the locker room, walked over the Heights and down into Newhaven to score some grass from Mad Rikki, a friend of Holland's who grew his own.

Rikki answered the door on tiptoe.

'Come in, yeah?' he said.

'Do we have to be quiet, man?' asked Holland in a low voice.

'No. Do you want, you know? . . . some tea?'

'Yeah, cheers, man. This is Cats.'

'Nice to see you, yeah?' Mad Rikki tiptoed into the kitchen, leaving Cats and Holland to watch *Four Feather Falls* on the video, the sound turned down to nothing. He tiptoed back with a tray, put it down, tiptoed over to his albums, chose *The Plan* by the Osmonds, tiptoed across to the stereo, put the record on, and tiptoed across to his chair.

'Why are you dressed like a cunt, yeah?' said Mad Rikki.

'I've been playing golf. Why are you walking everywhere on tiptoe?'

'Oh, because I want to see what it's like to be a cloven-hoofed animal.'

So Cats and Holland drank their tea, scored some grass and took it up to Newhaven Fort, there to discuss their predicament, sitting on the clifftop in the last of the autumn sunshine.

'What are we going to tell her?' said Cats.

'Who cares, man? You're not scared of her, are you?'

'Yes, I am.'

'Me too. We can't tell her it hasn't worked. We got to do something.'

'But what? What?'

'We don't have to decide yet. There's still a fortnight before her folks arrive. If we keep coming out here, then at least we can put off the shit till then.'

For Holland, shit postponed was almost the same as no shit at all. So every day Cats and Holland would get dressed in their costumes, haul the golf bag on to the bus and hang out in Newhaven until four, when they would catch the bus back to Brighton. If it was fine, they would walk down by the harbour, or up at the Fort; if it rained, they sat in the Morocco or the Fishmarket cafés, waiting for the pubs to open, or they would hang with Mad Rikki and smoke his good grass, and watch Gerry and Sylvia Anderson videos and listen to some of the worst albums ever recorded while Rikki tiptoed around.

Once, for a change, they stayed on the bus, and carried on as far as Eastbourne, but they found that the tide of life had left the town many years before, if indeed it had ever got so high. Everyone was eighty-two if they were a day, and all the men were dressed like Holland. So they didn't repeat the experiment. And then, two days before Frances's parents were due to be met from the plane at Gatwick, it all fell apart. One of Frances's colleagues, a woman who had met and been repelled by Holland at numerous faculty parties, returning from a day trip to Dieppe, had spotted him from the deck of the ferry, sitting on the end of the Breakwater with Cats, drinking lager. She had phoned Frances from the harbour station and asked, did she know that her husband was out enjoying himself in Newhaven? When Cats and Holland got home that night, she went spare at them, and the whole gaff was blown. They stood, pathetic in their golfing threads, and took it like men: they made excuses, they whined, and each tried to pass the buck to the other. Seething with anger, Frances ordered Holland to get out of her sight in case she killed him. As patiently as possible, she and Blossom debriefed Cats.

'It wasn't my fault, really it wasn't. I tried, I did. But he was so . . . hopeless. It was as if he didn't care.'

'I'll make the little fuckwit care, don't worry.'

'Now, darling,' said Blossom. 'You must stay calm. It was always a long shot.'

'The longest shot he managed was into the stream,' said Cats.

'Yes, very funny,' said Frances, witheringly. Cats withered.

'The thing is,' said Blossom, 'your folks arrive the day after tomorrow, and we need to present them with a first-class golfer as a son-in-law. We have tried, and failed, to turn Paul into that golfer. The question I must ask you now is this: have you ever shown your parents a photo of your husband?'

'Yes. Once, I think. Wedding photos, maybe. It was a long time ago.'

'So do you think they could recognize Paul from those photos?'

'I doubt it very much. He'd had a bath for the wedding, and everything.'

'So, if you need a golfer for a husband, and your parents could not recognize your husband . . .'

'A ringer! That's what you mean, isn't it?'

'Exactly. We substitute a golfer for your husband.'

'But who?'

Blossom looked pointedly at Cats, who was wringing his hands, and muttering about how it wasn't his fault. A broad smile crossed Frances's face.

'Cats,' she said in a sing-song. 'Oh Cats.'

'What?'

'Cats, how would you like to be married?'

'I don't know, really. If she didn't mind me playing in Wurmsbreth, I suppose.'

'I wouldn't mind. I like Wurmsbreth, especially "Jeffrey Dahmer's Dead".'

'Yes, everyone likes that one.'

'Smashing tune,' said Blossom.

'And,' continued Cats, 'if she didn't want me to mend stuff all the time.'

'I've just bought a brand new video. It's still under guarantee.'

Cats looked puzzled. 'Why are you telling me this? You're married already . . . to Paul.'

'But as far as my parents are concerned, I'm married to a golfer.'

'And you, Cats,' said Blossom, 'are a golfer.'

'But . . .' said Cats.

'No, Cats, don't you see? It's perfect, much better than trying to teach that spastic to play. All you'd have to do is pretend to be Paul for a couple of months, and play golf with my dad. And they won't be staying here the whole time, anyway; Dad wants to get up to Scotland to visit the McCade ancestral home and stuff like that. So you'd only have to pretend to be Paul when they're around.'

'Let's face it, Cats, pretending to be Paul is hardly an arduous task. You just have to sleep a bit, and watch lots of TV,' said Blossom.

'What about Er and Um? Wouldn't they notice that their dad had changed?'

'Don't worry about them. They're young, they're gullible. After all, they've believed that Paul is nice for all these years.'

'I'm really not sure. I do have a life of my own, you know,' said Cats.

'That's debatable,' said Blossom.

'The business. Who'd run the workshop? I've got a huge pile of things waiting to be repaired already, since I've been playing golf every day for the last three weeks.'

'Or not,' said Blossom.

'You know what I mean.'

'Details, Cats, details. We'll think of something,' said Frances. 'What do you say?'

'I don't know. Can I sleep on it?'

'Of course. Good thinking. I'll come up in the morning. Ten-ish. I'm sure you'll see it's a great idea. Thanks, Cats. I knew you'd help.' And, as when he had agreed to teach Holland, Frances leaned across and gave him a kiss before she went back to her own flat. Cats and Blossom tried to watch television after she had gone, but found it difficult to concentrate because of the violence which they could hear being perpetrated through the floor.

That night both Frances and Cats were visited by dreams. Frances was forced by her father to snog a disgusting green toad wearing a red tam-o'-shanter and a pair of black silk knickers. Mashie Niblick, said the toad. Mashie Niblick, he said, exploring her mouth with his long grey tongue. Er and Um were watching, and singing 'I saw Mummy kissing warty jaws.' She awoke at seven, the sheets soaked with cold sweat.

Cats, however, passed a pleasant night; he and Frances and the two children were wearing bathing costumes, laughing together in the sunshine as they played crazy golf at a caravan park, which seemed to Cats to be located near Aberystwyth.

By the morning, both had resolved what must be done. Frances realized that if the thing was to be carried off, she would have to sleep in the same room as Cats when her parents stayed, and she would have to show him signs of affection; she might have to snog him. The walls in the flat were paper-thin; if she didn't once hear the sound of shagging in the course of her extended stay, Frances knew that her mother would worry, and ask if everything was all right on that front. Frances thought maybe she could bang the headboard against the wall and make some appropriate noise, but she found herself disgusted by the notion. She could not allow Cats to touch the children in any way, which her parents would find very odd. The thing was impossible.

Cats had a more positive spin on it. Cats had also realized that he would have to sleep in the same room as Frances, and that this might mean that he could really see Frances's tits for once, and not just a hint of nipple under her shirt in the summer.

Both prepared for their meeting. Cats took a bath and, borrowing Caroline's toothbrush, even went so far as to brush his teeth. Frances smoked ten Silk Cut, drank six cups of coffee, and read the *Telegraph*. At ten she phoned upstairs, and Blossom answered.

'Is he up?' she asked.

'He's up, and washed and dressed.'

'Washed?'

'Yep. I think he's going to agree.'

'Oh shit. I'm on my way.'

Cats leaped across to the door at Frances's knock, flung it open enthusiastically and said, 'Yes! I'll do it,' at exactly the same moment Frances said, 'I'm sorry, Cats. No can do.' Both paused and looked at each other.

'Oh, darling Cats . . . you're disappointed.'

'A bit.'

'Was it the thought of having a real home? Being part of a family?'

'A bit . . .'

'Or was it the thought that you might get to see my tits?'

Cats giggled.

Frances looked at him with her head on one side. 'Do you know, Cats, you've been so kind, and I know you really tried to help . . . I'm going to give you a present. Blossom!'

Blossom had been reading the paper and pretending not to listen.

'Yes, my bold and buccaneering colonial chum?'

'Look out the window, and don't turn round till I say.'

'OK.'

'Cats . . . here.' And Frances lifted her shirt and her bra and showed Cats her tits, while she counted to five and he boggled, and then she lowered her shirt again, and Cats slumped back in his chair.

'Was that nice?' said Frances.

'Yes . . . thank you. Thank you so much.'

'It was my pleasure, Cats. And thank you. There aren't many of you left.'

'Many of what?'

'Gentlemen, Cats.'

Cats blushed. 'I should get back to the workshop,' he said.

'You do that thing. And thanks again.'

'Thank you.' And Cats put on his donkey jacket and hurried out.

Frances said to Blossom, 'A good idea. I'm sorry. I couldn't have him that near for so long. Sorry.'

'Don't apologize. It's pretty disgusting having him in the room next to you. I understand. But . . .'

'Yes. But. This time tomorrow my folks get here, and they're going to find out the truth.'

'Never say die. We must be able to think of something. We've still got, what, twenty-six hours or so.'

'But what?'

'There has to be a way. Can't we persuade your father that Paul can't play golf temporarily?'

'How?'

'I don't know. We could fake an injury, pretend that Paul has broken his arm or something. Put it in a sling.'

'Brilliant! Brilliant! It's what we must do! Yes! Yes! Yes . . . No.'

'No?'

'No. Don't you remember what my father does?'

'No. Oh, hang on, isn't he . . . ? Oh, yes, that's right, he's a doctor. Of course. Well, he wouldn't have to examine Paul, would he?'

'He's a fucking orthopaedic surgeon. He'll be examining him every five fucking minutes. No, it won't do . . .' A dreamy look came into Frances's eyes. 'Unless . . . unless . . . unless we do him in.'

'What, kill him? I don't think we should . . .'

'No, not kill him. Injure him a bit, that's all. Break his arm. Or his leg. Or both. It'd be fun.'

'He's not going to put up with that.'

'We're not going to tell him, are we? We're going to set a trap . . .' Frances's voice fell to a conspiratorial whisper, and Blossom moved his head closer to hers to listen.

The plan involved the help of Cats, who was phoned at the workshop and asked to bring home some flex. Caroline, whose term had begun, and who had found an evening job in a local macrobiotic restaurant, would be home from the university to wash and change for work; she must also be warned of the existence of a tripwire. The idea was quite simple: Blossom would lure Holland up to the flat that evening with the promise of some free drugs (which Frances stole for the purpose from Holland's own stash) while Cats and Frances fixed the wire across the top of the stairs. Next Cats, by now Frances's devoted slave, would remove the light bulb from the landing, and 'come home'. Blossom and Frances knew that Holland would not budge until the drugs had all gone and Caroline was home from work, because, as Frances had predicted, he had begun the attempt to seduce her. So she would come back, knock on Frances's door, and then Frances would guide her over the wire with the aid of a torch. Finally, at about one, Holland would leave the flat, find the light on the landing extinguished, trip over the wire and fall down a flight of stairs. This would surely, Frances reasoned, be more than enough to keep him out of action for a month or two. It was a thrilling and audacious plan, and Frances and Blossom hugged themselves with glee. Blossom phoned Holland at the pub and invited him round for the evening, making sure to tell him that it was one of the rare occasions when he had got himself a little bit of spliff together. Holland readily agreed, and he turned up at about nine. Blossom put a Buzzcocks' Greatest on the CD player, to mask the sound of Frances and Cats erecting the tripwire and removing the light. Cats duly 'arrived home'; he winked at Blossom and sat down next to Holland, who passed him a number. At about eleven, a blushing Caroline came in.

'Hello, doll. You're looking guilty. Have you been smuggling meat into your punters' nut roasts?' asked Holland.

'No. No. No . . . I . . . er . . . I met a homeless old man and he asked me for change but I didn't have any, so I couldn't give him anything, and now I feel guilty. That's all.'

'Don't feel guilty about that, doll,' said Holland. 'All them beggars and tramps are on a fucking fortune, you know what I mean. They are not homeless, they all live in bastard great big houses in Withdean and drive Astras.'

Caroline narrowed her eyes as she looked at Holland, and felt glad that he was about to be launched down the stairs. She made drinks while Blossom rolled the last joint.

'This is good gear, man,' said Holland. 'It's not unlike a bit I've got myself. Did you get it off Black Barney?'

'Yeah,' said Blossom.

'His stuff is all right really. People complain, but he does right by me.'

'Me too,' said Blossom. They drank their coffee and finished the spliff; Caroline made her excuses, and began her preparations for sleep; as predicted, Holland took this as his cue to leave.

'Well,' he said, standing up, 'this won't buy the baby a new bonnet.' He dusted the tobacco and blims from his sweater, and grasped the handle of the living-room door. He was halted in his progress by the sound of a heavy crash and a loud shout from the landing.

'What the fuck is that?' said Holland.

'Don't know,' said Cats.

'We'd better look, man,' said Holland.

'I suppose we better had,' said Blossom, opening the living-room door and going out into the hall. 'It sounds very much as though someone has had a nasty fall.'

Rock 'n' roll, as Mott the Hoople remarked many years ago, is a losers' game, and for every bloated megastar or *NME* darling there are a million no-hopers whose dreams are fed by a monthly gig in their local. Cats's outfit, Wurmsbreth, fell into this latter category. But there are those who manage to hack a modest living from the Great Game, and Sailor Dave was of their number; he was a drum technician, quite a good one, and he spent at least half of the year away from Bloomsbury Place on tour. But those who are convinced that the road is one long round of drugs and sex parties are sadly mistaken; often Sailor Dave worked on tours of shattering dullness. The last month had been no exception, as he had been on a European tour with Johnny Mathis. But to Sailor Dave's everlasting delight, Mr Mathis had contracted a throat infection and had been forced to cancel the last three nights. Sailor Dave had helped to pack the drums into an artic and rushed to Budapest airport (to Johnny's great regret, it was his many Eastern European fans who were to be disappointed) to book himself on to the first available flight to Gatwick. From Gatwick he had caught the train to Brighton, and at Brighton station he hailed a taxi, which had taken him home, a good week earlier than expected. The journey had been effortless and incident free. He opened the front door, bounded up the stairs with his grip bag and, to his surprise, fell sprawling on the darkened landing outside the flat, where Blossom and Holland and Cats now stumbled on him, rolling around and holding his knee.

'You're home early, Dave,' said Blossom.

'Good trip, man?' asked Holland.

'Did you get Johnny's autograph like I asked?' said Cats.

'You fuckers! I've done my fucking knee in!'

Frances, who had been waiting and listening from just inside her door, came up to see if she had got lucky. 'Hello!' she shouted. 'What's all the noise? Has someone had a fall?'

'Yes! I fucking have!' shouted Sailor Dave.

'Dave! You're not supposed to be here! You're supposed to be in Ruri-fuckin'-tania or someplace.' Frances arrived at the top of the stairs, and stared accusingly at Sailor Dave.

'Oh, *sorree*,' said Sailor Dave, sitting up. The light from the open door to the flat showed Dave that he had tripped over a length of flex tied to the banisters at the top of the stairs. 'Who the fuck put that there?' he asked.

'Don't know,' said Frances and Blossom.

'Not me,' said Cats.

Frances stared wildly about her. As the Sailor got to his feet, still holding his knee, Holland took hold of his wife's arm and led her carefully over the wire and down the stairs.

'Come on, dear,' he said. 'Someone has been very careless, leaving that there. If Dave hadn't've come home when he did, there might have been a nasty accident. I might have fallen down the stairs myself, and then I wouldn't have been able to come with you to the airport tomorrow. I think we'd better leave the blokes to sort out what happened here.'

And Frances allowed herself to be led away, a meek little New Zealand lamb.

And so the morning dawned. Er and Um were packed off to school, despite their protestations that it wasn't fair, that they should be allowed to meet Grampa and Grandma at the airport, that Daddy didn't even know them and he should go to school instead. But why delay it? It would seem very odd to her parents if Paul did not accompany her to the airport, and they might as well find out now as later. No golfing son-in-law. It could not be done. She had tried, and she had failed. As she drove up the M23 in her gun-metal grey Golf GTI ('That's a funny way to spell Git,' Blossom had remarked when she got it), Holland, oblivious to the gravity of the situation, chattered away beside her, while she reflected on the consequences of telling one little white lie all those years ago in Christchurch. And as she drove, she thought, 'It's not *so* grave, when all is said and done.' No, really. It wasn't so bad. Her parents would loathe and detest Paul, even if he could play golf, and it was highly likely that they would have been at least as horrified by Cats. Her father, when he found out the truth, might even see the funny side. So Paul was only a professional arsehole – who cared? She was the successful professional, the breadwinner, and her father should be proud of her for that, and not worry if she chose to keep Holland. There were the children anyway, who adored and were adored by their grandparents in turn. That was what mattered. She would maintain the lie no longer. She would face the truth, instead of running away from it all the time. The time was now. Frances pulled into the arrivals car park at Gatwick, and prepared to face the future with an open heart and a clear conscience.

The flight was delayed, but only by an hour; the Hollands sat in the Country Kitchen Cafeteria, and each of them had some tepid water with a brown tampon in it which slowly leaked colour into the cups. They also had a whortleberry jam doughnut each. The bill was a modest £12.

'What *are* whortleberries?' said Holland.

'The sort of thing you get in airport doughnuts, but nowhere else in the world.'

'They're fucking disgusting anyway. Are you eating yours?'

'No.'

'Can I have it, then?'

'I thought you said it was disgusting?'

'Yeah, it is, but I like disgusting things.'

'I've noticed.' Holland ate the remaining half of Frances's doughnut, and stared from the window of the Country Kitchen at the taxiing airliners. Frances took a deep breath and prepared to admit to her husband that she was wrong, for only the third time in their relationship. The first time was when she had accused him of sleeping with her best friend, when in fact he had been sleeping with her best friend's sister; the second was just before Um had been born, when Frances had insisted that she was carrying another girl, and Holland had bet her a tenner that it was a boy. So it was not an easy matter to admit that she shouldn't have deceived her parents about Paul's ability as a golfer, or gone to so much trouble to bring her lie to life. As the arrival of her parents' flight was announced, she still hadn't summoned up the courage.

The Hollands walked together from the Country Kitchen to the first class arrivals lounge. Frances felt her mouth go dry, and her nails digging into the flesh of her palms. The lump in her throat was not from the excitement of meeting her parents, but from her pride, stuck in her gullet as she tried to swallow it. As they entered the lounge, she turned her head to address her husband and to eat humble pie – but Paul turned his head too, to look at an air stewardess's arse. So she saw what he did not: the empty luggage trolley left carelessly in the doorway, where anybody could trip over it. He raised his foot, and put it down on to the trolley with sufficient pressure to send the thing rocketing across the lounge and him sprawling on to his side. It certainly looked like an awkward landing, Frances thought, as she watched her husband writhe in agony on the floor.

'AAAAAAAAAAARRRRRRGGGGGGGGGGHHHHHH!!!!!! MY WRIST!!!!!! I'VE DONE MY FUCKING WRIST!!!!!! AARRRGHHHHHHHHHH!!!!!!!!!'

'Oh dear, darling,' said Frances. 'You really must look where you're going.'

'Hello! Sweetie!' called a man's cheerful voice.

'Frannie! Coo-ee!' called her mother. They were here. The truth must be . . .

'Golf!' hissed Frances. 'Talk about golf!'

'MY WRIST!!!!!! WHAT ABOUT MY FUCKING WRIST??????????!!!!!'

'Fuck your fucking wrist, you selfish cunt! Just remember you're a golfer . . . Mum! Dad! Thank Christ you're here. Paul has fallen over . . .'

Frances's father put down his Air New Zealand bag and forced his way through the small crowd which had gathered around the stricken Holland, while Frances and her mother stood anxiously by.

'Here, let me through. Hello, Paul, I'm Jack, Frances's father. Let's have a look . . . I know it hurts, just let me have . . . keep still, son . . . tut, tut . . . can you move your fingers? No? Well,' he said straightening up, 'I'm afraid there's going to be no golf for you for a month or two. You've got a rather nasty compound fracture of the wrist.'

Frances held her breath. A slow grin spread across Holland's face, paper white with pain.

'No! Bad one!' he said.

And as the airport paramedics carted him off on a trolley, Frances saw him raise his good hand and give her the thumbs-up. She took the arms of her parents, and they followed behind to the airport aid station. And to think, she thought, that some people wonder why I love the little bastard. Which, at that moment at least, she did, with all her heart.

Small is Beautiful

'Bit fat ugly bastard,' muttered Caroline to Blossom after another evening spent with Porky sprawled all over the couch, his pig-fatty eyes bulging at the telly, their telly, drinking their booze and coffee, eating their biscuits and cake, sounding off about immigration and young offenders, and what he'd do with them if he were in charge.

'Why do you put up with him? He's not funny, he's a fascist, he's a pathological liar, he smells . . .'

'Yes,' said Blossom, 'but he's our mate.'

'Your mate? You all hate him.'

'Not hate . . .'

'You spend all your time bitching about him when he's not here.'

'That's because he's our mate. It's OK for your mates to have a go.'

'Why? Why the fuck?'

'Why what?'

'Why is he your mate?'

'Well . . . he's rich.'

'He's not . . .'

'Thirty-five thousand a year. That's doing OK by our standards.'

'But we never see any. He ponces our food, our drink, our spliff; last week, he went into the fridge and nicked a whole bowl of my soya pudding. I wasn't even here to ask!'

'So, yes, I admit it. He is a bit of a sod. We all go back a long way, that's all.'

'Loyalty is one thing but, in Christ's name, look at him!'

Blossom watched as Porky scratched at his genital area through his suit trousers and then sniffed his fingers.

'It's disgusting.'

'I know. But we can't stop him coming round. He's our mate.'

'And that's it, is it? He's your mate? He might be a rapist or a serial killer or the host of a daytime TV chat show, but everything is forgiven, because he's your mate?'

'That's right.'

'It's sick.'

'If I had to choose between betraying my country and a friend, I hope to God I'd have the courage to betray my country.'

'Even if your friend was, I don't know, a Nazi spy or something?'

'Porky's hardly a Nazi spy.'

'No, but he is loathsome.'

'But he's our mate.'

'Oh, for Christ's sake. But *why* is he your mate if he's so horrible? Was he nice once or something?'

Blossom's face momentarily contorted; with fear? Caroline wondered.

'Who told you about that?' he said.

'About what?'

'About when Porky was nice.'

'So he *was* nice, then? That's why he's your mate?'

'Come into the kitchen.'

'Why?'

''Cos I'll tell you.'

'Why Porky's your mate?'

'No. Not really. No, I'll tell you about when Porky was nice.'

Blossom led and Caroline followed; they sat at the kitchen table drinking coffee, while Blossom told his tale. Blossom's Phil Spector tape banged away on the kitchen ghetto blaster.

'Have I ever told you how long I've lived here?'

'No.'

'Fifteen years.'

'Really?'

'Really. Fifteen years. I left university in the early eighties and moved to Brighton with my student band. We thought we might make it big.'

'What were you called?'

'The Dub Liners. We were a kind of Irish Reggae band. Of course, it was all bollocks; six months later we'd split up. It didn't really matter; I was pissed off with it all, so I started working on *In Southern Waters* and Kate and I had found this place, sharing . . .'

'Who was Kate?'

'Oh, didn't I say? Kate was my wife. We got married when we were students. We lived here.'

'Ahhh! Young love! Married too young though, wee Bobby.'

Blossom smiled.

'When did you split up, or do you mind my asking?' continued Caroline.

'No, not at all. We didn't split up. She died . . . no, please, don't be embarrassed. You didn't know.'

'I'm so sorry. What happened? If . . .'

'No, I don't mind. She had a brain haemorrhage. In here, actually. She fell down in a fit. Died four days later. They had her on a life support machine, then they told me she was brain dead and that they were turning it off.'

'Oh, I'm so sorry.'

'It was a long time ago. Ten years.'

'How old was she?'

'Twenty-nine. Anyway, that's not the point. The point is, when we moved in, the people we were sharing with were Paul, a guy called Bruce who moved to Liverpool to look for work, and Porky. So Porky's just been here as long as I can remember.'

'And was he nice back then? When you moved in?'

'No, that was later. Understand, O Queen, that Porky is not a nice man. Fat, aggressive, stupid, yes, but nice, no. There was a time, however, before he got fat, years ago, before Holland and Frances got the house and moved out and sold the house and moved back in, before Kate died and all, when Porky had something of a reputation as a wit.'

'I didn't know Paul and Frances had a house.'

'Yes. They moved back here about five years ago when old Miss McKernan downstairs went to live with her niece in Sidcup. Anyway, Porky: The Years of Struggle. Back then he was washer-up at the Pizza Pizza place in Preston Street, and although even his mother would have been forced to concede that he was essentially unpleasant, he was at least funny, in a bitchy kind of way. And you will have noticed that we can forgive much in return for a cheap laugh at the expense of those less fortunate than ourselves. But as he grew more involved with Pizza Pizza PLC, and progressed from his menial position to short order chef, to deputy under-manager and so on, right up to his current lofty status as regional director, his semi-legendary bons mots shrank in proportion to the growth of his big fat gut. Holland suggested that his name be changed from Porky to the Fat Cunt, and this has pretty much been taken on behind his back. His fabulous wage and company car—'

'Hang on. Isn't he called Porky because he's fat?'

'Good Lord, no. What sort of people do you think we are? No, he's called Porky because of all his lies, though Kate used to insist that it was because he fucked pigs.'

'I find it hard to imagine that even pigs would want to . . . would . . . ugh! Errr!' Caroline started giggling.

'Anyway, his fabulous wage and company car meant that nobody ever had the nerve to call him Fat Cunt to his face, just in case he might buy them a drink, which he never does. Well, Frances calls him Fat Cunt, but then she calls everybody a something-or-other cunt at some point, so he never takes offence. Truth be told, he never takes offence at anything, except being touched for money. Only Holland has ever succeeded at this, but then he owes everyone on earth twenty quid.'

'He owes me thirty.'

'Whatever. What I'm trying to impress upon you is that Porky is tight with his money. He does not spread it around and he does not give it to charity, or good causes of any kind. Take Live Aid; even Holland gave twenty-five pence. Porky just said that he wasn't giving any money to a bunch of skinny nig-nogs, and that they should go out and get jobs, as he had done.'

'No!'

'Really. So it was with . . . shall I call it some surprise? . . . that I reacted one evening, years ago now, when Katie was still here, when Holland came back from the pub and told us that Porky had put ten bob into a collection box that came round the lounge of the Eastern Star. I didn't want to believe it at first, but Holland's pale face and shaking hands showed that something out of the ordinary had happened, and I came to accept his story as the truth. We sat him down and made him some tea, and he told us all about it. Holland had been sitting with Porky, Black Barney and Bruce when a Greenpeace tin had appeared, being rattled in front of their faces.

Holland, Bruce and even Black Barn had all put a little coin into the box; Porky lifted his face from his beer, preparing to tell the collector to go get fucked, when he saw . . . her.' Blossom paused, and a beatific smile crossed his face. 'I can see her now. She was, I suppose, the prettiest girl I have ever seen. Pretty, mark you, as opposed to beautiful. It is an important distinction. Her name was Dorelia; she was about five foot three, with a face like an angel, and a cute little figure, and a halo of golden hair which framed her lovely . . .'

Caroline made gagging sounds.

'Yes, all right, I'm sorry. Only it is important that you get some idea of the force of her loveliness. She had that doll-like prettiness which women always assume men instantly go for . . .'

'Well, they do.'

'Not necessarily. I prefer what one might call handsome women. I am attracted to women with large noses. And you . . . you are, if you don't mind my saying so, while very attractive, not strictly pretty, and yet from what I hear, you don't do so badly.'

Caroline blushed, and looked at the floor. 'Who told you?' It was true. No one was quite sure how it had happened, or when, but the Bloomsbury Place rumour mill hummed with suggestions that Holland had somehow succeeded in his wooing of Caroline.

'Never mind that. I'm telling you about Dorelia and Porky. A couple of nights later Porky came round to see me. Now, at that time, before I had become fully aware of the futility of political action, I was a member of the Brighton Green Party. More than that, I was information officer for the party. As a consequence, the small library of books that the party possessed was kept here. Porky had come round to find out about environmentalism.'

'Fucking hell.'

'I know. I was a bit taken aback myself. Still, another recruit to the cause, I thought, and I gave Porky some stuff to read . . .'

'I didn't know he could.'

'After a fashion, yes. He used to boast that the only thing he'd ever read was the warning on a packet of fags, and that he never took any notice of that. But I've seen him reading the *Sun*, too, and poring over reports from work. But no, I don't think he'd ever actually read a book before I lent him *Small is Beautiful*. He asked me lots of questions, too. I was impressed. The next Saturday it was the Peace Centre Fayre in the Corn Exchange, and I was running a stall for the Greens. Mid-morning, Porky comes over to the stall, wearing a Greenpeace badge. "Christ," I said, "you have moved quickly." "I'm a member," he said. And he was. He had joined Greenpeace, that morning, at the Greenpeace stall. "I'm pleased," I said. "How are you getting on with the book?" "I've finished it," he said. "Come and meet Dorelia." So he took me over to the Greenpeace stall, and introduced me to the divine Miss D. She was seventeen, and still at school, and pretty as . . .'

'Yes, yes, you've told me. Get on with it.'

' "Kenny told me that you were in the Greens," she said.'

'Who is Kenny?' asked Caroline.

'Porky. That's his name. "Yes," I said, "and he tells me that he's joined your outfit." "We're lucky to have him," she said. "I'm helping Dorelia with the stall," he said. And he was. Porky, the most hate-filled son of a cunt that I've ever met in my life, was helping at the Greenpeace stall. It knocked me back a bit, made me think. About my own politics. I date my own inexorable drift to the right from that morning. And then that night in the pub, Porky came in with Dorelia. Kate and Frances looked at each other, and I thought that they were going to be funny. But they weren't; they were almost as nice to her as was Porky himself. And that was saying something, because Porky was being quite incredibly nice. He listened to what she said, he laughed at her jokes, he didn't tell any of his jokes, he bought her drinks, he looked serious as she spoke of her concern for whales . . .'

'That must have been difficult for you to sit through.'

'No, not really. I hardly ever bothered to explain about *In Southern Waters*. Now I come to think of it, Porky did tell her that I was very keen on whales too, though he didn't go into it. So the evening passed very pleasantly, with none of the screaming matches between Porky and Frances that we've all come to expect and not always enjoy on a night out. And after the pub Dorelia came back here and had her first-ever spliff, and still Porky was as solicitous as anything, and he drove her home. After they had gone (by this time Porky had moved out of here and up to Elm Grove) Kate and Frances started pissing themselves. And for why? Because, they claimed, Dorelia was quite clearly a virgin, and they declared that Porky had no chance with her; no chance whatsoever. I must admit that I agreed with them at first, but over the next month or so, I became unsure. Porky was so sincere. He never went anywhere without his Greenpeace badge, he tutted at the news, he insisted to Frances that men needed to be more in touch with their feelings; I can't say for sure, but I think he even voted SDP at the 'eighty-three election, held about this time. I came to believe that Dorelia had changed him for the better, and for six months or so they seemed inseparable at weekends, though at night, of course, she always retreated to her parents' place in Woodingdean. They held hands the whole time, and Dorelia would allow Porky to steal a chaste kiss on occasion. In her holiday from school, they went away together and spent a week at the Peace Camp at Molesworth, sharing a tent. Just before they went, I asked Porky if he hoped to shag her at last on this trip. "She's not that sort of a girl, Bob," he said, and Kate told me that Dorelia had told her that Porky had never once lunged at her, or even so much as tried to force his hand up inside her bra. It was becoming frightening. They returned from the Peace Camp, and Kate reckoned from Dorelia's eyes that she had now fallen in love with Porky, though she guessed that they had still not done the deed. Dorelia began taking Porky back to Woodingdean to meet her folks, and she told us that her parents were charmed by Kenneth. No one here, with our many years of knowing Porky, could easily come to terms with the idea of anybody being charmed by him; but there it was. Dorelia clearly trusted him implicitly, as did her parents; and so when, in the August of that year, we decided to hold a birthday party for Kate, Dorelia's parents were quite happy for her to stay at Porky's flat, so that Porky could have a few ales. It was a great party; everyone was rat-arsed, or stoned out of their tree, or both. Everyone danced, there were no fights, only one sad fucker lost a contact lens, and everybody seemed to be having a great time. Dorelia was the belle of the ball; her lovely face was flushed red with excitement and drink; I remember watching as she danced around the front room to ABC,* looking really young and joyous and full of life. And she had eyes only for her man; for Porky, who seemed to be drinking nothing but orange juice. They left at about two, Dorelia clinging, I should say merrily rather than drunkenly, to his arm; I watched them get into a taxi. Kate insisted that it was all about to go off, and she was right. Four o'clock the next afternoon, Porky comes round, and Kate lets him in. Porky walks into the kitchen and sits down, grinning all over his face. He winks at me, and picks a virtual pubic hair from between his front teeth. "Gone off then?" I asked. "Fucked her! Blood all over me fucking sheets!" he said. "All

* 'Poison Arrow' – still quite a good record, I think.

right, Porky, there's no need for that," said Kate. "Where is Dorelia?" "Dunno. She got the bus home." And it was true. He'd fucked her, and then told her to fuck off. And that was it. He never saw her again; refused to speak to her, though she used to ring in tears, pleading with him. And as for the environmentalism, that went right by the board. It was back to the old Porky. Instantly.'

'The fat cunt. The fat cunt!'

'And she loved him, you know. But really. He was her first real full-blooded love. And he'd been so kind; he had waited for her, he'd let it all happen at her pace, he was so thoughtful and so sincere. And do you know why? Why he did all that? Played all those games?'

'No.'

'For a bet. The night after he'd met her he was boasting he could shag her, and Holland bet him a tenner he'd get nowhere.'

Caroline looked up at Blossom.

'Paul's not like that.'

'Oh, little one. Conchita. You know perfectly well that Paul's just like that.'

'Yes, but it was Porky who took the bet. Paul says anything for a laugh.'

'Yes, that's right. Paul says anything at all for a bit of fun.'

'Poor Dorelia,' said Caroline quietly.

'Have you ever really lost someone you love, irretrievably and for ever? Where you can never see the person again, where you can't ever say anything that might make things right, or at least bearable? Have you ever lost someone you loved so much that you wake up in the night, and you have to go and throw up, and empty the fridge into your aching empty gut, throw up again, and then sleep all day? That never goes, that kind of stuff. And that's how it was for Dor. I know because she used to come and talk to Kate, who tried to tell her the truth, but she wasn't having any. It was her fault; she should have let Kenny sleep with her earlier, she shouldn't have let Kenny sleep with her at all . . . and so on. She stopped coming after a bit.'

'Poor Dorelia,' said Caroline again.

'I saw her a couple of years ago, at a wedding. She said that she'd heard about Kate, and was sorry; she was married now, and she was a sculptress, quite a successful one. There was a picture of her in the *Sunday Times* last year, standing in front of a vase full of dried twigs at her place in Suffolk. I showed it to Porky. He smirked, and called her a little scrubber.

' "I still got the stain on my sheet," he said. And I hit him.'

'You didn't?'

'I'm afraid I did. Hit him in the face. I enjoyed it, he needed it; it was a mutually beneficial experience.'

Caroline looked at Blossom as he wandered across to the ghetto blaster and turned over his tape. She smiled at him and lit a cigarette, a new affectation without which she could no longer imagine finding the will to live. And then her brow furrowed, and she took a short hard drag on her bifta, and said, 'So why the fuck DO you put up with him?'

Blossom sighed.

'I told you,' he said. 'He's our mate.'

'Oh but why? After all you've told me?'

'Because women love men, but men love their mates. And that's it.'

'That's it?'

'That's it.'

The Free Baby

'That's it?'

'Yup.'

'I hate men sometimes.'

'Probably a wise move.'

Caroline stood, and put on the kettle for more coffee. She did not speak, and Blossom watched as she moved about the kitchen, rinsing cups, spooning in Gold Blend, fetching semi-skimmed milk from the ancient refrigerator. He was aware that she had been upset by the story about Porky, and he was aware too that it was the fact that he had accepted the bet from Holland that had upset her in particular. He did not want to enquire too closely as to what exactly was going on; nor did he wish to see Caroline hurt. She sat down opposite him again, and handed him his mug of coffee.

'Tell me about Paul,' she said.

'Oh no, please don't make me do that.'

'Please. Why doesn't anyone trust him?'

Blossom sighed again. 'Oh come on, Caroline. Leave it out.'

'No, please. You tell me why. Frances has told me why. Please.'

The Spector tape had finished; instead Blossom and Caroline could hear Porky being ejected by Sailor Dave, who joined them in the kitchen.

'David,' said Blossom. 'Caroline has asked me why nobody trusts Paul.'

Sailor Dave smiled grimly.

'David, what can I tell her?'

Sailor Dave shrugged. 'What about when Holland looked after Erica?' he said.

Blossom looked puzzled. 'What . . . Oh! Yes! I remember. All right, come on, David; skin up, and I'll tell Caroline.'

So Dave made a little number, while Blossom laid out his second tale of the evening.

'Now there came a time – about, oh, eight years ago or so – when Paul and Frances lived in the little house on Southover Street, when a few people came to believe that Holland was not so black as he was painted. So long as it was nothing to do with drugs, money and cars . . .'

'Or wives, daughters and girlfriends,' said Sailor Dave.

Blossom inclined his head in acknowledgement. 'Quite. So long as it was nothing to do with any of the above, it had begun to seem as though there could exist circumstances, theoretically at least, where Holland might, to a limited extent, be trusted. For example, a friend who had been foolish enough to lend Holland *"Slade Alive"* when they were at school together was so moved when Paul turned up on his doorstep to return it that he lent him ten pounds. Then again, Frances had come home from college one day – this would have been, I suppose, the first year of her Ph.D., when she was still working to fund herself – and found Paul looking through the jobs vacant column in the *Argus*. It was little things like this that began to lure Frances into a false sense of security; and despite her best instincts, she felt the faintest stirrings of trust. She'd taken to sending him to the shop, with cash, to buy bread and milk, and sometimes he even handed over the change. One evening, after he'd taken Frances out on the proceeds of her grant cheque, she allowed him to walk the baby-sitter home; he was only gone ten minutes, and on his return showed no obvious signs of having been slapped. On a couple of occasions, Frances had allowed Holland to take the baby up the park in her buggy, and these excursions had been largely incident free.

'So when, on a particular Saturday in July, Frances's agency phoned offering a day's work demonstrating sausages in a local superstore, she turned after a moment's hesitation to Holland and asked if he would look after the baby. Old Dolly downstairs who often looked after her was away; there seemed no alternative but to entrust Holland with the task, or lose fifty quid. He was, after all, the child's father. Much to his own surprise, he agreed.

'"I'm a New Man, me," he asserted.

'"Yes, dear. I'll be home about five. You'll have to give her lunch – please, not at the pub."

'"Nothing to it."

'"You'll have to change her nappy."

'"I've done it a thousand times."

'"Well, twice anyway, with me helping."

'"It seems like more."

'Frances sighed. "Are you sure you'll be OK?"

'"Course. You go and enjoy yourself." Holland has always viewed going to work as an indulgence, something done for pleasure.

'Frances contained her temper, instructed Holland in his duties, showed him where everything was, picked up her bag with her costume, and set off for the bus.

'Holland was a bit put out when the baby yelled for its mother, but he soon discovered that Jaffa cakes applied liberally stemmed the flood of tears, and he spent a not unpleasant morning attempting to entertain the thing. The baby had learned to walk a couple of weeks before, and would launch itself off on unsteady trips without any awareness of danger. It liked to climb up on to the armchair, and then to step off the arm; Holland had to move quicker than he normally preferred in order to catch the child. Nonetheless, by remaining alert, he managed to keep it from flinging itself off chairs and tables; and, as lunchtime approached, he felt an increasing self-confidence.

'The baby needed its nappy changing before Holland could tie it down in its high chair for lunch; so taking his courage in both hands, he persuaded the baby to toddle along to its room. He had not allowed for the baby wriggling quite as much as it did, nor for the fact that its arse was totally vile; but he managed to get the filthy nappy off and the baby's bum cleanish, at the cost of shitty hands. He smeared most of it off on the carpet and by pinning the baby down with one hand had managed to get the clean nappy half-on, when the doorbell rang.

'"Oh shit," said Holland.

'The doorbell rang again.

'"Oh fuck," said Holland. "Look," he said to the baby, "you wait here, all right?" And he hurried off to answer the door.

'It was Black Barney . . .'

'Why *is* he called Black Barney?' asked Caroline.

'Because he has a heart as black as coal. Shh. As you know, Barney is Holland's dealer – but he is also his mate; he tries not to rip him too often, or too badly, and if ever he feels like a convivial blow he knows that he's always welcome round at Paul's. This particular day, he had brought along a piece of draw as big as a baby's fist, which he held up for Holland's approval.

'"Come in, Barn," gasped Holland, "but quick. I've got a crisis upstairs." And much to Black Barney's surprise, Holland sprinted up the stairs. Barney had never seen Holland so animated before; he followed him up the stairs and into the nursery, where he was just in time to prevent the baby from launching itself from the open window.

'"Oh what!" said Barney. "You've got a baby!"

'"Yeah. Had it over a year, I think."

'"I remember Frances saying something about it, yeah. So shall I skin up, or what?"

'"I dunno really, Barn. I've got this baby to look after."

'"No, it'll help you, man. I'll skin up."

'"All right then," said Holland, his already crippled responsibility circuits closing down altogether. Somehow he managed to finish sticking the baby's nappy on, despite the child's best efforts to escape.

'"It nearly got out the window," said Paul. "It's fuckin' mad. It flings itself off things."

'Paul Holland, Black Barney and the baby trooped downstairs, the baby holding its father's hand, insisting that it knew how to walk down the stairs, despite very good evidence to the contrary. Holland strapped the child into its high chair and went off to heat a jar of goo, while Barney started to roll a major spliff on the kitchen table.

'"Where's Mum then, Paul?" asked Barney, sticking the papers together.

'"Demonstrating sausages."

'"So you got stuck with the nipper?" said Barney, sprinkling tobacco the length of the papers.

'"Right."

'"What, do you mind, or what?"

'"Nah. Women expect it these days, now they've got careers, and all that."

'"Well, so have you," said Barney, lacing the tobacco with dope.

'"No I haven't!"

'"No, I suppose not," said Barney, rolling the joint, inserting the roach and lighting up.

' "It's modern – not like in your day."

'Barney is – what – ten years older than Holland? He likes to tell of going busking with Clapton up Ladbroke Grove, dropping acid with Brian Jones, selling smack to Hendrix, and other such tales of the sixties, which Holland doesn't believe. Holland in turn tells of seeing the Pistols at the Hundred Club, fighting with Sid backstage at the Screen on the Green . . .'

'. . . pissing over Iggy Pop,' said Caroline.

'Yes, you've heard them all. All Holland's "Punk Rock, I Was There" stories. Of course, Barney doesn't believe him either, but they like yarning, and they shared a joint while Holland fed the baby its goo, another while he attempted to spoon yoghurt down its neck, a third while the baby rubbed food into its face; and a fourth as Holland released the baby to wander about the room.

'Holland and Black Barney felt themselves begin to unwind from the stresses of the morning, and as Barney rolled the fifth joint he told Holland of his experiences as a father.

' "I got kids," he said.

' "Is that so?"

' "Oh yeah."

' "How many?"

' "Difficult to say for sure."

' "I've seen a couple of them at your place."

' "Yeah. Di had two of 'em. But I've got others, I know."

' "Where are they?"

' "With their mothers, I expect. One of 'em's twenty-one."

' "No!"

' "Really. She's a student or something."

' "Where?"

' "Newcastle? Birmingham? Exeter? Somewhere like that."

' "Wow. What's she studying?"

' "Electrical engineering? Art? Sociology? Something, any-way."

'Holland was impressed by Barney's experience of parent-hood. The baby had been troubling Holland's ankles for some time, so he gave it another Jaffa cake while Barney skinned up.

' "Give it the fuckin' packet, man," said Barney.

' "What? The whole packet?"

' "Yeah, go on. Then it can get Jaffa cakes for itself when it wants to. It's never too early to start giving 'em indepen-dence."

' "Yeah, but it'll eat the whole lot," said Holland doubt-fully.

' "No it won't! Have a little faith. It'll take what it wants and leave the rest. Trust. That's what babies want. No one trusts the little fuckers."

'Well, Barney was clearly the expert: Holland put the packet on the floor and accepted the spliff.

' "Yeah," said Holland, "but you can't trust this baby too far, 'cos it's fuckin' daft. It just throws itself off things. You saw – it was trying to get out of the window."

' "Bollocks," said Black Barney. "Have you actually seen it fall, or do you just think it's going to?"

' "I seen it fall down the stairs," said Holland.

' "Stairs are different. They're made to be fallen down and tripped up. They project space downwards. Everyone falls down stairs. Your spatial awareness gets thrown all to fuck on stairs. No, most of the time you just reckon that baby is going to fall because you don't trust it. Man, you are *teaching* that baby to fall."

' "How do you reckon that, Barn?"

' "Well, as I see it," said Barney, absent-mindedly rolling another jay, "we get conditioned into all these straight, uptight roles, yeah, and out of all our free, natural, childlike stuff. You think that baby is going to fall out the window, but maybe if you didn't stop it, it would walk on the fuckin' air!"

'"Yeah," said Holland. "I can see what you're getting at."

'Holland and Barney looked down at the baby. It had a Jaffa cake stuck on its forehead, one in each hand, another stepped into the carpet, and one smeared up the wall.

'"There!" said Black Barney triumphantly. "What'd I tell you?"

'Holland was impressed; just as Barney had predicted, the baby had not pigged itself.

'"You see!" said Barney. "You just have to have faith! Trust! Believe in yourself! This baby does. If it believes it can walk on the air, then who are we to slap it down and tie it to the ground? Your baby can fly!"

'"Yeah! I bet you're right! I bet loads of things . . . like ESP . . . and . . . and . . . what were we talking about?"

'"Astral Projection!" shouted Black Barney.

'"Yeah, right! Out of body experiences and all that! I bet we have all that when we're babies and that, but we lose it when we get older 'cos it's all repressed out of us. And that."

'Holland picked up the baby and smelt its bum.

'"Right!" he said. "It's time this baby went upstairs for a nappy change . . ."

'Between them, Holland and Barney managed to propel the baby to its room; and while Barney held the screaming creature down, Holland cleaned it up and stuck on another nappy. This time it was more successful, Holland reasoned, because he was stoned. Black Barney let the baby go; it stood up, toddled across the room and started to climb on to the bed beneath the open casement. Holland and Barney smiled benignly at each other, and sat on the floor to see what would happen. The baby bounced across the bed, and pulled itself up so that it could lean from the window.

' "Yeah!" said Holland.

' "You can do it, man," said Black Barney. "You're free!"

'The baby climbed on to the window sill and edged along it. Holland and Barney stood to watch. It came to the open window, and stood with one hand on the frame, supporting itself, looking out and down – and then, with two quick steps, the baby took its first walk in the air . . .'

Blossom arched his eyebrows, and drained the cold coffee from his mug. Sailor Dave, who had heard the story a thousand times before, sat with his arms folded, staring at the ceiling.

'Yes?' said Caroline. 'What then?'

Blossom cleared his throat and continued.

' ". . . bad one," said Black Barney, looking at the squalling infant on the flower bed beneath the window.

' "There's going to be ructions about this, I reckon," said Holland, leaning out beside him.

' "Yes. I'd . . . I . . . I told Di I wouldn't be long."

' "Right." They looked down again.

' "I suppose it's all right?"

' "I guess. It's making enough noise."

'Leaning from the window, Holland noticed a bus pulling up at the stop down the road, and was struck by a horrible thought.

' "What time is it, Barn?"

'Barney looked at his watch.

' "Five past five."

' "Oh fuck. I think you'd better go."

' "Yeah. I think you'd better go and see to the baby."

'Holland and Black Barney hurried down the stairs. Barney plucked his much diminished stash from the table and pocketed it on his way past. He and Holland hurried out into the small front garden. Holland picked up the baby and wriggled its limbs about; nothing appeared to be broken; the rubbery qualities of babies and Holland's famous luck had prevented a major disaster.*

'Or so it seemed. For, as Holland had begun to realize when he saw the bus, Frances was home from work, and now she was coming through the gate. She saw her baby, covered in soil, a Jaffa cake stuck to its forehead, screaming. She saw Holland, flaccid with fear, and with the vacant grin she had come to associate with massive drug intake. She saw Black Barney.

' "Hello, dear," said Holland.

' "Right! Fuck off NOW, Barney!" screamed Frances.

' "I was just passing," said Black Barney. "I told Di I wouldn't be long." He hurried out through the gate.

' "OK, *bastard*, give me my baby, and *get in here*!" said Frances. She snatched poor Er back from her father, and marched through the front door.

' "Jesus!" she yelled. "Look at it in here! Where did she get all these Jaffa cakes from?"

'Holland mumbled. It had occurred to him that perhaps the Jaffa cake stuck on the baby's head had saved its life; or maybe it had somehow interfered with the energies from its third eye, and had thus caused the flight to fail. Either way, he didn't think it wise, under the circumstances, to say anything.

' "Right. Get cleaning," said Frances through gritted teeth. "And let me tell you that this is the last time I trust you with anything!"

'And, sorry to report, it was. The End.'

'Bollocks,' said Caroline.

Blossom laughed. 'No . . .' he said.

'It's bollocks. It's very funny, but you made it up.'

'I embroidered. But it's true. Holland told me.'

---

* If you want to try this with your own baby, it might be advisable to put down a mattress first.

'Ah, *you* trust his word, then?' said Caroline.

Blossom looked at Sailor Dave, who shrugged his shoulders.

'What can I do with her, Dave?'

Dave shrugged again.

'There's no telling some folk, is there?' said Blossom, to no one in particular.

'He's not like that now,' said Caroline.

'Anyway, hon,' said Blossom, 'truth is a social construct. Always make sure you pick your beliefs well, that's all.'

'Yes, but if truth is a social construct, how am I to discriminate between good and bad beliefs . . .'

This kind of talk always sent Sailor Dave to bed: he left Blossom and Caroline in the kitchen, attempting to unmask fundamental metaphysical truths so that Caroline could continue to overlook the facts of her situation.

Bad science, thought Dave as he climbed the stairs.

Weekender

Caroline knew that it had been a mistake to tell her flatmates about borrowing her father's car. She knew that the thing to have done would have been to park it around the corner, and sneak out to it, and generally keep it as her little secret.

'It's right here, I think,' said Blossom from the back seat. Sailor Dave, who sat beside her in the front, was snoring loudly.

Oh well, thought Caroline, I've never been to Wales before. That's something. It's a shame it's so dark. And pouring with rain. She took the turning as instructed.

'How much further?' she asked.

'Oh, about twenty, twenty-five miles,' Blossom replied. Which didn't sound like much, but she had been driving since three o'clock in the afternoon, and now it was eleven at night. She stared with sandpaper eyes at the road which wound in front of her up into the mountains. How had she been so weak as to let Blossom talk her into this trip? She could have gone anywhere this weekend. Christ, she could even have taken the ferry from Newhaven and driven down to Paris, and spent the weekend with Mary, her sister, who was married to an engineer at Renault. Oh, but no. Not she. She had to drive the breadth of England and Wales with a narcoleptic, unromantic drum roadie and a 'writer' who had never had one word published and who lived from betting on horses. And for why? And for what? So that Blossom and Dave could go and stay with some loonies who she didn't even know, had never met, and had only heard of that morning. Why why why why why why why?

'It's a shame Paul couldn't come,' said Blossom from behind her.

That was why, of course. She had planned to spend some time with Paul. Frances was taking her parents and the kids up to Scotland for a week, Cats had a gig with Wurmsbreth in Leamington Spa and wouldn't be back till Monday, and Sailor Dave and Blossom were planning to hitch down to Wales to stay with some old friends. She and Paul were going to have the flat to themselves for a wild three-day shagfest, *and* her father's car if they wanted to drive out for some quiet country-pub lunches in those moments when her thighs were chafing too badly. But at the last minute that hateful old bastard Jack, Paul's father-in-law, had insisted that Paul should accompany his family to Scotland, so that Paul, broken wrist and all, could pass on some of the benefit of his experience over the Royal and Ancient, and Turnberry, and so on. And there she was this morning in tears after Paul had phoned her sotto voce to say that it was all off, and dear old Bob Blossom, he never hassles her, never asks her why, he just does something nice.

'Stop your fucking whingeing, bitch, pack a bag, and drive me and Dave to Wales for some fun in the country. We leave at eleven,' he had said. With weary familiarity, Caroline now accepted that this was a textbook example of a project that had seemed like a good idea at the time.

She did as she was told, and at ten to eleven she was sitting in the front room, all nice and ready, when she realized that at eleven Dave would still be asleep, and Blossom still in the bath. She did a few bits and bobs, and was ready again by half twelve, when Dave got into the bath, and Blossom went for a lie down. By two she was becoming psychotic and by foaming at the mouth she had managed to get them out of the flat; though only as far as the Drive-in Café, where they ate fried bread, bubble and squeak, sausage, bacon and egg, and she ate margarined toast. Only bursting into frustrated tears had persuaded them into the car, a little before three.

Eight hours later, her eyes full of birdseed, her mouth as dry as Crockford's *Clerical Directory*, she was feeling a bit hacked off. Murderous, even.

It had been lovely through mid-Sussex, fascinating as they passed by Gilbert White's Selborne, Betjemanesque over the Berkshire Downs, enchanting through the Cotswolds and down Birdlip Hill into Gloucester and through the Forest of Dean, and majestic in the Black Mountains at sunset, but it had all been ruined when, driving in the dark past the Llynn Brianne Dam, Blossom finally admitted that it would have taken five hours less on the M4, but that this was, you know, the nice way.

It was almost over now. The last few twisting miles over the Empty Quarter of the Cambrian Mountains down into Llanstephan, Britain's smallest university town, passed almost too quickly. Caroline realized, as they drove at last from the alien dark into the homely sodium glow of the town, that she might feel intimidated by her hosts for the weekend. She was nervous. What little she knew she had gathered on the way down.

They were called James and Geraldine. They were married. They had a three-year-old daughter called Polly and a lurcher called Toby. She taught para-psychology at the college; he was a part-time lecturer in philosophy and a part-time second-hand record salesman. Both of them appeared occasionally on the television: he, apparently, had got only as far as Channel 5 and BBC2, whereas she had already done *This Morning with Richard and Judy*, talking about UFO abduction stories, *and* had co-hosted a Hallowe'en Special for Yorkshire with Michael Parkinson. Most thrilling of all, she was booked to do a *National Lottery Live* in the spring with her bit about intuition. She was Scottish. He had been at school with Holland; was, in fact, his oldest surviving friend. Blossom and Dave had met him through Paul, and had already been several times to stay at the Atkinsons' large farmhouse on the edge of the little town. Fine wines, vegetarian cooking from Geraldine and Nepalese Temple Balls courtesy of James would be freely available. And, as Blossom had insisted, late November is still really autumn, and it would be pretty and all.

Force-fed prettiness all day long, it seemed a bit intimidating at this late hour; what was worse, Geraldine and James sounded like her parents' friends, earnest liberals who didn't believe anything they read in the paper, unless they'd read it in the *Guardian*; although, Caroline was forced to admit, her parents' friends didn't take drugs like James Atkinson did, if what Blossom had told her that afternoon was anything to go by.

'He's the spliffing king. He gets up in the night for a joint. He puts all his roaches from the day before in his cornflakes, and eats them for breakfast. He's the only man in the world who ever tried jacking up grass. He appeared on *The Late Review* with a teenth up his arse as a slow-acting suppository. He taught Holland everything he knows about altering the human consciousness; turned him on when they were thirteen. Maaaaaan.'

They drove through the town.

'Which way?' Caroline asked.

'It's only about half a mile. I'll show you.'

A short way beyond the edge of the yellow zone, perhaps a little under a mile, Blossom ordered Caroline to slow down and look out for a track on the left; she spotted it, he hopped out to open the gate, and they bumped down a rutted and muddy lane for several hundred yards before they came to a halt in front of a large red-brick farmhouse, the light from the porch shining a welcome out over the yard.

Caroline poked Sailor Dave awake; he sat up with a grunt as a very tall man dressed like a rich skinhead advanced smiling towards the car, holding the hand of a little girl in a tartan frock. She was carrying a bicycle pump. They were followed across the yard by a dog that looked only slightly more aware of its own existence than Wuzco Thunderflash, Holland's moronic greyhound. Caroline felt herself tensing, hoping that she wouldn't say anything naff. Hoping that she wouldn't say naff, for example, which she was very much afraid was now naff in the exalted circles in which she felt the Atkinsons must move.

The weary travellers climbed from the car.

The little girl let go of her father's hand, and advanced on Blossom with her bicycle pump. She held it up to his arm, pressed home the lever, and said, 'I inject you with methadone.' Then she toddled round to Caroline, repeated the performance with the pump, and said, 'I inject you with thpeed.' Finally, she turned her attention to Sailor Dave; she drew back the lever of her pump and was preparing to inject him, when her father spoke.

'Hey now, Pollie-wollie. What are we not allowed to do?'

Polly thought for a moment; then her face brightened. 'Share needleth.'

'That's right, Polly-wobblers. Share needles. We must never share needles, even with a friend.'

Chastened, Polly backed away from Sailor Dave, while her father shook hands with Blossom.

'Hi. I'm James. This is Polly,' he said to Caroline.

'Hi,' said Caroline, nervously.

Blossom, ever the gentleman, carried Caroline's bag into

the house, leaving her to lock the car door and carry his bag in for him.

'I can tell you haven't been here before,' said James to Caroline as they entered the house.

'Oh? How?'

'You've locked your car doors. Not much car theft out here. Very little crime altogether.'

'How lovely. Did . . . I hope you don't mind my asking . . . did . . . is it Polly?'

James nodded.

Caroline rubbed her eyes. 'It's been a long drive. I'm sorry,' she said.

'For what? Here, let me take your bag.' James led her to a large room lined with bookshelves. A CD ghetto blaster stood on a large pine table in the centre. He deposited the bag on the flagged floor.

'It's Bob's. Thank you. No . . . it's just that I rather thought that Polly pretended to inject me with speed.' Caroline laughed brightly.

'Here, let me take your jacket. Yes, she did. We've been talking about drugs. I don't want her picking up nonsense at school.'

'Thank you. How old is she?'

'Well, she's three and a half, but it's never too early to start. Is it, Polly-Anna?'

'No, Jimmy,' said Polly, still holding his hand.

'Sit down, I'll put the kettle on. Geraldine's not back yet. Meetings.'

Caroline and Sailor Dave sat down.

James turned to the kitchen, and nearly tripped over the dog. Polly stared at Caroline. Blossom followed James into the kitchen at the opposite end of the room. Sailor Dave yawned and looked at the ceiling. The dog put his head in Caroline's lap.

'Toby likth you,' said Polly.

'Good.'

'But I don't,' said Polly.

'Oh dear,' said Caroline, with whom the feeling was becoming mutual.

'Do you know why?'

'No,' said Caroline, her patience fast dissolving.

'You thmell.'

'I do not!'

'Yeth you do. Dothent she?' said Polly, appealing to Sailor Dave, who shrugged.

'Dave!' said Caroline.

'Dothent she, Dave?'

Sailor Dave shrugged again, and nodded. Caroline was mortified.

'Told you!' said Polly.

'Cheeky little cow . . . you should be in bed, shouldn't you?'

James came back into the room with a tray. Blossom followed, laughing at a joke.

'Hey, Caroline,' said James. 'We don't like laying those kind of trips on Poll, do we, Polly-Olly?'

'No, Jimmy,' said Polly, who smiled up at Caroline.

Caroline pulled a face back. 'Doesn't she call you Daddy?'

'Hey! The last thing she needs is a patriarchal role-model.'

A car pulled up outside.

'Oh Christ! Polly! It's Mum. Bed!'

Polly shot from the room, and could be heard clattering up the stairs.

An attractive strawberry blond woman bundled in a fake fur who Caroline realized she had actually seen on *This Morning* came through the door and dumped a bursting briefcase on the table. She took off her specs, which were slightly misted, and rubbed them on her sleeve. She radiated unfocused smiling goodwill around the room, narrowed her eyes and looked at Caroline.

'Hi,' said the woman in an Edinburgh accent. 'Caroline, isn't it?'

'Yes. Geraldine?'

'Yah. Hiya, Bob! Dave!' She kissed them both. 'I'm sorry I wasn't here when you came. I was conferencing with a colleague in Manila on the net.'

'Not to worry,' said Blossom. Geraldine sat next to Caroline, and helped herself to tea. James put a CD on the ghetto blaster, and sat down himself. They chatted for a few minutes, while Geraldine drank her tea, then she said, 'I'll go and see if Poll is asleep.'

'She should be. She's been in bed for hours,' said James.

Blossom watched Geraldine leave, and then he said, 'Hey, Jimmy. I can't help noticing . . . I mean . . . we've been here twenty minutes or so, and you haven't skinned up.'

'No, man. I'm clean.'

Sailor Dave spat a mouthful of tea over the table; the colour drained from Blossom's face.

'You . . . you can't be,' said Blossom.

'Yeah, I am. Since the summer. I go climbing instead. And, of course, there's the computer.'

'Of course,' said Blossom.

'I feel great. Really. I'm really getting on with some work. You should try it.'

'What are you working on, James?' asked Caroline.

'I've been commissioned to write about the philosophy of the management sciences. It's fascinating stuff. I'm rattling through it. Don't miss the drugs at all. Hey, in fact, I'm going up the Brefi valley tomorrow, just for a bit of rock-climbing. Anyone fancy it?'

Blossom demurred, as did Caroline, but Sailor Dave said he wouldn't mind. Geraldine came back from kissing Polly and said that she'd take Caroline and Blossom into town to show them the admittedly limited sights, while James and the One-Eyed Sailor pitted their designer outdoor wear against the elements. She asked Blossom about *In Southern Waters*, Dave about his forthcoming tour with the Stranglers, and Caroline about her course. James talked about crampons and e-mail. In this way they spent a half hour before Caroline started to yawn, and Geraldine, intuitive to a degree, showed her up to where she was to spend the night. It was a tiny whitewashed room, obviously at one time the boxroom. There was a little icon of Christ above the single bed, a Clarice Cliff pitcher on an old washstand in the corner.

'It's very nice. Thank you.'

'That's OK. Bathroom's along the hall. 'Night.'

'Good night.' Ignoring the bathroom, Caroline took off her army boots, her long home-knitted black sweater and her fatigue pants and got into bed. She lay thinking about Polly. How dare she say she was smelly! She always had a wash, when she needed one; anyway, how could you be a real traveller if you smelt of Wright's Coal Tar soap all the time? Besides, Paul didn't seem to mind. With this reassuring thought, Caroline fell asleep.

She spent a somewhat disturbed night. Sailor Dave and Blossom were sharing the room next to hers, and they came up noisily and chatted loudly long into the night; or at least, Blossom did. If Dave ever replied, she never heard him. Much later she awoke to the sound of Toby barking, and her hosts shouting at him to shut the fuck up. Finally, when the sun was in the sky but her watch showed her that it was only seven thirty, she thought she heard Polly laughing, and what sounded like a motorbike pulling away. And at eight thirty she was woken for good by the sound of James Atkinson calling in the yard.

'Polly! Polly-wobbles! Where are you hiding? It's breakfast!'

Caroline tried to go to sleep again, but Atkinson continued to call.

'Polly-wolly-doodle-all-the-day! Where are you? If you're hiding that's very good, you've done very well, and you've won! Hooray! And your prize is a lovely breakfast! Polly!'

Caroline's bladder insisted that she should get out of bed and hurry along the landing to the bathroom. She could hear Atkinson calling agitatedly from the bottom of the stairs.

'Ger! Geraldine! Quick!'

Caroline enjoyed her piss, hurried back to her room to get dressed and then, curious as to the cause of the excitement, went downstairs. She found James sitting at the table with his head in his hands; from the kitchen Caroline could hear Geraldine whistling tunelessly. Atkinson looked up at Caroline.

'Morning,' he said. 'I hope you slept well?'

'OK, thanks. I heard shouting.'

Atkinson pushed a note across the table at Caroline. 'I found this letter in the letter box just now. Read it,' he said.

Caroline did as she was instructed:

Dear James and Geraldine,
   I have the kid. By the time you read this she will be hidden from you. You know what you have to do. You have until 6 this evening - and then...

love and kisses from
The Owner x

Caroline stared in horror at Atkinson, who looked at her intensely in return.

84

'Oh Jesus!!' said Caroline. 'Oh shit! Have you phoned the police?'

'The police?' said Atkinson with a bitter laugh. 'The police! What good are they? Anyway, it's Saturday.'

'What's that got to do with it?'

'Well, they'll be off fishing at Aberaeron with Hywel.'

'Who's Hywel?'

'The chief superintendent. No, the police are no good . . . listen, go and get Blossom and Dave. Quick. And tell them what's happened.'

Geraldine came into the room, dressed in a robe, a rolled-up newspaper under her arm, and a mug of coffee in her hand.

'Morning,' she said brightly.

'Oh, good morning. I'm so sorry . . .'

'Why?'

'The note . . .'

'He's got lovely handwriting, hasn't he?' said Geraldine.

'I hadn't really noticed . . . I mean . . .'

'Oh, please go and get the lads,' said Atkinson. 'Then I'll explain.' Caroline ran up the stairs, hammered on her flatmates' door, and by shouting loudly at their recumbent snoring forms managed to persuade them that they were needed downstairs in a hurry. Sailor Dave had even managed to get dressed; Blossom stood in his mackintosh, smoking, while Caroline sat at the table biting her thumbnail. Blossom and Dave were shown the note.

'Who is "the Owner"?' asked Blossom.

'He was my landlord before we bought this place.'

'And why has he taken your daughter?'

'It's war.'

'War?' said Caroline. 'War? Your little girl has been snatched away, and it's war? It's kidnapping. I'm calling the police!'

'Please don't,' said Geraldine. 'Listen to James.'

'The Owner and I have been at war for months. I managed to sneak into his camp and stick crow-scarers on to the roof of his palace . . .'

'What?' said Caroline.

'Then he came out here one night with some of his people and painted all the windows black. We slept till eleven in the morning,' said Atkinson.

'Which was a pisser, since I had a telly in Glasgow that night, and had missed the train,' said Geraldine. 'So I put a hex on him. He's very superstitious. I made him believe that the Lord of Cthulu was coming to eat his soul. The Witch showed me how. That was very funny!'

'So he hired actors to pretend to be police, and do a bust on us. They came and kicked in the doors at 4 a.m. That wasn't funny at all,' said James.

'So we nicked his Harley and had it hoisted to the top of the town hall,' said Geraldine. 'And now this. And she's left Lamby-Blue-Blues.'

'But what does he mean in the note? And who is Lamby-Blue-Blues?' asked Caroline.

'He means that if we can't get her back by six this evening, our army has to buy his army a pint,' said James. 'This is very bad news as there are . . . five . . . eight . . . eleven people in our army at best, and ninety or a hundred or so in his. And Lamby-Blue-Blues is her knitted kangaroo.'

'He's blue,' said Geraldine, by way of explanation.

'That doesn't seem very fair. It'll cost a packet if you lose,' said Blossom.

'Who cares whether it's fair or not? What about poor Polly?' asked Caroline. 'Won't she be scared?'

'Not she,' said Geraldine. 'She loves the Owner. The kids out at the City all have a great time. She'll miss Lamby-Blue-Blues though.'

'So what are you going to do?' said Blossom.

'You mean, what are *we* going to do. I counted you three as part of our army. Well, the first thing is, I'm going to get my emergency stash. My straight days are over, at least while we fight this battle. It's clear that we must get into his head space, as far as possible. And while we share several large cannabis cigarettes, I shall tell you the nature of the problem we face.'

James hurried off to get his secret stash from his office in one of the barns outside, and Geraldine made everybody toast. In twenty minutes they were all breakfasted and sharing a sorely needed spliff while James and Geraldine told their visitors about the Owner.

'His name is Geraint Tudor ap Llewellyn. He is an earl . . .'

'Really. He really is,' said Geraldine, clearly impressed.

'The fifteenth Earl of Maesyfed and, as he always insists, the rightful Prince of Gwynedd and Powys. He has a big estate over Radnor way but his younger brother runs all that, on behalf of a trust for the Owner's eldest boy, Two Dogs Fucking—'

'That's not true,' said Blossom. 'That's a joke.'

'An old joke, yes, but it is true. The Owner has, if nothing else, the ability to see a joke right through to the end.'

'I mean, essentially he's an acid casualty,' said Geraldine. 'As he tells it, he was at his college's May Ball in 1956 . . .'

'Chris Barber *and* Lonnie Donnegan headlining . . .' said James.

'When Rolando May . . .' said Geraldine.

'No!' said Sailor Dave.

'Yes! *The* Rolando May . . .' said James.

'Who's Rolando May?' asked Caroline.

'Man!' said Sailor Dave.

'A jazz saxophonist. Black, blind, and cool as fuck,' said Blossom.

'You tell it, hon,' said Geraldine to James.

'So the Owner is part of the Ents Committee, and he's trying to tell Rolando May, who has been playing at the May Ball, that he is cool too, that he even smoked a little "tea" at a club in Chelsea once, so Rolando May says, here, man, try this, and he puts a lump of sugar in the Owner's hand, and the Owner downs it. Soaked in CIA-issue acid. That was it really. The Owner forswore haircuts and decided not to try for the Bar after all,' said James.

'He did all sorts of stuff, though. He even spoke in the Lords a couple of times in the sixties, once proposing a bill to legalize blow, and once opposing the '67 Broadcasting Act,' added Geraldine.

'He had a pirate radio station, Radio Free. He financed it, bought the boat, kitted it out and all. He made a packet actually.'

'They broadcast from off the Welsh coast. Simon Dee started with them.'

'But now he lives on about fifty acres of land, up in the hills on the other side of the valley. You've heard of the Teepee Village?' James asked.

Everyone nodded assent.

'Well, the Owner lives in Bender City. It's like the Teepee Village, only much weirder. It's his land, so there's no hassle. Anyone who wants can go and build a bender on the land, and grow food up there and stuff; all they have to do is accept the Owner as their liege lord, and swear to give him military assistance in times of war. You see, a holy and righteous war against the forces of darkness is inevitable. According to the Owner, the world is controlled by demons. This was made clear to him when he heard "Out, Demons, Out" by the Edgar Broughton Band. He is protecting his people; they protect him.'

'Wow!' said Caroline. 'How cool!'

'Yes, it is, kind of. There's no homeless people around here, thanks to him. He lays on water, and there's some wind generators so they have an intermittent electricity supply, and he helps find all the materials for building the benders if people need them, and there's a little school up there.'

'It sounds medieval,' said Geraldine, 'but it's not. It's quite futuristic, in a way.'

'So Polly will be in this . . . city?' asked Blossom.

'Yes. He's got the granddaddy of all benders, with quite a few rooms, all turfed over. It's called the Palace. She'll be in there with the Owner, who she likes,' said James.

Geraldine nodded her agreement.

'Ah, but,' said Blossom, 'if that's the most obvious thing to do, then won't he have double bluffed you?'

'Maybe,' said James, 'maybe.'

'So what are we going to do? How are we to know?' asked Caroline.

'Ah!' said James, becoming increasingly enthusiastic as the first joint for five months started to work on him. 'We are going to apply the DIME shape to the problem.'

'The what . . . ?' asked Blossom.

'DIME shape. It's a model for problem solving. Management scientists use it.' James was talking very fast now. 'All problematic concepts, C, can be mapped against the DIME shape, where D equals domestication, demythologizing, defanging, demotion and desiccation, I equals irreducibility, the indefinable, the inexplicable; M equals the magical, the mythological, the mysterious, the miraculous and the mad; and E equals—'

'Excrement,' interrupted Geraldine. 'You're full of management school bullshit since you started doing your book. We know she's in the Palace, because it's right in the middle, and that's where the Owner will be.'

James looked disappointed and started to roll another spliff.

'What's to do about it, then?' asked Blossom.

'Well if we can't attack them and win, and assuming that they have her banged up at the very heart of their evil empire, then we need to try another method. We need a Trojan horse,' said Geraldine.

'Oh, what?' squeaked Caroline, excited.

'Or, to be more specific, my dear Caroline, we need a Trojan hippy. We need you,' said James.

'Me? You need me?'

'I know. Thank you. Now listen. This is what we're going to do . . .'

Caroline walked down the single-track road over the shoulder of the mountain, Pendollau. She looked the part in her clothes from the day before and her old biker's jacket with a lizard painted on the back. She carried a foul old rucksack that Atkinson had found in the back of his van. Her blue hair had been carefully matted by Geraldine, using a mixture of lard and dirt from the yard. Geraldine had also found at the back of the bathroom cabinet an almost empty bottle of artificial suntan, which had been applied to Caroline's face to give her a weather-beaten appearance. She was feeling nervous to the point of panic; but happy too, manic even. The rainclouds had rolled away; the sky was a brilliant blue. Rowanberries decked the trees; sheep grazed in the barren little fields. From the map that Geraldine had drawn up on her PC, Caroline estimated that she must be a little over half a mile from the Watchtower, the majestic 300-year-old oak which marked the gateway to the Owner's demesne. According to Atkinson, at least one of the Owner's people was permanently looking out from the little house which had been built in its branches; in the present crisis, Atkinson estimated that the Owner might have as many as ten of his myrmidons stationed in and around the tree. The first part of his plan was the simplest. When Caroline was in position, she was to signal with a hand mirror a little way down the valley to where Atkinson and his troops were waiting at their dispersal point in two Land-Rovers. Where the Owner, much like the People's Army of China, had a labour-intensive approach to problems of security, Atkinson Force was capital intensive, and trusted that they could overcome superior numbers with superior technology. The Land-Rovers were to come screaming up the track and pull up in front of the tree, whereupon Atkinson Force would emerge, wearing hard hats supplied by Bloke, Atkinson's builder chum, who was to drive the foremost of the vehicles. They were all armed with large pump-action water pistols full of piss; all except Nest, the Tree Surgeon. She, flanked by Atkinson and Bloke as cover, would be carrying her chainsaw, merrily whirring away. Atkinson calculated that the sight of this would scare away those of the Owner's people gathered around the base of the tree. Nest reckoned she knew enough about the Watchtower oak so that she could hack away at its base without doing any real damage,* but so that those Bender-folk left in its spreading boughs would abandon tree and make off towards the Palace, pursued all the way by Atkinson Force spraying them with piss.

Nest and Bryn, Atkinson's doctoral supervisor, who was in his late sixties if he was a day, were to turn the vehicles around, and have the engines gunning against the inevitable moment when Atkinson Force would come in retreat from the raid on the Palace. Because, of course, the scouts coming back from the tree would have alerted the Owner, and he would have released a large party to repulse the attack,

---

* Because, of course, Nest knew that it is silly and irresponsible to hurt a tree.

armed, Atkinson hoped, with nothing worse than cow-shit bombs and pine cones. Still, their numbers would be overwhelming, and it was Atkinson's desire that his force should retreat in some disarray, even perhaps losing one of the piss guns in order to give the Owner the impression that he had bloodied their noses a little. Atkinson needed the Owner to feel a temporary elation, to receive the impression of a breathing space.

The road bent a little to the right. Caroline could see the half-tumbled cottage from the overgrown garden of which she was to signal her readiness, and in which she was to wait and listen. Before she pushed aside the rotted gate hanging off its hinges which marked the entrance to the garden, she pulled a hand mirror from her rucksack and flashed it down the valley as instructed.

She could hear engines starting up beneath her. She sat on a stump by the gate and listened to the sound of the cars coming up the road, the screaming of the chainsaw and, a little fainter, the screaming of the Benderfolk; she heard the yells of Atkinson Force as they ran towards the Palace; the much louder yells of the Owner's rapid response strike force, the Land-Rovers retreating down the road. Caroline didn't know what had happened, but she did know that she must assume everything had gone according to plan. And that she must therefore wait half an hour before walking on down the road to the Watchtower and demanding to see the Owner. She prepared carefully. She hid her memorized instructions and the map that Geraldine had prepared. She let the half-hour pass, took off her watch and hid that too. Then she strolled as nonchalantly as possible down the road to the Watchtower tree.

Four Bendies stood around its base; in one of the roots, just visible above the ground, there was what looked like a nasty wound. Caroline's instincts took over and, unscripted, she ran across to the tree, hugged it, and said, 'Oh you poor thing.'

The Bendies muttered approval.

'Did you do this to the poor tree?' asked Caroline in an outraged tone.

'Aw, man. No way, man,' protested the Bendies.

'Who did this to the poor tree?'

'Some well bad cats,' said tribesperson A.

'The army of the demons, man,' said tribesperson B.

'They attacked our sacred tree with a chainsaw,' said tribesperson C.

'How bad?' asked tribesperson D.

'Well bad,' replied tribesperson A.

'That's horrible! How can anybody hurt a tree? I'd like to string them up!' said Caroline.

The tribespersons nodded their assent.

Caroline looked around her; in the tree she could see the little guardhouse, with more Bendies hanging out.

'Where is this place?' she asked. 'I'm lost.'

'This is the Bender City, man,' said tribespersons A and C together.

'Oh what!' said Caroline in delight. 'I've been looking for this place. I heard about it in Bristol and walked here! It's taken me a week! Oh wow! The Bender City. This place is . . . like . . . legendary.'

'You have been looking for us?' asked tribesperson B.

'Yes. In Bristol they told me that I might find somewhere to live . . . and a place in the tribe.'

The Bendies looked at one another.

'Then you must meet the Owner,' said tribesperson D. 'Come with me, man.'

'The Owner said that we were all to stay here,' said tribesperson A.

'It's OK. The Demon Army will not try anything like that

for a while. Anyway, you have the pissgun. Come.' Caroline followed him down the track which wound down through the valley, away from the Watchtower Tree and deep into the Owner's territory.

'I am called Star,' said tribesperson D. 'What are you called?'

'Caroline,' said Caroline. 'Wow, this place is amazing.' Here and there among the trees were benders, ramshackle houses made from polythene and wood. Some had been turfed over. All were surrounded by little areas of cultivated ground. Every hundred yards there were groups of hippies, standing around, or up in the trees which overhung the track, armed with sticks and piles of cow shit and pine cones. As they ventured deeper into the Owner's strange territory, the benders came thicker, as did the hippies. At last Star brought Caroline to the largest of all the benders, turfed over completely. In front of it there was a clear space, with an elaborately carved totem pole in the centre. This Star described as the Dancing Place. In this space, at least twenty Bendies were sitting, smoking grass, braiding one another's hair, and playing the bongos. Two extra-large tribespersons stood beside the sacking door to the Palace, like a Praetorian Guard. They each had a catapult in their belt.

Christ, thought Caroline, no way is anyone getting past this lot.

'This is the Owner's Palace,' said Star. 'You must tell him that you have come as a seeker. He will welcome you into the tribe; and tonight, when we have won the war with the demons, we will receive you as one of our number.'

The larger of the guards spoke. Caroline was struck by his resemblance to the Chief in *One Flew Over the Cuckoo's Nest*.

'I am Kelvin. What is it that you seek?'

'The Owner. I'm told I must speak with the Owner. I have walked up from Bristol to join you. If you'll have me.'

'I would have you any time, pretty little blue-haired one,' said Kelvin, 'and normally you could go straight in and see the Owner, but in times of war we must be careful. Wait here. I shall see if he will receive you.'

'What *is* going on?' Caroline asked Star. 'What is the War against the Demons?'

Star smiled. 'This is an exercise, really. The demons are those who run this country; who run all countries of the world. Anyone who lives in the world of the demons is on the demons' side. There is one, known as Atkinson, who was once our ambassador to the demons, who we thought we could trust, who has now joined forces with them. In preparation for the final day of reckoning, we have been skirmishing with him all this year. Now we have taken his daughter hostage.'

Caroline began to feel frightened. She still trusted that these people did not intend to hurt Polly, but she began to see them as potentially dangerous; wackos whose beliefs might one day take them over the edge. The Millennium had a lot to answer for.

Kelvin emerged from the Palace.

'The Owner will receive you. He says that we need all assistance in the fight against the demons. Follow me.' He ducked his head and led the way into the Stygian darkness of the Owner's Palace. Caroline followed.

The Owner's Palace was essentially three interlinked benders. In the first Caroline passed five or so women, dressed as though punk had never happened, some of them clearly preparing food; through a crawlway into the second where three naked men sat cross-legged, meditating silently, a bong between them; and then into the third, hung with tapestries, a Persian carpet of great quality spread on the floor.

The oldest and fattest hippy Caroline had ever seen, and who could only be the Owner, sat on a large cushion in the centre of the floor, wearing a three-piece suit, with a Hawaiian shirt covered by his vast beard, his immensely long grey hair topped with a flat cap. Polly sat on his lap as he read her a story. They both looked up when Kelvin and Caroline crawled into their presence.

'Ah,' said the Owner. 'This must be the traveller you told us of, Kelvin. Caroline, Kelvin tells me.' Caroline had learned to recognize this voice from Jeremiah's visits to Bloomsbury Place. Undisguised by forty years of fast living, the Owner still spoke in the unmistakable tones of an Old Harrovian. 'How may I help you?'

Caroline gulped, just once, and batted bravely on, realizing that everything now depended on a three-year-old child. For the moment, Polly sat silent on the Owner's lap.

'I heard of your camp . . .'

'Ah, now we call it the City, you know.'

'I'm sorry; I heard of your city in Bristol from some friends; and they told me that you were trying to build something that was . . . real, and natural – and that you are the sworn enemy of the demons who have taken everything over. And I don't have a place to live.' Polly remained quiet, but her eyes widened.

'Ah . . .' The Owner sounded content. The line about demons had been an inspired choice. 'Then, my dear, we must see if we can't find you a little something here with us. Tonight, of course, you shall stay here with me in the Palace; tomorrow we shall set about helping you build a little place of your own. And we shall explain what it is that we expect in return.' He licked his corpulent lips. 'You have no, ah, partner?'

'No,' said Caroline.

'Then, once our little skirmish with the demons is over, we shall have to set about finding you one of those. There are several single men in the City and, of course, for a pretty little

96

blue-haired thing such as you, there would always be a place among my retinue. If you so wished.'

'Yes,' said Caroline quickly, choking back vomit, 'people have been telling me about today's war. What's it all about?'

'A game, my dear, nothing more. This child here has been removed from her parents. They are trying to get her back. If they fail, they must buy us all drinks at the Black Lion this evening. If they succeed, which they will not, then we must buy them drinks. It's just a game. We like games, don't we, Polly?'

'Yeth,' said Polly, speaking for the first time. 'But I do think my daddy will win.'

The Owner beamed. 'Isn't she sweet? So loyal. Do you like the blue-haired lady, Polly?'

'Oh yeth,' said Polly. 'Sheeth niyth.'

Caroline smiled at the little girl, and said, 'Well, I think you're nice too, Polly. Hey, I think I've got something in my bag you might like. Shall I go and get it?'

'Oh yeth pleath! Can she, Uncle Geraint?'

'Of course, my dears. You must stay here with me, Polly, while Caroline gets this thing. Not for much longer now.'

Caroline crawled through the rooms of the bender; past the meditating trio, past the hippy chicks, one of whom was now playing an acoustic guitar and singing of freedom, and out into the autumn sunshine. Star sat next to her bag; Kelvin stood guard over the entrance once again; others of the Benderfolk were gathered around in the Dancing Place, some of them preparing cowpat bombs. Far away in the sky, over the top of Pendollau, a brightly coloured speck was circling.

'Are you in ?' asked Star.

'I think so,' said Caroline. 'Has anything happened?'

'No, not yet,' said Kelvin. 'We gave them and their machines a beating. They will be trying to get more people. They are few; we are many. We shall win, I think.'

'Good,' said Caroline. 'I just came to pick up this . . .' She rummaged in her bag and produced Lamby-Blue-Blues, adding, 'I thought the little girl might like it.'

She crawled back into the bender. From what she had seen in the sky, she guessed that there must be about another fifteen minutes before the next attack.

Back in the throne room, Polly played happily with the blue knitted kangaroo, while the Owner asked Caroline about her walk from Bristol.

'It is a long time since I was in that city,' he said.

Caroline thought, me too, and said, 'It's changed.'

'Everything has changed,' said the Owner, 'and not for the better.'

Caroline felt her mouth drying. It had all been fine so far, but now she must keep him talking for another ten minutes or so. He must not send her away, or decide to move Polly to somewhere else in his camp. So she talked of traffic and crime and the export of live animals and hunt-sabbing and festivals and the essential evil of the scientific age and how crap science was and how machines and computers were taking over everything and how important it was to meditate and practise aromatherapy and not allow unnatural products into the temple of your body, except drugs, and how you must always wear natural materials next to the skin, until she sounded like George Bernard Shaw on acid, and all the while the Owner nodded and grunted in assent and Polly sat beside Caroline playing with the kangaroo.

At last the Owner spoke: 'I will lie with you tonight, I think, since it is your first night, and we shall be celebrating our victory over the demons. You will accept this honour?'

Before Caroline could say anything, shouting started from outside the Palace.

'Ah,' said the Owner, 'the demons are trying again . . .' and suddenly very loud bangs started sounding on the roof of the palace, and Caroline shouted 'Demons' and the inner sanctum of the Palace was filled with a terrible mechanical howling, for which even Caroline, who had known roughly what to expect, had no rational explanation. The Owner rolled from his cushion and lay on the ground covering his ears as he screamed in terror, and there were more bangs from the roof, and Caroline grabbed Polly's hand and guided her back through the bender, past the meditating hippies, one of whom had opened his left eye in surprise, through the first room, empty now of hippy chicks, and out into the afternoon sunshine.

There were panicking hippies everywhere. Overhead Maria, Bloke's lady, manoeuvred her microlite, leaning from the trapeze to drop fireworks on to the Palace, while a little further up the path the bulk of Atkinson Force sprayed the Benderfolk with piss. Atkinson himself had set up a large crow-scaring cannon, which he used as a mortar to shower the Tribe with cow shit. Once he fired, then he reloaded as his commandos covered him, and he fired again. But, as Kelvin had pointed out, Atkinson Force was small, and the Bender Tribe was large; the Tribespersons gathered their shitballs and charged Atkinson's position. Only Kelvin and Star had the presence of mind to stay by the Palace, where Caroline and Polly now waited watching the action.

'Daddy!' shouted Polly. Atkinson waved, but his situation appeared desperate. The hippies did not like being covered in piss, and they were frightened of the cannon, but they bore down on Atkinson, and he was forced to abandon his turd mortar. The bulk of the hippies chased Atkinson Force, once again, back up the path towards the Watchtower Tree and the waiting Land-Rovers. Her fireworks exhausted, Maria found a thermal, and guided the microlite down the valley and away from the Bender City. Kelvin turned to enter the

Palace, to see how his leader was. A firework still smouldered on the turf roof.

'Follow me,' he ordered Caroline. 'And bring the child.'

'No, it's . . . it's . . . it's not safe. It might catch fire,' said Caroline.

Kelvin turned to look at her. 'You will do as you are told. Bring the child.'

'Fuck off, freaky,' said Polly, still gripping Lamby-Blue-Blues, whose tail seemed to have become detached from its body in the midst of all the excitement.

'Polly!' said Caroline, in genuine surprise.

'Don't call me freaky,' shouted Kelvin, advancing on Polly and Caroline. Polly screamed.

'Don't you dare touch this child,' said Caroline. Where was phase three? Had something gone wrong? Stragglers were returning to the Dancing Place in triumph from the second rout of Atkinson Force. Was Caroline supposed to cope alone, to improvise?

No. At last she heard the roaring engine from behind the Palace.

'Quick!' shouted Star as he came back from the chase. 'There are more of them coming up the back way.' He was right. Bloke had an old jeep, which he had piloted up the deserted track from the other side of Pendollau. As Atkinson had hoped, the Owner had neglected to post sufficient guards on this overgrown green road. Bloke skidded into the Dancing Place in front of the Palace. Geraldine and Sailor Dave leaped from the back of the jeep and advanced towards Kelvin, who was still trying to grab Polly. Even now, Caroline could not see how Geraldine and Sailor Dave would be able to snatch Polly back and get her into the jeep in the face of the rapidly growing crowd of Benderfolk who were bearing down upon them. But she had underestimated Atkinson's insight into hippy psychology.

Before the hippies could grab Geraldine and Dave, they produced their secret weapons. Geraldine brandished a pork chop, while Sailor Dave whirled a string of sausages around his head. Meat to a hippy is like kryptonite to Superman. If they come too close to it, they lose all their powers of double thinking, prevarication, procrastination and vagueness.

'Look out!' screamed Star. 'They've got meat!' The tribespersons fell back in fear.

'Quick!' shouted Bloke. 'Into the jeep!' Shielded by the meat, Caroline and Polly made for the jeep; Geraldine and Sailor Dave hopped in after them, and Bloke drove as fast as he could up the track towards the Watchtower. As Caroline turned for the last time to look back at the Palace, she could see the vast bulk of the Owner crawling from the entrance.

'Hello, Poll,' said Geraldine. 'Had fun?'

'Oh yeth, thank you, Mummy. Uncle Geraint *ith* funny!'

'I didn't like him much,' said Caroline. 'He wanted to sleep with me.'

'Ever shagged an aristo?' asked Geraldine, as the jeep passed the Watchtower Tree and turned back on to the road.

'No,' said Caroline.

'Me neither. I wouldn't mind, though.'

Caroline laughed. 'Not with the Owner, surely?'

'No. No, perhaps not.' Geraldine leaned across and kissed Caroline on the cheek. 'Thanks, Caro. You were brilliant.'

'I didn't tell, did I, Caroline?' asked Polly.

'No. You were very good.'

'I like you now.' And Caroline hugged Polly, and gave her a kiss.

Back at the dispersal point to which Caroline had signalled with her mirror, Atkinson Force stood, pissguns hanging by their sides, covered in cow shit, cheering as the jeep pulled into view. In a little field, Maria had landed her microlite, and Bryn was helping her from the harness. Atkinson lifted Polly from the jeep, while Blossom and Nick Drugs, Atkinson's dealer, lofted Caroline on to their shoulders and carried her through the cheering crowd.

Atkinson called for hush and Caroline hopped down, smiling and blushing.

'And now,' said Atkinson, 'to the Black Lion. The drinks are on the Owner!'

Later that evening, the Owner stood with Atkinson and Caroline at the bar.

'You were very good,' he said to Caroline. 'If ever you feel like coming back . . .'

'No thanks,' said Caroline, 'but thanks all the same.'

'The meat trick was a bit nasty.'

'Oh well,' said Atkinson, 'all's fair in love and war.'

'You are right, of course. There is just one thing I don't understand.'

'What's that?'

'In the Palace, as the first of the bombs fell, there was a terrible high-pitched screaming. Scared me shitless. How did you do that?'

'Yeah, I didn't know what that was, either,' said Caroline.

'I'll show you,' said Atkinson. 'Polly! Come over here.' Polly, who had been sitting by the fruit machine with Bryn and Nick Drugs sipping Coke from a bottle through a straw, hopped off her stool and toddled over. She was still carrying her blue knitted kangaroo.

'Darling, show Uncle Geraint Lamby-Blue-Blues' little secret.'

Polly smiled, and pulled off the kangaroo's tail; the terrible howling filled the bar.

'It's her My First Rape Alarm. We hid it in the kangaroo in case she ever got into trouble.'

Caroline looked at Polly. 'Did you have this in bed with you last night?' she asked.

'Oh yeth.'

'So why didn't you pull his tail off when the Owner came and kidnapped you? Then you'd have woken your mummy and daddy up, and they could have rescued you straight away.'

'Yes. Very good point actually, Caroline,' said Atkinson. 'There are several useful models which might enable us to map these kinds of informal decision-making processes, including SPUM, PLUF diagrams, and Balochevsky-Horowitz analysis . . .'

'Shut up, darling,' said Geraldine.

'Coth I didn't want to,' replied Polly.

'CIDWaT,' said the Owner, helpfully.

The Gay Deceiver

Blossom usually spent Christmas with his mother in Northamptonshire, but this year she had phoned him on the twenty-first to announce that she had been offered a special seasonal pensioner's break in Torremolinos with her friend Mr Evans, all paid for, and would her only begotten child mind terribly if she went off to the sun instead of labouring over turkey and sprouts and pudding all day? Oddly, Blossom found that he did mind. He went 'home' only once a year now, and he always looked forward to having a drink in the Plough with some of his old schoolmates on Christmas Eve; not to mention his mother's cooking, and to taking the dog for walks along the canal. And the canal would be frozen, probably; he enjoyed his native landscape, which would at least be enjoying a seasonal frost, unlike damp Brighton, where it now seemed inevitable that Blossom was doomed to spend the break. But, of course, he expressed himself delighted that his mother had the chance. He teased her a little about her growing intimacy with Mr Evans, and she told him that she would ring on the day.

Cats was going to his married sister's in Stowmarket, Sailor Dave was in Germany with the Stranglers, coaxing Jet Black's kit through another trans-European slog, and Caroline was already back in Haywards Heath. The Hollands were staying with Frances's parents in a hotel in London, Jeremiah was temporarily unavailable, and the Atkinsons, who Blossom phoned in desperation, already had a farmhouse full of Japanese anthropologists who were studying the behaviour of British academics at Christmas. He seemed to have a choice between going round to Porky's or spending the day on his own.

So he planned to spend the day on his own. He told himself that it would be fun; that he could live without all the hoohah, that he would eat baked beans and drink Veuve Cliquot and read and watch the telly and enjoy a bit of time to himself. Nevertheless, when Dolly Ashbrook from the ground floor flat phoned on the morning of Christmas Eve to say that she had heard of Blossom's predicament from Frances Holland, and would he like to have Christmas lunch with her and Bill and the family, Blossom jumped at the chance.

After a fairly bruising night in the Eastern Star, Blossom awoke late on Christmas morning. He had three parcels: one, a bottle of Denim aftershave from his mother, two, a mid-price CD of Gene Pitney's *Greatest Hits* from Caroline, and three, from Frances Holland, a newly published critical biography of Claude Lévi-Strauss. Blossom, suspecting a conspiracy, breakfasted on coffee and cigarettes, washed and dressed, and walked down the stairs to knock on the Ashbrooks' door at the stroke of one.

The Eel, as was his annual custom, was staying at a small hotel in Budleigh Salterton; but a fairly large company had assembled in his absence. There was Geoffrey the landlord and his sister Jemima from the basement, Bill and Dolly and their two sons plus spouses and five grandchildren, and a gentleman of perhaps seventy-five who was introduced as Vernon, an old RAF pal of Bill's. Dolly and her daughters-in-law were busy with a goose and a rib of beef in the kitchen, and Bill charged glasses with sherry. After some polite talk with Geoffrey and Vernon about the advantages of the pre-decimal currency system, Blossom quickly attached himself to Jane, the Ashbrooks' eldest granddaughter. Tall, coltish, sulking in a black minidress, she was aged, or so Blossom fervently hoped, sixteen. He hadn't had much luck on that front recently, unless you counted an ongoing flirtation with Frances, which Blossom didn't. He made little headway with her before lunch, but he did not lose heart. He hoped that as the afternoon wore on he might be able to lure her up to the flat, there to pretend that he liked Blur and Oasis, and would she consider a meaningless sexual encounter of some kind with a man (at least) twice her age? Lunch, as so often at this very special time of the year, appeared at teatime. Blossom made sure that he sat next to Jane, from where he was able to ply her with the little jokes and compliments which he felt sure would do the trick. The fact that she did nothing but sulk only served to inflame Blossom's lust, and he wished that Vernon, who sat on her other side, would lay off the unending stream of antediluvian jokes which Jane seemed to find much funnier than his, Blossom's, own.

He managed to get her to pull his cracker with him, and to smile at his paper-hat joke, but even the light of Blossom's almost pathological optimism began to fade in the shadow of her utter indifference; and at six, when the puddings and mince pies had gone and the brandy was coming out, he gave it up as a hopeless cause. He sat back in his chair, lit the cigar which Bill had offered him, and consoled himself with the thought that he had at least tried, for the first time in a good while. Now that he was able to relax again, he could take in some of the conversations from around the table. They were not especially edifying: Bill and his sons were talking about long ago family holidays on the Gower; Dolly and Jemima of footballers' legs; Geoffrey was noisily asleep; Jane sat on the sofa, sipping a Bailey's and regarding the world of adults with instinctive teenage contempt, while the younger children played around the table with the boxes that their new toys had arrived in. Old Vernon disappeared into the hall, and returned with a black holdall.

'Would anyone like to see some magic?' he asked.

Everyone agreed that they would – Jemima poked her brother awake, and the children, even Jane, no longer strictly one of their number, returned to the table. Blossom was only three feet away from the old man, close enough to see his hands, and he felt sure that he would catch him out. As he went into his patter, Blossom started to pay more attention to the old conjuror, and he noticed that he habitually spoke through his tightly clenched yellowing dentures, and rolled his eyes to emphasize his points.

With a flourish, Vernon produced two small plastic cups and eight old pennies, worn shiny with age, from his holdall.

' 'Ere we are, ladies and gentlemen. I 'ave 'ere eight pre-decimal pennies. If you would care to examine them, madam?' Blossom felt a momentary twinge of jealousy as Vernon held up the pennies for Jane's approval. 'I think you'll agree that those are quite ordinary pennies?' Jane nodded. 'So, I lay 'em art in two lines of four, all overlappin', like so . . .' He counted out the pennies. 'Now if you'd care to inspect these cups?' These he showed to Dolly, who peered inside them. 'In point of fact, they're just the caps off of some old medicine bottles . . .' Dolly seemed to agree, and she handed them back. 'Now I'm going to transfer one penny from this pile . . .' and, as he spoke, he scooped up the first row of pennies by covering them with one of the cups, '. . . and transfer it into *this* pile . . .' and he repeated the performance with the second row. 'Now I just get a pinch of woofle dust . . . it's four thousand pounds a ton . . .' and the old man reached into his pocket and sprinkled the cups with a little of the invisible 'dust', '. . . give the cups a little magic swirl . . .' and he moved the cups around the surface of the table with an insouciant motion of the wrist '. . . and, *voilà*, under this cup there are . . .' and he lifted the first of the cups '. . . how many pennies?'

'Three!' shouted the assembled company.

'Which means that under this cup there are . . . ?'

'Five!' came the reply.

Vernon pushed the second cup to the edge of the table, let the concealed pennies drop into his hand, and counted them out on to the place mat in front of him. 'One, two, three, four, five pennies!'

Everyone around the table clapped, even Jane, and her younger brothers and sisters and cousins squeaked appreciatively.

'Now,' Vernon continued, 'you should never do a trick twice, but if you watch carefully, you'll see how it's done. How many on this pile?'

'Three!'

And Vernon went on to repeat the trick, until there was only one penny left on the first pile, and there were seven in the second.

Blossom had sat with his eyes glued to the cups, and to Vernon's hands, and for the life of him he couldn't see how it was done. As the old man continued with his repertoire, which involved dice and gloves and packs of cards, Blossom decided to attempt another seduction, seeking this time, not Hot Teeny Sex Action,* but the conjuror's secrets. Blossom would never admit it, but he was a closet fan of TV magic shows. Try as hard as he might, he had never worked out how a single one of the tricks was done; accordingly, when the act was finished and the younger children were playing around

* For three-hour video, please make cheques and postal orders payable to 'Specialist 1-2-3', PO Box 23, Skelmersdale, Lancashire. Allow 21 days for delivery.

the table again, and while Dolly cleared away and Bill made sure that everyone's glass was full, Blossom tore his eyes away from Jane, who sat with her knees prettily together and her hands between her thighs, watching the television, and turned to Vernon, who was packing away his accoutrements in the holdall.

'That was very good,' said Blossom.

'Thank you. It's the speed of the hand that blackens the eye.'

'Were you a pro?'

'Bless you, no. I was in advertising. No, I used to do it for fun, for concert parties in the war. I was known as the Gay Deceiver.'

Blossom laughed. 'You couldn't call yourself that these days, could you?'

'Why?'

'Well . . . gay.'

'Oh . . . I see what you mean. No, I don't suppose I could.' The old man seemed annoyed that Blossom had spoilt the memory of his performing days and, sensing this, Blossom attempted another tack, one which in his experience had never failed to bring these old military types round to his side.

'So . . . er . . . were you in the RAF with Bill, then?'

'Sort of. We were in at the same time but we met after the war, through the RAFA. Bill was in bombers, I was in Coastal Command. I trained with the Yanks.'

'Really?' said Blossom.

'Yes, yes. I flew out of Gib, then later on Iceland. Protecting the poor hods on the convoys.' Blossom noticed that whenever Vernon cursed, he did so from the side of his mouth, so that the blue-pencil words, already clipped by his terrible dentures, all sounded as though they began with an aitch.

'There was a hole in the middle of the Atlantic where we

couldn't go with 'em. That was where the U-boats used to wait for 'em. Poor hastards.'

'People forget that thousands died in the convoys. Just imagine, even if you survived the torpedoes or whatever, being stuck out in the middle of the Atlantic, not knowing if you're going to be picked up, or, if you are, picked up by the Nazis,' said Blossom.

Vernon cocked a swivelling eye at him.

'Yes. Yes. I lost five.'

Blossom began to feel uncomfortable.

'Yes. Yes. I lost five of my crew. We ditched, didn't we?'

'No.' Blossom felt himself becoming interested and, reaching for the brandy bottle left by Bill in the middle of the table, he filled the old aviator's glass.

'Thank you.'

'What happened? That is, if you don't mind my asking?'

'Not at all. Yes. Well, it was after VE Day, as it happens.' Vernon laughed. 'After VJ Day too, for that matter, so it could have been worse. It was February forty-six. Funny, really, if you think about it; coming all through the war, and then . . .' Vernon sipped at his brandy. 'Yes. We had to go out over the Atlantic on met flights. Flying the old American B17s. That's what I trained to do with the American Navy. Anyway, we had to fly out so far at twenty thousand feet, taking temperature and pressure, and just seeing what it was like, and so on; and then we had to drop to sea level for a bit and do the same. Cor, that was huddy terrifying, that was, the old spray against the props. Used to keep the old landing lights on, watch the old waves. This time, I still don't know why, it all started to go wrong. Terrible huddy night, terrible. The engine packed up, didn't it, starboard engine, and we started to drop, didn't we, a thousand feet a minute; that meant we had twenty minutes. Yes, and I heard screaming, screaming from the wireless op, or the met boy, or someone

110

in the back – I never knew who it was, he sounded so terrified I couldn't recognize the voice. And me and old Paul, he was the other pilot—'

'Oh, you were the pilot?'

'One of 'em, yes. Yes. Me and old Paul, as I say, he was the other pilot, we're fighting 'er, fighting 'er in this terrible weather, this storm, and old Paul, the flight engineer – another Paul, two Pauls, funnily enough – old Paul the flight engineer, he's got out of his seat and he's standing between us and now he's screaming at us. Hrist, and I put on the landing lights and I watch this . . . terrible sea . . . I'd never seen a sea like it . . . we watch it in the lights, watch it, huge waves coming up towards us, and the flight engineer is screaming, and someone's screaming in the back, and then we clip the top of a wave, and old Paul the flight engineer falls forward and smacks his face on the instrument panel; and he's got a really bad cut, all across 'ere.' Vernon indicated his forehead.

'But, of course, there's nothing we can do, nothing. And then SMACK, we've ditched, we're in it, and all the lights go out. And the noise . . . yes. Yes, and the tail starts to go under, and the waves, the waves are thirty and forty foot, so I open the cockpit window, and I start to crawl along the huddy fuselage. 'Course, I can't swim, can I?'

'You are kidding,' said Blossom, more as statement than question.

'No. I can't swim. Can't swim to this day. So, I'm crawling along the fuselage, and it's blackest night, and all these waves breaking over us, and then I feel something with my hand, and it feels round, like one of the radio domes might, but then I realize it's the dinghy.' Vernon sighed, rolled his eyes, and took a slug of brandy.

'Yes. Yes, it's the dinghy. So nothing is going to make me let go of that, is it? Then, who else comes crawling along the huddy fuselage but Paul the other pilot, so I shout, "I got the dinghy!" And he and I get it free, and it's February, remember, and we're in the middle of the Atlantic, and if we go in the water, we've got maybe ten minutes, that's it, we're dead, dead of cold. And then, hugger me if old Paul the flight engineer doesn't call out, and he's on the huddy wing tip, isn't he? Though how he got there, I don't know, and we shout and shout and he comes crawling over. Hrist only knows how he didn't fall off. He's got a cut head, remember, but he stays on, and he gets to the dinghy too. Yes, me and the two Pauls.' Vernon paused again.

'Yes, and the waves, the huge waves. And the old plane starts going down, so we cut the dinghy free. And the others, five of 'em – they go down, they never got out.' Vernon stopped again, and Blossom saw tears welling in his red-rimmed eyes.

'They drown. Drown. But me and the two Pauls, we're in the dinghy. Full of freezing water, it is, you can imagine how cold that is on your backside?'

'Jesus.'

'Yes. And at first we're thinking, they know where we are, they'll find us, they'll come in and drop a flying lifeboat . . .'

'What's a flying lifeboat?'

'Oh, right, a flying lifeboat is a proper wooden lifeboat, with proper food and a radio transmitter where you just turn the handle and it sends out Dit Dit Dit, Dah Dah Dah, you know. They fly 'em out under an old Warwick and drop 'em upwind, so that they drift down on you. Well, of course, we heard later that they'd sent out a Warwick – later this is, when we got back – but the weather was so bad, it had to turn back halfway. So . . .' Vernon finished his brandy; Blossom leaned across the table and freshened his glass again.

'So, there we are, Paul and Paul and me, in the mid-Atlantic, a hundred mile north of the shipping lanes, in

February in a dinghy full of freezing water. Not funny. There's a tin box thing in those dinghies, but we couldn't get it open at first, it's all sealed down. We're supposed to do ditching drill once a month, but, of course, we never bothered, we just sign the sheets. And Paul the flight engineer, he's drifting in and out, because he's got this knock on the head of course. But me and the other Paul, we're trying to open this tin box thing, which is sealed with tape, and at last we get it open, and there's some iron rations and a desalination kit, and lots of stuff, and there's a Verey pistol, and a tin with three cartridges. But what's the huddy use of that? No point in firing 'em, is there? Nothing to do but wait. So we wait. Yes. And we wait. Maybe an hour. Yes, and then old Paul the flight engineer starts going "Lights, lights!" But he's a bit doolally by now, and we don't take no notice. Then he goes, "Lights!" again, and he's right; there on the horizon we can see mast lights. So I load the Verey pistol and POW! I fire it, up it goes. Heh, heh, course, in my hurry, I didn't really think, did I, heh, heh, heh, I fired him upwind. Course, the cartridges are on a parachute, gets blown back at us, heh, heh, lands about three feet away from us, fizzing in the waves. That would have been funny, wouldn't it? If we'd been sunk by a cartridge from a Verey pistol?' Vernon's face was alive with a kind of savage joy, revelling in the irony of his situation, celebrating his survival.

'Then we couldn't see the lights, because we're going up and down and up and down with these huge waves, but when we see the lights again, they've gone one over the other, we can see her port and starboard lights, and we know that she's found us, or at least seen our flare. So I let go another, making huddy sure this time I fire it downwind. But the weather is so bad, she can't find us. And we've only got one cartridge left. We watch her as her lights turn away

113

again, and old Paul the other pilot, he starts going mad, starts rooting through this tin box, and hugger me if he doesn't find another three boxes of cartridges. So I let them blast . . .'

Blossom realized that around them was silence, and that only he and Vernon were left in the sitting room. He looked at his watch – it was eight thirty. From the kitchen he could hear Bill and Dolly talking over the sound of washing up. Everyone else, including Jane, seemed to have gone.

'I'm not boring you, am I?' said Vernon. 'I go on a bit, I know, since my darling wife died . . .'

'No,' said Blossom. 'No, I'm gripped. What happened next?'

'Well, of course, eventually she finds us. She's eight thousand tons, a Liberty ship. Now, the biggest ship that ever gets into Shoreham is four thousand max, so you can imagine how huddy big that is.' Vernon rolled his eyes.

'Yes. Yes, and the captain brought her alongside a rubber dinghy in a thirty-, forty-foot swell, but she's broadside on to the wind, so as to shelter us from the storm. But, think, that's a big ship, and when it keels over towards us – Hrist! We're nearly sucked under, and when she rolls the other way, SQUARNCH, the old barnacles scrape against the dinghy and I'm sure we're going down. They've got a couple of lines down to us, but we've been in that dinghy three hours or more, and our hands – they're frozen, we can't grip, can we? And as the ship rolls those freezing ropes are running through our hands. Took the skin off. And old Paul the flight engineer, he's in no state to climb up the side of an eight-thousand-ton ship anyway, even in a dead calm. And we're dragged along the side of her, back towards the stern, towards the props. Hrist, that was it, you know? That was the worst moment of all.' Again the old man gulped at his drink.

'Well, the old captain, Thomas A. Hudson, in the end he

114

come down from the bridge, left the wheel, and they threw a rope ladder over the side, and the old captain climbed down that ladder and he came right down, right to the bottom, and he held on with one hand, and with the other he pulled us out, one by one on to the ship. Now, what do you think of that?' asked Vernon, his eyes rolling again.

'I think that's amazing,' said Blossom. 'Was she heading to the States?'

'No. Antwerp. She was overloaded, that's why she was so far north – he wanted that wind up his harse, not over his quarter. The SS *Edith Tubman*, she was. We were three days at sea, and old Thomas Hudson, as we came past Dover, he radioed, and a cutter came out and picked us up. Yes. Yes, and do you know, we put the captain up for a Humane Society Medal, and they wrote back and said that he wasn't entitled because he hadn't risked his life. Hanging on with one hand over the side of a Liberty ship in a forty-foot swell, and he hadn't risked his life!'

'Incredible.'

'Yes, and here's a thing. A few years ago, somebody showed me a copy of *Jane's Merchant Shipping*, and there she was, the SS *Edith Tubman*, mothballed in the Mississippi. So she's still around, too, like me. Though maybe it's time I was mothballed.'

With that, Vernon looked at his watch, drained his brandy, stretched and prepared to leave, and since everyone else had gone, Blossom too went to say goodbye to Dolly and Bill, who were just finishing the drying up.

At the door, Blossom shook Vernon's hand, and told him that it had been an honour. It was only later, as Blossom lay reading in bed, that he realized he had forgotten to ask how the trick was done.

The next morning, Blossom was just coming to when there

115

was a knock at the door. He put on his mac and hopped across the freezing floor to answer it. It was Bill with a plate of cold beef for Blossom's lunch. Blossom invited him in and, over tea, he asked about Vernon.

'Told you about ditching, did he?'

'Yes. A staggering story.'

'It is, isn't it? Hope you weren't too bored?'

'Not at all. I loved the tricks, too. I hoped he might tell me how he did the one with the pennies.'

'Not he. He's in the Magic Circle, you know. Funny, when you think about it, what people choose to tell, and what to keep secret. Five of his crew died, and he'll put himself through it again and again; but he'd rather have gone down with 'em than tell anyone how he does the conjuring. The Gay Deceiver!' Bill laughed, and rose to go.

'Thanks for the beef.'

'The missis and I'll never get through it. Bring the plate back when you've finished. Oh, and there was a message . . .'

'Yes?'

'My granddaughter Jane rang. Said that you'd offered to lend her an LP record of some kind: the Blurs, was it? They all sound the same to me. Very kind of you to take an interest. Look, here's the number – she said perhaps you could give her a ring?'

Bill left, and Blossom leaped about the room triumphantly, flapping the piece of paper and feeling that he was still hot, hot, hot. But as he sat to dial the number, he began to feel ashamed. Millions of guys like Vernon and Bill – and what, after all, was his story? – had given everything, or bloody nearly, just so that guys like Blossom could sit on their arses and seduce their sixteen-year-old granddaughters. It hardly seemed fair, somehow. He replaced the receiver, walked over to the window, slid up the casement

116

and threw the scrap of paper with Jane's number on it out into the wind, watching as it blew down Bloomsbury Place towards the sea.

Dynasty

Still dressed in his uniform, Jeremiah lay on the old bed that pulled out from the wall of his little bedsit up by Brighton station and shivered. He had just come off shift from his cash-in-hand job at Kemptown Fried Chicken, and so he had a little money, but had forgotten to get a fifty pence for the gas meter which had run out that morning while he was trying to make breakfast. He would go and get one in a while, from Mr Shah's on the corner, but now he was tired and wanted to put his feet up for a couple of minutes before venturing out again. It was cold in the flat, yes, but at least it was out of the bitter January wind. Blossom had assured him last week that Brighton station was the coldest place on earth, next to the Scott-Amundsen base at the South Pole, and Jeremiah had not laughed.

He didn't talk to his friends about his job much. Not that he was ashamed, far from it. That, for Jeremiah, was the whole point of his being here, to work so that he could pay for his Ph.D. in International Relations. In a free market he felt free to take low-status, low-paid work to keep body and soul together. He was rather proud of the fact that he was the first member of his family to get through college in this way. But it was not interesting work, frying chicken all day, and he had huge amounts of reading to get through, so when he saw his chums, he liked to argue politics, not talk poultry. To argue with one's friends, to learn from Mr Luff; he might be cold and tired but life, for Jeremiah, was good.

Mrs Norbury called through the door.

'Mr Farafan! Phone!' He hopped off the bed, opened the door, and followed his landlady down the hall to a payphone by the front door.

'Who is it, Mrs Norbury?'

'A lady. Very grand. Didn't give a name,' said Mrs Norbury.

'Hello, Mother,' said Jeremiah into the receiver.

'Hello, sweetheart! You'll never guess where we are?'

'London.'

'Oh. How did you guess?'

'Because Father always comes to the UK on one of his jute and orange junkets in January. You go to Dundee, you come down to London for the new year sales, you phone me up and invite me to lunch, I come, Father and I argue, you go home. Every year for six years. And you always say, "You'll never guess where we are?" How are you?'

'Well, things are a little difficult, to be honest. Your father and I were wondering if we might come and stay with you for a few days?'

'Mother, it's impossible. I only have a bedsit.'

'Oh, but darling, we must. You see, we're in the most terrible spot – Daddy's been deposed!'

Christmas out of the way, things had returned to normal in Bloomsbury Place. Frances's parents had gone back to NZ, the Eel had frightened Dolly's friend Josephine by shouting at her for sitting in one of his chairs, and several pairs of Caroline's knickers had gone missing only to turn up mysteriously in Cats's laundry bag. Sailor Dave was still off somewhere with the Guildford Stranglers, but otherwise God was in his heaven and all was right with the world.

With the new university term still a week away, the kids

already back at school, Frances had little to do in the afternoon but sit with Blossom in the top floor flat drinking coffee and running over the finer points of her parents' visit.

'It was OK, but the old man will talk politics with me, and he says stuff that he knows will wind me up.'

'Like what?'

'Oh, stuff about immigrants, and how lucky NZ is not to have any . . .'

'Hello? Isn't everyone an immigrant?'

'Yeah, even the Maoris really, if you think about it. But he won't have it. I try not to rise to his bait, but he's such a bigoted old cunt I can't help it.'

'I used to argue with my mum all the time about politics. During the three-day week, when my dad was still alive, we used to sit there by candlelight, the three of us, screaming about Mr Heath, and the unions, and all that. It's funny, when you think about it, 'cos old Ted was a bit of a hero in the 1980s, wasn't he? I mean, who else was standing up to the Milk Snatcher? It was Ted Heath, Harold Macmillan, the Church of England and the Prince of Wales. Very strange, really.'

'Do you still argue with your mum now?'

'Nah, life's too short. Anyway, she stopped voting Tory after the Libya bombing. Said that it was wrong to treat this country like an aircraft carrier.'

'Good for her.'

'Yes, but the horrible thing is, the older I get, the more right wing I get. It's annoying. My old man used to say that one day I'd grow out of Deep Purple and Uriah Heep, and like real music, by which he meant jazz. And he was right. And he used to say that I'd end up a Tory too. And maybe he was right about that as well.'

'No.'

'Maybe. It's talking to Jeremiah and the Eel. They make sense.'

'Oh, but they're not Tories. Libertarians, yes. But that's different.'

The phone rang. Blossom answered.

'Hello? Hi! We were just talking about you . . . What? . . . Oh, I see . . . well . . . yeah, Dave's still away . . . yeah, and Frances's folks have gone . . . hang on, she's with me now . . . yeah . . . I'll ask.' Blossom put his hand over the mouthpiece. 'It's Jeremiah. He's got some people from home stuck with nowhere to stay, and he was wondering if . . .'

'Of course,' said Frances. 'We can put up a couple, no problem.'

'Hello, Jeremiah? Yeah, Frances can do two . . . yeah, I'm sure that's fine. The Sailor's not due back for a fortnight . . . OK . . . now? That's cool . . . see you in a bit. No, it's no hassle. OK, see you in a bit.' Blossom put the phone down and explained to Frances, 'He was calling from the station. Turned up out of the blue, they have, looking for somewhere to crash. There's three. I said one could have Dave's room.'

'I'll nip down and get the spare room ready. Are they coming straight here?'

'Yeah, I said it was fine.'

'OK. Give us a bell when they get here.'

Frances and Blossom knew that despite Jeremiah's avowal of the unfettered free market, his own economic position was parlous in the extreme. He worked in a fast chicken place and received a tiny grant from a shadowy organization called the John Galt Foundation in order to pursue his post-grad studies at the university, but life was sometimes quite hard. There certainly wasn't floor space in the tiny bedsit which Jeremiah called home to accommodate unexpected guests. What little they knew of Jeremiah, they had learned from the Eel, who had introduced him into Bloomsbury. He was a political exile from a tiny African state and so they assumed that his friends must be fellow refugees, escapees from some foul regime. Both Blossom and Frances felt kinda cool to be putting up asylum seekers. Blossom poked his head round the door of Sailor Dave's room, just to satisfy himself that it was in its usual Spartan state. Not that any of the weirdos who occasionally turned up looking for somewhere to crash would care if there was fungus growing up the walls, so long as they could smoke spliff all night and sleep all day. Still, it was as well to check. Perhaps African political refugees were fussier than hippies.

The intercom rang, and Blossom pressed the bell to admit them. He rang Frances to tell her that their guests had arrived, and she came running up. They could hear the sound of voices coming up the stairwell.

'I've never met any of Jerry's friends from home,' said Blossom.

'No, neither have I. I'm intrigued,' said Frances.

Jeremiah arrived at the top of the stairs, carrying some expensive luggage; behind him came a very smart middle-aged couple and, behind them, a smiling white-haired gentleman in his sixties.

'Thanks, people,' he said, putting down the cases. 'I really appreciate this. So, Bob, Frances, allow me to introduce you to my parents. Their Serene Highnesses Martin and Maria, King and Queen of Farafangana.'

The smart middle-aged couple nodded.

Blossom stared open-mouthed at the couple; Frances went white, and dropped a curtsey.

'Oh, my dear, there really is no need,' said the queen. 'Jerry's only pulling your leg. We've been deposed.'

The king winced.

'And this,' continued Jeremiah, 'is Grand Vizier Cornelius, First Secretary of the Marxist-Leninist Party of Farafangana.'

'How do you do?'

'I'M DEAF!' shouted Cornelius.

'He's deaf,' said Jeremiah.

'Deposed?' said Blossom to Jeremiah.

'It's my brother, Martin,' said Jerry. 'He's organized a coup, the crafty old sod.'

'Where the fuck is Farafangana?' whispered Frances to Blossom.

'Off the east coast of Africa. South of Zanzibar,' said Jeremiah, overhearing.

'He's a traitor, that's what he is, a traitor to the principles of International Marxist-Leninism,' said Jerry's father with some bitterness.

'Don't be too harsh, Martin. Democracy does seem to be very much the thing these days,' said Queen Maria.

'Democracy. Oh, yes, we all know what that means, don't we? The hegemony of a deeply ingrained ruling class, serving their own interests and the interest of multi-national capitalism. He's a liberal bourgeois traitor to the class struggle, that's what he is. Little sod.'

Blossom and Frances helped with the cases, and got the ex-royals and their grinning son and their faithful old retainer around the kitchen table drinking cocoa and lemon tea, while Martin V fulminated against his eldest boy.

'Father! Calm down! What's happened?'

'You tell him,' said the king sulkily.

'Well,' said Queen Maria, 'we got into King's Cross from Dundee, and usually there would have been someone from the embassy to meet us, but there wasn't, so we phoned but it was busy. We thought, funny, so we got an *Evening Standard* and went and had a drink and your father sat and read the paper, and he saw this.'

The queen pulled the paper from her bag, and showed it round.

'What, "Portugese Premier in sardine talks"?' said Blossom.
'No!' snapped the king. 'Look!'
It was just a short piece:

Island Coup

A non-violent coup has taken place on the idyllic Indian Ocean island of Farafangana. Crown Prince Martin, heir to the throne, has been proclaimed king by the speaker of the island's parliament in the absence of his father, the despotic Martin V. A spokesperson for the new ruler says that full democracy will be established on the island paradise. Elections are expected soon.

'Despotic! Little fuckwit! He's a power-crazed little toad, always was, always will be.'

'So what did you do?' said Jeremiah.

'Well, we hurried off to the embassy, and the ambassador demanded the return of our passports, so your father hit him.' When the queen said this, the king smiled for the first time. 'Then the ambassador told us that all our assets were frozen, and we went off to the bank, and they said we couldn't have any more cash. All we had was the £200 I got out to get some new duvet covers for the Royal People's Bungalow. So we phoned Jerry. And then,' the queen said, dabbing at her eye with a tissue, 'if that wasn't awful enough, we had to come down to Brighton by Connex South Central.'

'And here you are now,' said Frances, 'and very welcome too.'

The ex-king turned to his son. 'I bet he abolishes the People's Militia and sets up a standing army.'

'No, there'll be no demand for it,' said Jeremiah (now revealed to Frances and Blossom as His Royal Highness the Prince Jeremiah of the People's Second Administrative Division).

'Demand?' said the king. 'Demand? What's demand got to do with it?'

'Well, you're the one who always goes on about the people's will. I mean, what could be a clearer indication of their will than the expression of needs in a free and open market?' said Jeremiah.

'Market, market, market. That's all you ever care about, isn't it, the bloody marketplace. People have needs beyond the acquisition of material goods, son,' said Martin.

'Do they argue all the time, your majesty?' whispered Frances into Maria's ear.

'I'm afraid so. It's even worse when Marty's about. They see things so very differently. It's their education, you see. My husband went to Eton and Cambridge back in the fifties, so of course he's a terrible old-style communist. He didn't believe in his children getting a privileged education, so we sent Marty to Fettes and Oxford, and I'm afraid he's turned out a screaming Social Democrat. Blairite revisionist scum, my husband calls him. Well, realizing his mistake, Martin insisted that Jerry be sent to Harrow and the LSE, which were regarded as quite sound in my husband's day, but that was the worst of all, and he's turned into a fervent free-marketeer. If only they'd listened to me.'

'What did you want for them?'

'Gordonstoun and St Andrews. Rough 'em up a bit. But it wasn't to be . . .'

The ex-king and his son argued on, with Blossom, who fancied himself as a barrack-room political philosopher, trying to keep up to speed. Unfortunately, Blossom was a mild agnostic in every area of human existence except whaling, and so although he could understand most of the argument, the passion which the protagonists brought to the debate was quite beyond him, and he felt excluded. After a hopeless attempt to engage Cornelius in conversation, he sat silent in his own kitchen while father and son raged, Frances and the queen whispered and Cornelius smiled at the wall. Finally, Blossom managed to get a word in.

'I hope you don't mind my asking, Martin, but how did you square Marxism with being a hereditary monarch?'

Martin looked at him. 'Well . . . it wasn't easy at first. I thought about giving up the throne and becoming President-for-Life instead at one time. But Maria talked me out of it. She liked all the dresses and everything.'

'Anyway, there was no demand in the market for your abdication, was there? The consumer preference at home has always been, quite clearly, for a monarchy of some kind,' said Jeremiah.

'What's that got to do with anything?' said Martin.

Blossom gave up, and made some more cocoa.

'Excuse me,' said Frances, 'but I expect you're all hungry. You're more than welcome to eat with us tonight. You too, Bob.'

'Er . . . thanks,' said Blossom, who was already dreading having to sit through hours more debate.

Maria and Martin nodded their thanks, but Jeremiah said, 'Listen, Frances, I hope you don't think I'm being rude, but could we ask the Eel as well?'

Frances was not particularly surprised as she knew that the Eel was Jeremiah's mentor, so she agreed, and left the debate to start preparing dinner. She had never cooked for royalty before, even ex-royalty; it was exciting, like that dream everyone is supposed to have where the Queen comes to tea. She phoned down to the ground floor flat, where the Eel in his turn was unsurprised at being invited; Jeremiah had already apprised him of the situation, and he had taken his dinner jacket to the One-Hour Dry Cleaners on St James's Street.

'It's not going to be formal, Edgar,' said Frances into the

receiver, a little shortly. She was happy to entertain, but she did like to know before everyone else who was going to be invited.

'My dear, I'm very much afraid that I'm going to come as a bit of a shock to their majesties. I'm hoping the old penguin suit will mitigate to some extent.' Frances didn't ask why the Eel was going to come as a shock; instead, she went and woke Paul, who had been enjoying his early mid-afternoon snooze, in order to preserve his strength for his late mid-afternoon nap, a nap which he regarded as essential if he was going to gather himself in time for his late afternoon doze in front of *Fifteen to One*. He was not pleased at being rudely awakened and sent out for some essentials.

'Oh, maaan. Who's coming to dinner? And do I have to come too?'

'Yes you do, you useless piece of shit. We're entertaining the king and queen of Farafangana. And then they're staying for a day or two.'

Holland gave the uncertain, crooked little grin that had persuaded so many young and gullible women that he was a sweetie, despite very good evidence to the contrary.

'Who's coming really?' he said.

'I told you. The king and queen. It turns out they're Jeremiah's mum and dad. And a batty old loon they've got with them, and Jeremiah, of course, and you and me and Blossom and the Eel. Now, here's the list.'

'Straight up?' said Holland.

'Yes! How many fucking times? Now, get going.'

Holland did as he was told, feeling self-important. It was not, after all, every day that you got to go down Asda at the Marina on behalf of royalty, albeit deposed ones.

Frances was preparing boeuf bourguignon from a recipe she had gleaned from *The Independent on Sunday*. The article said that boeuf bourguignon had been the great star of sixties and seventies dinner parties, had fallen from grace during the eighties, and should now be due for a revival. Frances, ever the back-street post-modernist, could not resist serving something so knowing; she cooked her ingredients as slowly as possible and got herself dressed, thinking her little red mini-dress would do the job. At seven thirty the king and queen arrived, and Frances showed them to the spare room. Um and Er were allowed to shake hands with the illustrious guests, and were then plonked in front of a Disney video to keep them quiet; by eight all the guests were assembled except the Eel.

'What a lovely flat,' said Queen Maria, as she sat in the front room sipping Tio Pepe.

'Thank you,' said Frances. 'It could do with a lick of paint, though.'

Holland and Blossom looked at each other; every January, Frances started to think about redecoration; and every March, the two men were railroaded into spending a week with paintbrushes and stepladders. The doorbell rang; Frances rose to admit the Eel. Choking with exertion from the climb, he was resplendent in his dinner jacket, his medals gleaming proudly on his breast.

'Mother, Father,' said Jeremiah, 'allow me to introduce Edgar Luff.'

'It's a pleasure, your majesties. After so long. The last time I saw you, indeed the last time I was in Farafan, was at your wedding. So long ago!'

The ex-king gawped, if royalty can do anything so undignified as gawp.

'Christ,' he said. 'Luff. I remember you. You . . . you're . . . you were my grandfather's adviser at the conference when we got independence.'

'I had the honour of serving your grandfather, your majesty, that is true.'

Cornelius was looking at the Eel suspiciously.

'Luff!' he bellowed.

'Yes?' said the Eel.

'Do you remember me? Cornelius?'

It appeared to Frances that the Eel blushed.

'Ah . . . Cornelius . . .'

'What?'

'YES! I REMEMBER YOU!'

'He remembers me. He remembers me. Do you remember my wife?'

'Yes,' said the Eel quietly.

'What? Do you remember my wife?'

'YES.'

'He shagged my wife,' said Cornelius, pointing at the Eel and smiling around the room.

'Edgar!' said Frances in surprise.

'She was a lovely woman. A LOVELY WOMAN!' bellowed the Eel.

Cornelius smiled and nodded.

'VERY GOOD LEGS!'

Again Cornelius smiled. 'How is she?'

'Eh?'

'HOW IS SHE?'

'Dead. Dead. Dead these last ten years.'

'I'M VERY SORRY TO HEAR IT.'

'Thank you. She always spoke very highly of you.'

'Yes, this is very touching,' said the king. 'But wasn't it you who advised my grandfather to license jute production to Britain at a rock-bottom price, in return for a once and for all payment, pocket the profit and have done? The deal that threatened to destroy our economic independence before we'd even begun?'

'Yes. Well, it was your grandfather's idea. He told me that he didn't want independence at all; couldn't be bothered with it. He liked the colonial life; playing golf, swanning around in his Roller, drinking Pimm's, sleeping with lovely women. He begged me to find a way to keep the cash rolling in. Of course, I was working for the UK government, so your grandfather's idleness and indifference to the fate of his kingdom were a godsend. Farafan was a smashing little stop on the way from Cape Town up to Calcutta, but it had long ceased to be valuable. So I swung the deal on jute.* Your granddad was happy, we were happy and the Farafanganese people in the excitement of independence neglected to read the small print. Sorry.'

'Sorry?'

'Yes. Still, I got this for me trouble.' He thrust out his breast, to show the king the Star of Farafan.

The king was dumbstruck. All these years of struggle, just so his granddad could live like a king. 'The old fucker . . .' he said.

'And now this, your majesty. It is a tragedy, a terrible sadness to us all. Especially Jeremiah and myself.'

'Why's that, Luff?' said the king. 'I should have thought that Marty's ideas are much closer to yours than to mine.'

'Good Lord, no, your majesty. We abhor wishy-washy pinkos like your eldest son. Now, if our plans for a coup had advanced a little further, we hoped to establish Farafan as the first genuinely free-market state in the world. But the bloody social democrats got there first.'

Jeremiah looked at the Eel, and then held his head in his hands. 'Your plans for a coup,' said the king. 'Your plans for a coup? Why, you treacherous—'

'Oh Jerry,' said Queen Maria, disappointment in her voice.

'Shall we go through?' said Frances brightly. 'We're eating in the kitchen, I'm afraid.'

* What *is* jute?

The party trooped into the kitchen, the atmosphere decidedly cool, and sat around the large stripped-pine table, where, inevitably, political debate raged on. Blossom chatted to Frances and the ex-queen, while Jeremiah, the Eel and ex-King Martin screamed at one another. Surprisingly, Holland was something of a hit with the king. As a man with all the political clout and insight of Dale Winton, he had little of substance to contribute. But he nodded when the king spoke, and said things like 'Right on' and 'Power to the People', and, implausibly, even gave a clenched-fist salute and chanted, 'Ho, Ho, Ho Chi Minh!' as Frances served the pudding.

Over coffee, the king spoke with approval of his new disciple. 'I'm glad to see that this young man, at least, does not suffer from false ideology.'

'Right on,' said Holland.

'Perhaps while I'm here you might show me something of the down-trodden lot of the workers, Mr Holland?' said the king.

This puzzled Holland. What workers? Holland didn't really know any, though he was aware that his wife staggered up to the university occasionally. Perhaps he could take the king to Cats's workshop, and they could watch him mend videos and hi-fis and stuff. Then inspiration dawned.

'I've gotta sign on tomorrow,' he said. 'You could come and watch that, I suppose.'

The ex-king beamed. 'I'd be delighted.'

And so it was that at eleven the next morning, Holland and the king went along to the social in Upper North Street. The king was a little taken aback by the plush open-plan offices, but he was cheered by the sight of beggars in the street outside. The lady behind the desk smiled at Holland.

'Good morning,' she said. 'How can I help you?'

'Gotta sign on,' said Holland with bad grace.

'Thank you, sir. And your name is . . . ?'

Holland handed her his signing-on card; she flipped through the envelopes in the box in front of her, and found his file.

'Here we are, sir . . . if you could just sign here? Thank you very much.'

Holland signed.

'Thank you very much, sir. Thank you for using the Benefit Agency. Call again soon. Have a nice day.'

Holland gave her the finger, and stalked from the office.

'What a nice lady,' said the king.

'She's a cow. She's got that false thing you were saying last night.'

'Er . . . eyelashes?'

'Nah! Wotsit. Thing.'

'Ideology?'

'That's him.' Outside the office, the ex-king paused to give money to one of the beggars.

'You shouldn't have done that,' said Holland. 'They're all fucking loaded.'

'Really?'

' 's a well-known fact. They all got Astras and big houses.'

'No!'

'You don't know much, do you, man? Stick with me and I'll show you what it's really like.'

Holland took the king round to see Black Barney.

'It's well hard, man, signing on,' said Barney, the king watching as he skinned up.

'That's why me and Barney, we're socialists.'

'Yeah?' said Barney. 'Why should some rich fucker have everything, when me and Di have to make do with stolen? We've got kids, and all.'

The king tutted. 'In my country, we had full employment,' he said proudly.

Barney and Holland shuffled in their seats.

'The Iron Marmalade Pot, they called the policy.'

'No, man, that's not what I'm saying,' said Barney. 'We don't want full employment, man, I've got a fucking business to run, I haven't got time to work, not with my sinuses. No, what I'm saying is that we should be able to live like decent human beings on the social, not scrimping and saving for stuff what's stolen anyway, and not under guarantee.'

'I expect the system almost demands to be abused . . .'

'That is right,' said Holland. 'It's like Gramsci said.'

'You know Gramsci?' asked the king enthusiastically.

'Course. Frances craps on about him.'

'Very sound on the hegemonic structure of ideology.'

'I know nothing about that bit. Frances just craps on about "the dismal failure of the left" and talks about Gramsci, and some other old Eyetie cat. Adorno?'

'Yes,' said the king excitedly. 'Er . . . but I'm not entirely sure that he was Italian.'

'They're all cunts anyway,' said Black Barney.

'Who are?' asked Holland.

'Eyeties. They're all cunts. What did they ever do for us? Perspective and banking. Stupid cunts.'

'Perspective is all right, though,' said Holland.

Barney thought for a painful second. Then he said, 'Yeah, perspective is fine. But banking, that's for cunts.'

'Oy, you shouldn't have money, anyway,' said Holland.

'No, no, that's right,' said the king. 'No, you don't need money at all, not in its present form.'

'No, you do,' said Barney, 'or you couldn't have a bet and that.'

'No, but you'd bet with your card, wouldn't you?' said Holland.

'Would you?' said Barney.

'Yes, man, of course. You have a special card, with everything on it, all your possessions and that, how much you're worth, and the card just takes it off on a machine. That was on *Horizon*.'

'You're full of shit,' said Black Barney.

'No, it was, it was on *Horizon*.'

The king said, 'Is there a Claimants' Union in Brighton?'

'Yah,' said Holland, 'but I don't go. It's in the Peace Centre, and Frances is against it.'

'The Peace Centre? It sounds admirable.'

'No, man. Peace. She doesn't approve of it.'

'I tell you another thing that is shit, and that is private property,' said Black Barney.

The king's eyes shone. 'Ah, Barney,' he said, 'now we're getting near to the core of the problem. Indeed. Private property is capitalism's secret weapon.'

'Yeah, that's right,' said Barney. 'You go out for a run in the country with Mum and the dustbins, and there's fucking signs all over the place – "Private Property", "Trespassers will be prosecuted" and all that.'

The king furrowed his brow. 'Well, I really meant private property in a somewhat wider sense.'

'That's right,' said Holland. 'It's wrong, not being able to walk where you like in your own country. If I had one of those bastard great big houses, I'd open the fucking grounds, let people come in and have a gander.'

'Yes!' exclaimed Barney.

'I'd charge 'em, like. Or have a theme park, or one of them drive-through zoos. Licence to print money, they are.'

If the ex-king had had the good sense to say no to the spliffs which were circulating freely, he might have realized that Holland and Black Barney were to socialism what Margaret Thatcher was to St Francis of Assisi. But, recalling his student days, and jazz clubs, and Soho in the fifties and the Colony Room, the French Pub, the Coach and Horses and all the rest of it, he remembered smoking a little 'tea' and feeling kind of good afterwards; and then he remembered for the first time in a long while what it was like to be free from care; and he remembered long, rambling discussions with fellow leftists and reading Marcuse by candlelight and what seemed like an impossibly faraway youth.

And so he forgot the burdens of high office and smoked right along with his new friends. And now he came to feel that although their ideas were perhaps a little muddle-headed, their hearts were in the right place, and heart was much more important than mind. Poor Princess Di showed that. He smiled and nodded and accepted joint after joint; then, at one o'clock, he went with them to the Eastern Star for a few beers. After that, of course, they all thought the best thing to do would be to go back to Barney's to finish off that little bit of blow that Barney had. By four thirty, the king, Black Barney and Holland were semi-conscious on Barney's new leather sofa in front of *Countdown*. At five, Di, Black Barney's lady, asked the king if he'd like some tea with her and Barney and the kids, and it came into his head that there was nothing he'd like more; they ate fish-finger sandwiches in front of *Home and Away*, and the king swore to Di that he'd never eaten anything nicer, and that he wanted nothing more than to sit here and put the world to rights and watch telly and eat fish-finger sandwiches for ever.

When, at eleven, Holland took the king back to Bloomsbury Place, Queen Maria was none too pleased, and she refused to speak to the king.

And now Holland saw it as his particular responsibility to show the king the dark underbelly of the welfare state. The next day he took the king to meet Matt the Bat, one of Black Barney's brothers-in-common-law, and his lady, Janet the Gannet. The meeting seemed to go smoothly enough; the king was fascinated to hear of Matt's run-ins with the Housing Benefit, while Janet told a doleful tale of her last court appearance. But the king noticed that his interest in social deprivation waned in direct proportion to the amount of cannabis he smoked; so that, after a very short while indeed, he was quite happy just to sit back and listen to Janet and Holland debate the possibility that our entire universe might just be an atom in a whole other universe, and that the amazing thing was, there was no way of telling.

As Holland and the king staggered up the stairs of the house, the king asked Holland, 'Why do you call him Matt the Bat?'

'Cos he can see in the dark, man. Very handy geezer.'

'I can imagine. And Janet? Why do you call her Janet the Gannet? Is it because she eats a lot?'

'No, man. It's cos when she gets pissed, she regurgitates her food.'

The next day, Holland said to the king. 'I know a guy you'd like to meet. Zom. He's a diamond geezer.'

'A diamond geezer?' said the king.

'Oh yes.' Holland paused. 'Well, diamanté anyway. Fancy it?'

'Why not?'

So Holland and the king went to visit Zom in St Martin's Place.

'We'll just walk up. Zom doesn't like it if you ring the bell.'

In Zom's flat the curtains were drawn; the only light came from the TV set. By this light the king could see an emaciated figure, seemingly dressed in rags, huddled on a mattress on the floor.

'All right, Zom?' said Holland.

Zom didn't respond.

'How are you?'

Zom was as still as the grave.

'Oy! Zom! This bloke's a king!'

Zom stirred not one muscle.

'I'll put the kettle on, shall I, Zom? I've bought some sugar!'

However hard the king looked, he could not see the rise and fall of Zom's chest by the hideous light of the cathode tube.

'Sit down, your majesty. Please,' said Holland.

'Oh. Ah. Thank you. Where?'

'On Zom's mattress. He don't mind, do you, Zom?'

Flies swarmed around Zom's mouth.

'Zom don't mind. Lots of people hang out here in the day. Zom's cool,' said Holland.

So the king perched nervously on the edge of the mattress, and tried to look at Zom. His eyes were wide open but they were not watching the TV; rather, they stared at the ceiling. The king looked, but Zom did not blink.

'I rather think your friend Zom is dead,' said the king.

'Who, Zom? Zom, dead? No, he's always like this, aren't you, Zom? He's a right laugh.'

'How do you know? That he's not dead?'

'Well, he don't smell,' said Holland.

'Actually,' said the king, 'he does a bit.'

'And he moves,' said Holland.

'When? Have you ever seen him?'

'No. I've never seen him moving. But I've seen evidence of his having moved. Sometimes when you come up, his mattress has moved, or the telly's on another channel. And there's always tea and milk.'

'So Zom goes shopping?'

'Well, no, not as such. He gets so many visitors, we all thought it was a bit tight, always drinking his tea or eating his biscuits. So people who come up always bring a little something, so as Zom don't have to worry.'

The king sighed. 'Has it ever occurred to you that it might be these visitors who move the mattress, or change the channel on the telly?'

'No, Zom wouldn't like that. People might hang out here a bit, but it's Zom's drum, and he gets to say where the mattress goes, and what's on telly.'

'And does he ever say?'

'Zom don't need to. He sets it all up before people come, gets it just how he likes it.'

'He's told you this, has he?'

'He doesn't need to, man. I just know.'

'Right.'

Another visitor arrived, who Holland introduced as Terry. In fact, there was no need for introductions, as he helpfully had 'Terry' tattooed on his forehead. Terry rolled a few spliffs, and when it came to Zom's turn, Holland held it in Zom's mouth. The king could not see the end of the joint burn any brighter. But as the king became more stoned himself he found Zom's company quite soothing, and he chatted to him about the problems of building a socialist state in one nation. People came and went, and the king became more stoned, and correspondingly more voluble; by the time he and Holland left, he felt that he and Zom were firm friends. When he took Zom's hand to shake it, it was cold and limp, but he was easily persuaded by Holland that this was because Zom had poor circulation.

On the fourth day after his arrival in Brighton, Holland took the king to visit Slim Jim. Slim Jim was fat. Very fat. Slim Jim was so fat that he looked positively American. Slim Jim indicated to the king that he should sit on a battered old sofa.

'You will no doubt be wondering, your majesty,' said Slim Jim, 'why my good friends, such as Mr Holland here, call me Slim.'

The king had wondered no such thing. He assumed that Slim was called Slim because he was fat. What the king was wondering was when Slim would skin up. But he nodded mutely.

'Allow me to demonstrate, your majesty.' Slim Jim reached behind him, with some effort, and produced a biscuit tin.

'In this tin, as you can see, I have all the doings which will enable me to roll a cannabis cigarette. However, you will have noticed that I keep this tin some way from my seated position. This produces an aerobic effect which helps me to keep fit. Now, if you will observe . . .' Slim took a Rizla from the packet with an exaggerated windmilling motion of his right arm, and then a second with his other arm; the third he pulled from the packet with both his arms, as though he were in a tug-of-war contest. The king was fascinated. When the time came to roll the completed joint, Slim did so on his stomach, rolling the spliff up and down for some minutes.

'By this means, I am exercising my arms and applying gentle massage to my stomach muscles. Now, I light the cannabis cigarette. You will notice that there is only one ashtray in the room, and that I have placed it centrally, so that in order to dispose of our ash we have to rise from our chairs. Also, you have no doubt noticed that our chairs are placed at a strategic distance apart. Again, in order to pass the number, both the passer and the recipient have to come to a half-standing position, once again providing us with all-important exercise.'

The king was gagging for his go, but it was Slim's dope, so he just nodded encouragingly.

'I have devised this programme in order to keep drug users fit,' said Slim. 'There is only one problem.'

'Oh? What's that?' asked the king.

'The Munchies. After a few spliffs you get fucking ank,* and have to eat biscuits. That is why, despite my ground-breaking fitness programme, I have put on a few pounds. I am currently working on this problem.'

* 'ank': short for 'ank (or 'Hank') Marvin; Brighton rhyming slang for feeling very hungry.

139

'Could you keep the biscuits on a high shelf?' asked Holland. 'So's you had to stretch for them?'

Slim Jim stared at Holland in wonder. 'Mr Holland! You are a genius. Have a cake.'

Queen Maria had not been idle either. While her husband was out investigating social conditions and getting off his face all day, she had been utilizing her own particular skills. By slow persuasion she had managed to enlist the help of the Eel, and it was his diplomacy, practised and patient, that saved the situation. Edgar Luff, assisted by the loyal Prince Jeremiah, had conducted negotiations by fax with their eldest son back in Farafan. On the sixth day of their enforced visit, when Holland, the plaster newly removed from his wrist, had decided to take the king bowling in the King Alfred Centre, the Eel, supported by Jeremiah, had puffed his way up to the top flat to tell Maria that these negotiations had reached a successful conclusion: they were now welcome to return home, where they could begin life anew in a grace-and-favour granny annexe that the new King Martin was having built on to the renamed Royal Democratic Bungalow.

The queen was delighted, but also a little nervous as to how her husband would react; to her surprise, when he rolled in late again, a beatific grin all over his increasingly relaxed face, he took it very well. He admitted that the strain had been getting to him lately, and maybe it was time just to kick back and let the kids run the family firm. He himself would do a little gardening, and he had acquired some skunk seeds from Barney to get him started. So it was arranged; Jeremiah went up to London to get his parents' passports back from the Farafan Embassy and to apologize to the ambassador for his father's having hit him. A flight was booked.

The preparations for a farewell dinner were set in train for the night before departure. Much to Frances's distaste, the king had asked that Barney and Di should be invited; Frances asked a couple of people from work, including Brad, an Australian post-graduate studying the socio-dynamics of tennis coaching, with whom Frances seemed especially friendly. The Eel and Jeremiah came again, of course, as did Cats and Blossom. Caroline came and sat through it all, sullen and blushing; Cornelius took an obvious shine to her, and sat next to her and did not seem to mind her silence.

At the conclusion of the meal, the king stood and made a little valedictory speech, in which he thanked his wife and Prince Jeremiah and Mr Luff for sorting everything out, and Frances and Di for their hospitality, and all his new friends for helping him to see that nothing really mattered that much anyway. He saved the best for last.

'Finally, I should like to say that, by way of appreciation for all the help that you have shown us in negotiating with . . .' here a little spasm of hatred passed over King Martin V's face, just one last time and never to return, 'King Martin VI and by the powers vested in me, I should like to confer upon Mr Luff membership of the Farafan Order of the Garter.' The Eel started to rise, to thank the king for his beneficent generosity. 'Please,' said the ex-king. 'That is far from all. In view of the extraordinary kindness and appreciation shown to my wife and me, and our old friend and counsellor Cornelius, by our hosts, Mr and Mrs Holland, I have decided to confer upon Mr Paul Holland the highest honour that it is within my powers to bestow. Mr Holland, from this day hence, you shall be regarded as an adopted Prince of the Royal House of Farafan, and an honorary member of the Fara tribe. When – and note I say when, and not if – you come to stay with us in Farafan, you shall be treated like the royalty you undoubtedly are. Ladies and gentlemen, I beg your indulgence: please give three hearty cheers for Prince Paul of Farafangana. Hip hip . . .'

And, to Holland's considerable embarrassment, the assembled party gave three if not hearty then at least audible cheers.

'Er . . .' he said. 'Thanks. And . . . right on!'

Byfield's Wife

Most Friday lunchtimes, if the weather was at least not bad, Holland and Blossom liked to take old Edgar Luff down to the Eastern Star for a few quiet beers. Friday was usually a good day for this, as the three avowed enemies of the state had drawn their benefit and pensions and were feeling flush. Holland and Blossom always enjoyed the Eel's company; he had been everywhere and met everybody, and they found his stories generally good value. Blossom's favourite was the one about how the Eel had met L. Ron Hubbard on a transatlantic liner just after the war, and had drunkenly suggested to him that setting up a new religion was a sure-fire method of earning big bucks; Holland never got tired of hearing how the Eel had given Neal Cassidy a lift south to New Orleans to see Bill Burroughs after spotting him hitching out of St Louis (or, at least, someone who claimed to be Cassidy; the Eel admitted that he couldn't be entirely sure but said he was 'a big healthy lad').

It was still winter, and the pavements were decidedly slippery. The Eel, dressed in his Astrakhan overcoat – 'Khrushchev gave me this at a conference in Novgorod in 'fifty-two. It still looks fine, too.' – clung to Blossom's mackintoshed arm for support as the three men carefully negotiated the short distance between the post office and the pub, where they settled in their accustomed corner seat, sucking pints of Sussex Ale through still chattering teeth.

'Ah, my dear boys. There is no finer beer than southern beer,' said the Eel. 'Northern beer is the most fearfully over-rated stuff – ah, but this . . .'

Blossom and Holland nodded, and raised their glasses in appreciation.

'If ever I had to get a job . . .' said Holland.

'Heaven forfend,' said Blossom.

'No, but if I had to, I wouldn't mind a job in a brewery.'

'Oh, don't be sad,' said Blossom. 'It would put you off beer for life. It's one of those jobs like being a dresser in a strip club that boys fantasize about. Get real. It would be a nightmare.'

'Oh right, and you know all about jobs.'

'I know the sort of thing I'd fancy, and that would be like Edgar. The Foreign Office. Travel. Glamour. Excitement.'

'Less than you'd think, old love,' said the Eel. 'And you have to glad-hand the most frightful shits. Besides, I'm very much afraid they wouldn't have you.'

'Ha ha,' said Holland pointedly.

'Whyever not?' said Blossom, a little hurt.

'Wrong school.'

'Oh, come off it. Maybe back in the thirties when you joined, but not now . . .'

The Eel cocked an eyebrow. 'Believe what you like, old thing. You might be right. I mean, I only worked there for forty years; perhaps I just didn't meet any of the grammar school boys. Perhaps they kept us apart, for some reason or other.'

Blossom said nothing, but sipped his beer.

'I tell you a job I'd hate,' said Holland, 'and that's being a dentist.'

Blossom and the Eel nodded their assent.

'Who the fuck wants to be a dentist?' continued Holland.

144

'What sort of person does all their "A" levels and that, just so they can go and be a dentist? Really though, who?'

'I don't know, I must admit,' said the Eel.

'Or a maths teacher,' said Blossom. 'There's a really scary job. Our maths teacher was called Mr Byfield, and he had to be the least attractive man in the whole world. He wasn't particularly ugly or anything like that, it's just that he didn't seem to have any kind of personality. Five years he taught me, and never once did he smile, or crack the feeblest of maths-type jokes. We used to watch him in the staff room; always on his own, never even reading a paper. He just used to sit, sipping his tea. He never raised his voice, he never got angry, he never did anything. Old Transparency, we called him.'

'Where did you school again?' asked the Eel.

'Wellingborough Boys' Grammar.'

'Yes. Yes, that would be the same Byfield,' said the Eel.

'Oh no! You're not going to claim that you knew Mr Byfield? You can't have done. He was teaching in North-amptonshire, for God's sake, and you were living in India, and the States. No, this one I refuse to believe.'

'I didn't live abroad my whole career, you know. I had a flat in Hove, used to catch the train up to the office for several years after the war. And old Derek Byfield moved up to Wellingborough in about 'fifty-one. Before that he taught at Lewes Grammar. Lived up Bear Road.'

Blossom stared at the Eel.

'My God. That was his name, Mr Byfield's, I mean. Derek.'

'Oh, it's the same chap, no question. Byfers. Well well.'

'This is incredible,' said Blossom. 'Paul, isn't this incredible?'

'I suppose so,' said Holland, who seemed unexcited by this little piece of synchronicity.

'Ah, but – how the fuck have you remembered Mr Byfield

all these years? Like I said, he was the least memorable man I ever met. That's how I remembered him.'

'Well . . . it was the business with his wife.'

'Oh, it can't have been the same bloke then. Mr Byfield wasn't married. That much I know.'

'He was once,' said the Eel, enigmatically.

'There's a story, isn't there?' said Blossom.

'There might be,' said the Eel, tapping his empty glass with his forefinger. 'There might well be.'

'Would you like another pint, Edgar?' asked Blossom.

'Uncommonly kind of you.'

'Thanks,' said Holland.

Blossom sighed, and bought three more pints. 'Come on then, Edgar. Let's have it.'

The Eel sipped his beer, cleared his throat, and began.

'Byfield was quite big with the ladies at one time. His wife was a plump blond piece, pretty enough, I suppose. An old bridge acquaintance, Arnold Collinson, pointed her out to me once at the cricket, years later; not because of her looks, but because she was Byfield's wife. I don't think you'd have noticed her in the street as anything remarkable; but nor, I think, would you have pushed her from your bed. She worked as a district nurse; and Byfield, of course, taught mathematics – even then, it was thought, to little effect. Even before the thing with his wife he was what one would call a colourless man; but he was quite good-looking, you know, and rather a useful dancer.

'Although your acquaintance with Byfield might make it seem unlikely, at the time of which I am speaking, which would have been, I suppose, some time after the war – 'forty-six or 'forty-seven maybe – he was keeping company with two young women, neither of whom was his lawfully wedded. One of the girls, who worked as a clerk at a transit depot in North London, had been attempting to persuade

146

him to leave his wife; Byfield was not keen on the idea, although he expressed himself as having at least an open mind, in order to pursue his relations with this young woman. In addition, he'd taken up with a little thing named Adele Patterson, with whom he used to dance at the old Regent. Byfield and Adele had won a medal in a foxtrot exhibition, and they had come to spend a great deal of time in each other's company. A very great deal of time. From what I gathered, Adele was married herself, and so was no keener to advertise the liaison than Byfield, beyond the display of the medal. Her husband, innocent soul that he was, believed that Byfield was nothing more sinister than a dancing partner; and Byfield's wife, for her part, betrayed no awareness of his carryings-on.

'One night, Byfield called on the girl in North London, expecting to stay the night, having told his wife that he was attending a talk at the Institute of Mathematics on the tricky subject of teaching fractions. Unfortunately, the girl had received a letter from Adele revealing that, far from considering leaving his wife, Byfield was enjoying her favours as well. The girl in North London – I'm sorry, I can't remember her name or where it was that she lived exactly, though I'm sure I must have known once – was forthright in her condemnation of Byfield, and ten minutes or so after arrival at her flat he found himself back on the pavement. Nothing daunted, he picked up a tart in Shepherd's Market and put up for the night at a hotel. The next day being a Saturday, he was due to dance with Adele; he caught the train, somewhat tremulously, back to Brighton, only to find a very aggressive Mr Patterson awaiting him at the Regent. Byfield told me that he hardly had time to put up his fists before Adele's husband laid into him; my feeling is that Byfield was more likely to have cowered, rather than put up any kind of defence; either way, Byfield returned to his wife with a marvellous shiner, some four hours earlier than advertised.

'As he came through the front door, his wife was standing in the hall.

' "Hello, Derek. You're a bit early." She pecked his cheek.

' "Yes. Adele couldn't make it."

' "Looks like you've been in the wars."

' "Bumped into the corner of a blackboard at the Institute. Hurts like hell, actually."

' "You poor thing. I thought you might have bumped into Adele's husband."

'Byfield felt as though his whole upper torso was being sucked into the pit of his belly, and he dropped his overnight bag in alarm.

' "No. Why?"

' "Oh, because I thought it might have been from him that you got your black eye."

'They walked into the front room and went to sit in their armchairs, which were on opposite sides of the fire, facing each other.

' "Whyever would you think that?" asked Byfield.

' "Oh, because I saw him today, and he told me he was going to beat the merry hell out of you."

'Byfield gulped.

' "Whyever would he do that?"

' "Oh, because I told him about you and Adele." Byfield's wife smiled benignly. "And I told Adele about the girl in Finchley," or wherever it was. "She said she was going to write. Cup of tea?"

' "Er . . . yes, please."

' "Why don't you go and freshen up while I put the kettle on?"

' "Er . . . yes."

' "And then we can carry on with our little chat."

148

' "Right. Righto."

'Byfield grabbed his bag from the hall, and scuttled upstairs to the bathroom.

'Now comes a part of the story which always seemed particularly distasteful to me, and if it were not for the fact that Byfield himself always used to insist that it was the nub of the whole matter, I might be tempted to leave it out.'

The Eel drained his glass and lit a cigarette.

'Oh come on, Edgar. Don't be squeamish,' said Blossom.

'Bad taste is my middle name, man,' said Holland.*

'Very well. I suppose you might miss the force of the story without it. If you'll just excuse me for a moment.' Leaning on his stick, the Eel made his way to the gents while Holland got another round in; on his return, the Eel settled back down and continued.

'Safely in the bathroom, Byfield took off his jacket, pulled down his braces, unbuttoned his trousers and sat trembling on the lavatory. He voided his bowels, stood to clean himself up: and let off the most tremendous fart, which, to Byfield's undying horror, sprayed a pint or more of disgusting, fruity-smelling shit out of his backside and all over the bath, all over the floor, right up the wall and all down the back of his trousers. Byfield could not account for this phenomenon; he swore that it had never happened to him before or since. It is my view that his stool had been loosened by fear, but you might have some other explanation. The point is that Byfield's arse had spontaneously stripped him of all dignity, just at the very moment when he could really have done with being dignified.

' "Oh Christ!" said Byfield. He mopped the foul liquid from his arse and stepped gingerly out of his trousers,

*This is true. Holland had it changed by deed poll at the height of the punk rock craze of the 1970s.

unfortunately getting shit all over the back of his knees in the process. He dropped his dripping trousers into the bath. He was filling the sink with hot water, preparatory to cleaning himself up, when his wife knocked at the door.

' "Will you be much longer, dear? Your tea's getting cold, and I really would like to press on with our chat."

' "No . . . I . . . I've had a bit of an accident."

'Byfield's wife entered the bathroom and surveyed the scene. "Oh dear! You have made a mess. Never mind, I'll clean you up."

'She flannelled down the back of his legs while he stood impotent in the middle of the bathroom; and as she washed him down, and as she subsequently cleaned the filth from the bath and the floor, she talked.

' "You see, I've known about the girl in Finchley" (or wherever) "for a while, and Adele too; but I didn't mind because it got you out of the house and out from under my feet. But in the end I told them both what was happening because I felt you were being a little unfair on them both, not to mention Adele's poor husband. Do stand still. Yes. And then, besides, I've decided to leave you."

' "Oh Joyce," said Byfield. "Please don't do anything so rash. Please. The girl in London, Adele – they meant nothing to me. Please. Please don't leave me now. You've put up with me this far. I'll change, I promise. Please, Joyce."

' "Oh, it's not because of them. There. You're clean. Go and put your pyjamas on while I deal with the bath. What *have* you been eating? No, dear, I'm leaving you because I've met someone else."

' "My God. Oh my God. Who? Tell me who."

' "Pyjamas first, please, and then you can come back and I'll tell you all about it."

'Byfield, the back of his legs still damp, walked into the bedroom. His pyjamas lay on the pale blue candlewick bedspread as usual; the framed illuminated address he had won at Sunday School for coming second in Scripture saying "And when the One Great Scorer comes to write against your name, He writes not that you won or lost, but how you played the game" still hung above the bed; the blue-and-white pitcher and bowl his aunt had left him still stood on the washing table by the window; all that was unchanged. Less expected was the sight of three packed suitcases by the door. He changed into his pyjamas and hurried back to the bathroom, where his wife was scrubbing away at the bath, Vim in hand.

'"Who is he?" demanded Byfield.

'"Well, actually he's one of my patients. I've been visiting him every day. I have told you about him, but I don't suppose you listened."

'"Which one, damn it?"

'"Squadron Leader Garman."

'"Garman. Garman? But isn't he . . . ?"

'"Yes, the poor old thing. He's a quadriplegic. He went right through the war unscathed, right through the Battle of Britain with not a mark on him, and then fell from the roof of a Nissen hut after drinking all through VE Day. Broke his darling neck."

'"But you can't leave me for a cripple! I mean, the man can't move. You'll have to do everything for him!"

'Byfield's wife put down her Vim and straightened up with a groan, her hand in the small of her back.

'"Well, Derek, if you don't mind my saying so, at least when Dennis makes a mess he doesn't spray it all over the walls."

'Byfield groaned. "But . . ."

'"What . . . ?"

'"Oh Christ, Joyce. What about sex? You're a normal woman. How will you manage without sex?"

' "Oh, I don't have to."

' "Do you mean to tell me that you've been sleeping with this . . . this cripple?"

' "Yes. Every day when I go round. Every day for the last six months. He's a randy old goat."

' "But . . . he's paralysed from the neck down?"

' "Yes?"

' "But . . . I mean . . ."

'Byfield's wife smiled. "Oh, there are ways and means."

' "But it can't be . . . satisfactory?"

' "Oh Derek, you'd be surprised. The squadron leader has made me feel like a real woman for the first time in many years." She picked up Byfield's trousers, still damp from where she had sponged them down.

' "I've done my best with these, but you'll need to take them to the cleaners."

' "Bugger the trousers. Bugger them. Bugger the squadron leader. Bugger it all."

' "Now, Derek, don't be like that."

'A ring came at the door.

' "That will be my taxi."

' "You're going? Now?"

' "Yes. Be a pet and help me down with my bags."

'Byfield meekly complied.

'As his wife put on her hat and coat, she said, "Well, goodbye, Derek. Look after yourself. You'll be hearing from my solicitors."

' "What?"

' "About the divorce."

' "Divorce? On what grounds?"

' "Your adultery, of course. No judge is going to believe what I've been up to with the squadron leader but I think he'll find the evidence I've collected against you more than convincing. Goodbye."

'She pecked him on the cheek, and disappeared off in her taxi.'

'Bloody hell,' said Blossom. 'How do you know all this, Edgar?'

'Byfield told me at the club. He used to tell everyone, actually. You couldn't shut him up about it. We called him "The Greybeard Loon". You know, he stoppeth one in three, and all that.'

'So you're saying that it was his wife leaving him that rendered him so utterly bloodless?'

The Eel sucked at his inhaler and lit a cigarette. 'Indirectly, yes. This is speculative, but old Arnold Collinson agreed with me. You see, as far as anyone could ever tell, that tart in London was the last woman that Byfield ever went with. He couldn't get it up, or so old Arnold and I thought. It was the sex thing. Byfield couldn't perform because he couldn't ever stop thinking about how the squadron leader, incapacitated as he was, had proved a much more satisfactory lover than himself. Enough to knock the wind out of anybody's sails. Don't you think?'

The Englishwoman Who Didn't Understand Irony

Ever since Frances had burst through the door of the top floor flat in Bloomsbury Place, her eyes shining with joy, and announced, 'Boring Paula is back!' almost the entire household had been overcome with excitement. Even the ground floor flat seemed to have been infected; the Eel had accosted Caroline in the hall and said, 'I hear Boring Paula is back. Marvellous!' Caroline felt herself being swept along on the wave of anticipation, and her pulse raced a little faster. Only Blossom did not contribute to the hubbub. He, it seemed to Caroline, was not excited. Caroline even felt that he was quite gloomy about the whole thing.

'What's up? Is it because Boring Paula's back?'

Blossom nodded.

Caroline started to say something about how it was going to be fun having her around again, and about all the great times they would share together; but just in time she realized that she was suffering from mass hysteria and didn't have a clue who Boring Paula was.

'Who is Boring Paula, anyway?'

'The hi-fi girl before you but two. She was my girlfriend.'

'Old flames give you heartburn, eh?'

'Not really. Everyone else is being a bastard. Poor old Paula.'

'How are they being bastards? They all seem really pleased that she's back. I should think she'll be made up that all her friends are so chuffed.'

'They're happy because they find her hysterically funny.'

'And you're upset because they find her funnier than you?'

'No. You misunderstand. They take the piss. They laugh at her. Poor old Paula has no sense of humour at all.'

'Oh. That's not very kind.'

'No.'

'Where's she been, anyway?'

'Germany. She lives in Germany.'

'Well, no one there will mind if she hasn't got a sense of humour.'

'There you are. You see? You're just as bad as the rest of them. You wouldn't take the piss if she had a leg missing or something, would you?'

'No, of course not.'

'Well, that's how it is for Paula. She's disabled.'

'Oh, come off it.'

'No, really, it is. Have you ever considered what it would be like to be English and not have a sense of humour? Not to understand sarcasm, allusion, irony, understatement? It was terrible for her. Terrible. I felt sorry for her.'

'Is that why you went out with her?'

Blossom sighed. 'No. I went out with her because I have the misfortune to have had a grammar school education.'

'I don't understand.'

'Would you like some coffee?'

'Go on then.'

Blossom rattled around the kitchen as he talked. 'I'm disabled, too. It's OK for guys like the Eel and Jeremiah. They went to public schools and they treat women like ladies, or like whores, or like both. They're polite, courteous, considerate and all the rest of it, just so long as they are not sleeping with someone; but as soon as they get into bed, they treat 'em as spunk receptacles.'

'That's horrible. What's OK about that?'

'Well, if you're a woman, nothing. But the men, at least, are all right. Women are aliens, and it doesn't matter what you do, they always will be. So, so long as you stick to a sort of Getting on with Aliens code, where you hold open doors for them and assume that they see sex as a disgusting violation, everything is fine. They feel no guilt. Remember, they all lose their virginity to other boys; sex, for them, is for ever associated with stink, and mess, and piles. It's something you have to do to keep the bloodline going, not something that nice girls could ever possibly enjoy. And so long as they are going out with women from a similar background, it seems to work. Look at all those poor cows who are married to members of the cabinet. They seem to like it.'

'You can't tell.'

'No, but it seems a fair bet. And then you have guys like Holland and Atkinson, who went to vast co-ed comprehensives. To them, women are normal. They treat women just like anyone else.'

Caroline was pleased. 'Do you think so? I think so. That's why Paul and I—'

'Hey! Watch it. I've told you before, I don't want to know anything. What I mean is, in Holland's case, at least, he is just as prepared to crap on a woman as he is to crap on a man, if it is to his short-term advantage. Yes, it works all right, too, I admit that. Both he and Atkinson are great with their kids, for example. I'm sure that's because all the girls in their class had babies when they were fifteen, and punched any of the boys who didn't want to know in the gob.'

'You exaggerate.'

'Of course. But I stick to my point. And as for the sex thing; they all started really early, and if they didn't perform adequately, all the girls would tell one another; it would get round the school and they'd never get a bunk-up again. You get the picture?'

'Yes, I see. That's why I fell for—'

'Ah ah ah. No tell me nothing. No, but you see, we didn't have any girls at all. We just didn't know any. Or at least we knew a few from the girls' grammar school, but they were all really nice and sensible, and if they went out with anybody, it was with older blokes with cars, and not with us. I mean, I was in the school cricket team, but it didn't impress them at all. But because we were in the world, instead of being locked up in a dorm somewhere, eating tuck and giving head, we knew that girls were real and had feelings, and all that stuff. And because we were clever and nice and socially aware, we knew that they had rights, and that it was not the done thing to stare at their tits on the bus, and because it was the seventies we knew that they had to have orgasms, and lots of them, too. But how you talked to a girl, or asked her out, or, having got her to go out, how you gave her an orgasm without trespassing on her rights, or feelings, we didn't have a clue. So I didn't lose my virginity until I was nineteen, and at university.'

'How did that happen?'

'Well, it was with Kate actually.'

'Oh, honey! How sweet. Your first love.'

'Yes. Yes, she was.'

'Oh, I am sorry. Oh how sad.'

Blossom lit a fag and drank some of his coffee.

'How did you ask her then? You managed all right with her,' said Caroline, to fill the awkward silence as much as anything.

'She asked me, of course. Women always choose, I know that now. At the time I thought she was being a bit forward. But if she hadn't made the first move, I'd still be sitting in her room stuttering with embarrassment. Except that I wouldn't, because she's dead.'

'Oh Bob. How sad.'

'You keep saying that. But it's not really. A bit poignant, shall we say? And I got better. After she died, I went out of my way to ask women out, lots of them, and to my surprise at least one in ten agreed. And out of them, a fair percentage went on to have orgasms. And so I thought I was cured. But then Paula moved into the flat.'

'What happened?'

'Paula was different. I was smitten. I really thought I was in love, for the first time since Katie died. Firstly, it takes a while to spot what it is that's wrong with her. I just thought she was deep. And, I suppose, meta-funny. I thought her sense of humour was so highly developed, I really did. We all did. It was too late by the time we discovered the horrible truth. But that wasn't the worst of it. I did something terrible.'

'Ooh, you lickle devil you. What did you do?'

'Well, it's the grammar school thing again. All the women I'd been out with, Katie too, were university-educated career women; intelligent, interesting. They were the girls from the grammar school grown up. But the girls that I had really lusted after when I was an adolescent were the girls from the secondary modern. All tight sweaters and lipstick on their teeth; the sort of girls that go out with squaddies, and despise soft-bodied intellectuals like me.

'And Paula, you see, was like that. She's from Leeds, and she's hard as fuck. She left school at sixteen with one CSE in geography, oddly enough, and worked in a factory. Making hi-fis. She'd worked her way up, and by the time she moved down here, to work at Ferguson's in Newhaven, she was production manager. But she was still so . . .'

'What?'

'You know. She was still from the council estate. Common.'

'Bob! You snob!'

'I know. I know. But I was making up for my lost youth.'

'So what went wrong?'

'You name it. We soon cottoned on that Paula didn't have a clue what any of us were on about – not because she's thick – she's not, she's very bright. I didn't mind at first; I didn't think it would matter. I was in love with her voice, and the way she could neck pint after pint of beer, and still be dull as ditchwater; I loved having sex with her – she didn't like kissing or foreplay, which I think she thought were middle class; I think I was going through a bad whore fantasy period myself, I can't account for it any other way. I loved it when she cooked chips. She didn't like to see men in pinafores, as she put it; she'd get home from work and cook me my dinner – which, although I have to admit it was appalling of me, I of course quite liked.'

'Now that really is sad.'

'Well, I suppose it was classic male behaviour. Your mum does everything for you; and remember, my dad died when I was fifteen, so it was just Mum and me; and although other women in your life love you romantically, they never replace that total love that a boy gets from his mum. So when Paula seemed to like doing all that stuff, it was great, even though she was so frighteningly ill-equipped for modern life.'

'Yes, OK, but what went wrong?'

'I laughed at an inappropriate moment.'

'Which was?'

Blossom sighed. 'You know how you're always harping on about how romantic it was between Kate and me? Well, it was, I guess; or at least it all seemed romantic after she was dead. But I wasn't entirely faithful to her, you know.'

'No?'

'No. I had a couple of affairs; I was kind of Holland in embryo . . . sorry. Sorry. But you know what I mean. Anyway, the most long-lasting of these affairs was with . . . well, I'll call her Sue. At the time, about three years after we'd left university, I was doing a bit of tutoring, to try and earn a bit of beer money. And Sue was one of my pupils. She was sixteen. Just. I was helping her with her history "O" level. She was incredibly sexy, and when she declared herself in love with me, I was unable to resist. I know it was wrong on every count but, as I said, until Kate came along I was a virgin. I'd never sown my wild oats, so to speak. So I lost control, and I fucked her. And then, to keep her happy, I'm afraid I told her that I loved her.'

Caroline frowned. 'Why do men do that?'

'Well, sometimes it's because they do. And sometimes it's because they think they do. But mostly it's just so that they get their knickers off; like with Porky and Dorelia. And that's how it was with Sue and me. It went on for about a year, until Kate found out. Then, of course, I dumped Sue, and I never saw her again. It was just like Porky and Dorelia, I guess, except that I thought I was behaving well, and Porky knew that he was being a cunt all along. Perhaps that makes me worse than Porky; ethics has never been my strong point. Still, Sue told me that I had broken her heart, and that she would never be able to trust another man again.'

'So, what has this to do with Paula?'

'Well, I thought it was funny. Paula and I had been going out for about six months, and it was getting weirder and weirder. She still did all the cooking, all the washing up and that, all the laundry. She still insisted that we fuck, rather brutally, with no real preliminaries, every night. But for all that, she was really distant from me. And one day I asked her why. So she got all upset and told me that when she'd still been at school she'd had an affair with an older man, a married man, one of her teachers. In fact, it was her geography teacher, which probably accounts for her success in that area. This affair had gone on for a year, when his wife found out. And, of course, he dumped her, and it broke her heart. Since that time, she told me, she'd never really been able to trust a man again. It was the Revenge of Sue. So I laughed.'

'That wasn't very kind.'

'No. It wasn't. But it was Merlin's laugh, you see; bitter, ironic. Another woman might have been able to see what it was that made me laugh. But for Paula, even Stan Laurel putting a custard pie in Ollie's face was puzzling; the humour of Merlin, of the cold spaces between the stars, was quite beyond her.'

'What did she do?'

'She slapped me. She packed up her hi-fi. And she left. I tried to explain, but it was hopeless. She stayed with a friend for a couple of months, and then she was promoted to run this plant in Germany. I saw her a few times and we talked, but she couldn't forgive me for laughing, just at the moment she'd decided to open up to a man for the first time since the geography incident. That's why all the others are such bastards. They'll get her in the pub and tell her jokes, and offer up one-liners and make barbed comments, and they'll all pass her by, and it will make their day. I think she deserves better.'

'Do you miss her?'

'In a funny way. I miss the cooking. I haven't been out with anyone since.'

'Why not?'

Blossom stretched and yawned. 'I've grown up a bit, I think. About time, seeing that I'm thirty-eight next week. I mean, what's the point of me getting into some kind of relationship? I'll laugh at the wrong moment, or she'll die

161

when I least expect it. I suppose I could have a one-night stand, but somehow I don't feel like using somebody like that, just for a lavatorial function. Wanking is ethical.'

'And will you go down the pub and see Paula?'

'Yes. I'll be able to ward off the worst of Frances and the Eel winding her up. Stupid, isn't it, feeling protective towards your exes?'

'No, it's nice.'

'Do you feel protective towards that bloke who dumped you in Budapest?'

'Prague. No. But he was a cunt.'

'And will you feel protective towards Paul, when he dumps you?'

'I thought you didn't want to know anything?'

'I don't really.'

'Anyway, I don't think he will dump me. I really don't. He's just waiting till after Easter, for the kids' sake, and then he says we'll get a place together.'

'And if he doesn't leave . . . if he stays with Frances . . . will you ever trust another man, as long as you live?'

Caroline thought for a moment. 'No. I don't think I could.'

And Blossom tried not to laugh, and failed. And Caroline tried, and failed, to get angry with him. At least, she thought, as she started to laugh too, she wouldn't be forced to move to Germany.

Chapter 23

How do you attempt to describe beauty? That girl on the bus last night, whose beauty left you breathless; how do you put that experience into words? And besides, she had amazing tits, didn't she, and she walked like the Girl from Ipanema – how can you detach her beauty from your lust, from your overwhelming desire? It hardly needs saying again: beauty is in the eye of the beholder. There is no way to objectify it, no SI unit of beauty. If, as most aestheticians agree, a work of art qualifies as such by consent of 'the art community', does that make such a community a legitimate arbiter of beauty? No; something can be 'art' without being 'beautiful'. Or maybe you are walking in a forest in May, an old deciduous forest, the Forest of Dean perhaps; sunlight comes dappling through the leaves on to the carpet of bluebells, leaves the brightest of green with joy at their release from winter into the mindless optimism of spring? How can you capture that moment of real beauty in the woods, really capture it, so that it can be experienced by your readers, if you have any? Besides, isn't it true to say that you walked in woods like this as a child, gathering primroses with your grandmother? And in another such wood you went with a girl for the first time, a deer watching shyly from behind a tree? Your description of the beauty of the wood is then bound up with nostalgia, woods remembered, trees recalled: is this a Kantian beauty that you are describing, some distillation of the Sublime, or is your memory filter acting like the vapour from a cameraman's hot breath on the lens? Your description is blurred, it is in the softest focus. The ignorant lout standing next to you at the bar and sounding off will assure you that 'Everything is Relative,' without understanding what he is saying; in the case of beauty, he may well have a point, though he knows not why. At the very least, we can say without much fear of contradiction that beauty is a social construct. Nevertheless we can still bring our own ideas of female beauty or natural beauty to bear on a piece of descriptive prose. Our ideas and the ideas of the author may not be identical, but they are at least *commensurate*. Our experience can be used to illuminate and understand the experience of someone else.

Cold is not like that, not entirely. There is an SI unit of temperature (Kelvin). It can be objectified and reduced to mathematics. It would be easy to say that on the Winter Journey the traveller encountered temperatures of -70 degrees Fahrenheit. It sounds cold. It is cold. But to experience something like it, really to know, to feel it in your marrow, to feel the moisture in your eyes start to turn to ice, to feel your breath freeze almost before it has left your mouth; that is something else. You have to have been there.

So it is my desire to attempt a phenomenological experiment. I should like us all to get cold together, as cold as we can. Because I want to understand, not just how it feels to freeze, but something of the imperial ideology which underlies the early exploration of Antarctica. If we could only feel as cold, as sick, as frightened as they did, maybe we could understand the heroic nature of empire building, of exploration, of the impulse to achieve something for its own sake. And only in Antarctica can we get close to the purity of those ideals without encountering economic or religious or racial or political considerations. There was nothing for Scott and his men in the Antarctic except the ideal of the British Empire. The reality was a long way off, in India, in South Africa. Out on the Barrier, where Amundsen had years of planning and experience, the Terra Nova expedition had only idealism to get them through.

What's the weather like with you right now? Here, it is early March. There is very little chance of any snow, not now, not so close to the sea. But it is not warm. This is a draughty room; cold south-east winds can seem like they are coming through the very walls. As I write, in this cold place, I wrap an old coat around me to stay warm. Is it like that with you, at this time of year? It's not so cold as it was in January, probably. OK. Let's assume that it is early March with you too. And that a freezing drizzle is blowing in from France on a Force Eight gale. Open the bathroom window and fill the bath with cold water. Now, go to your ice-box and get that stale ice-tray that's been sitting there, locked in frost. At the very least, you are reminded that it is time to defrost the fridge, so scrape out the accumulation of frost. Now take everything from the ice-box and dump it into the bath, take off your clothes and sit in the bath for half an hour. Then go outside. How does it feel? You're still warm.

Did you try the experiment by day or by night? Try it again by night, blindfolded. Can we begin to imagine, even now, what it must be like to feel that cold; and to walk 120 miles over the frozen sea? In total darkness? To sleep, feeling that cold and colder yet, in a tent, with nothing to eat but lukewarm corned beef and ship's biscuit, with a cup of tepid cocoa made from melted ice for comfort? I would say no.

And when Bowers and Wilson and Cherry-Garrard set out from Cape Evans for Cape Crozier at the darkest point of the year, in the very depths of the Antarctic winter, to find some Emperor penguin eggs, they too cannot really have imagined, even then, the cold and dark, the hunger and exhaustion. Because if they could, if Scott could, this most terrible of journeys yet undertaken by human beings would not have gone ahead. Scott's leadership of the Terra Nova expedition must be criticized, of that there can be no doubt; but on this charge, at least, we can exonerate him. Even though Scott and Wilson had overwintered in Antarctica previously, even though both Bowers and Cherry-Garrard were experienced sledgers, well used to the rigours of life on the Barrier, none of them could have conceived of what the Winter Journey really entailed. Cherry-Garrard's gripping account is called *The Worst Journey in the World*. And this journey, remember, was not the appalling hike across the Barrier, up the Beardmore

Glacier, across the Plateau to find the evidence of Amundsen's success; not the hike that killed Evans and Scott and Oates; not the journey that killed even Wilson and Bowers. This was the journey that, by some incredible miracle, both Wilson and Bowers (and, of course, Cherry-Garrard) survived.

Sitting in the hut at Cape Evans, it must have seemed like a bit of a lark. All the serious work of the summer and autumn had gone towards preparing for the assault on the Pole itself; all the laying of depots, the digging out of the encampment at Hut Point, the nightmares with the ponies – all of this was the main purpose of the expedition. The Winter Journey was a sideshow, Wilson's sideshow, which he hoped would show that Emperor penguins were, in a somewhat non-Darwinian way, the least evolved of all birds. And this is the first incredible thing about the Winter Journey: that Wilson had interpreted Darwin so badly.

(NB: Send this bit to Anya, see what she thinks)

To: Dr Anya Schacht, McMurdo Base, Ross Island, USARP.

Top Flat
23 Bloomsbury Place
Brighton
E. Sussex

Dear Anya,

Thanks very much for your last letter, and for the wonderful photographs of the hut on Cape Evans. One day I will have finished the book and made my fortune; then, perhaps, I shall be able to afford to come and see for myself. There is nothing I should like more in the world. But at the time of writing, the book is stalled. I sometimes wish that I had decided to leave the book on South Georgia, and to focus on whaling. But, in my mind, I stood at Shackleton's grave and felt that I had somehow to account for its being there, and so over the years it has grown and grown until it has become the sprawling monster that it now is.

I justify this by saying that there hasn't really been a definitive account of Antarctic exploration – also, I must admit, because Frances from downstairs pointed out to me that whaling in South Georgia was not really a commercial proposition. Sometimes I worry that even Antarctic exploration may not achieve best-seller status. When I took the decision to expand my theme somewhat, about five years ago, I nearly decided to turn it into a pot-boiler; a thriller, perhaps, set on Desolation Island, or a shopping and fucking blockbuster about turn-of-the-century Grytviken. Sometimes, like just now, I wish I had tried this.

I'm enclosing a few pages from what will eventually be Chapter 23 to give you a feel of where I'm up to. So far, I've managed to bury my overwhelming admiration for those men under a blanket of objectivity; but the Winter Journey still staggers me every time I come to think of it. Perhaps, dear Anya, you can help me again. You have over-wintered at McMurdo – perhaps you could send me an account of what it is like now, to work outside in June? I'd really be grateful if you could. I just need a line.

Meanwhile, life here goes along its merry way. The most important thing is the Flat Season, which starts in a couple of weeks. I need another reasonable summer in order to be able to spend the winter with *In Southern Waters*. I suppose I could have chosen a worse time to be stuck with the book, as following the horses really does take up a great deal of effort. And yes, since you ask, I do have a system; a really obvious and easy one that anyone could follow if only they could exercise a little restraint and were to spend hours reading the *Racing Post* (a daily newspaper here in England devoted to the subject of horse and dog racing). If ever you come to this country, I should be delighted to teach you, though whether or not it would work in the States really depends on what percentage of the winnings you get paid for a place.

The early spring is always a difficult time for mammals, as food can be scarce, and I am no exception. I have written before about Paul and Frances Holland, who live downstairs. Frances, almost uniquely among my friends (you excepted), has an actual job, and high standards. So every spring, in order to stretch the budget a bit, I paint their flat. Paul is supposed to help, but mostly he just skins up and makes coffee. Picture us kind of like Stan and Ollie, with stepladders and sheets and buckets of whitewash and all the other necessaries for decorating, but with nothing getting done except a bit of slapstick. Holland is not really interested in work of any kind, but it is his flat, so he feels that he has a proprietary right to help with the redecoration. As well as skinning up, he likes to read *Country Living* – a lifestyle magazine which shows you how to arrange sticks in tasteful vases and things like that. He sits and reads while I paint (though he tries to discourage me); and he keeps calling me over to look at some stencils he likes, or to suggest a distressed look for the spare bedroom. In fact, it is nothing to do with him at all; Frances chooses all the colours, issues all the orders before going off to work, and pays the bills. If I haven't covered a few square metres by the time she gets back I'm in dead shtook, so I have to stagger on despite Holland saying that dried hops look nice, and do I know where we could get some.

Rather oddly, I have had a couple of mornings' help from Caroline, the hi-fi girl in our flat, who has the room upstairs from mine. I say oddly because she is having an affair with Holland, so the atmosphere can get a bit strained when it's the three of us. God only knows what she wants to help decorate her lover's flat for. Well, I know really. Because on both occasions she's come to help, she's wielded the brush for about an hour before going off with Holland for a fuck in his wife's bed. She thinks that Holland is about to leave his wife for her, though how she explains his enthusiasm for redecoration, I don't know.

I find it difficult to explain why women are attracted to him. Frances says it's because of something in his eyes, but I don't see it myself. In fact, I don't know why women are attracted to men at all. If I was a woman, I should be a lesbian. Everyone agrees that women have lovely bodies, and that men's are ungainly and dangly. The only problem I have with homosexuality is why? Why shag blokes when you could sleep with girls? I mean, if you want to sleep with blokes, that's fine. Thank God some people do, or I would never lose my mess. But what the attraction is, I can't begin to say.

And Holland in particular, while a great personal friend of mine, is also a useless lying piece of turd. And mad. Last week, Her Majesty Queen Elizabeth Two came down to Brighton, to open a new extension at the Marina. What this means is that she comes down on the Royal Train, goes to the Marina, presses a little underclass flesh and unveils a plaque. In order to achieve this modest end, she is forced to drive from Brighton station down to the seafront and along

Marine Drive. It was a nice day (the day before my birthday, as it happens – by which time the rain had returned. Thank you. I am thirty-eight), and so the Queen drove in an open-topped Landau, in order that she might wobble a regal glove at the citizenry. Holland, hearing of this, and being, as usual, more than a little stoned, devised what he saw as a highly amusing wheeze. He and Dave, another of my flatmates, who has just returned from a tour of Europe with the well-known pop group the Stranglers (who are from Guildford), got hold of two spud guns. Do you have spud guns in the States? Do you have anywhere that equates to Guildford, I wonder? No matter. The point is, Holland and Dave got these spud guns and climbed out on to the roof of the flat, where Dave keeps his boat. Our roof is linked to all the other roofs in the street, and merely by climbing over some low walls it is possible to get down to the house at the end of Bloomsbury Place, from where you look down on to Marine Parade. And the plan? Why, to shoot at the Queen with spud guns. So Holland and Dave climb up and hurry along the roof, preparing to take up their places. Luckily for them, the police marksmen who are on the house on the other side of the road don't notice them, though I feel that their dereliction of duty has implications for our monarch's personal safety, and for national security in general. Also, very luckily, Holland and Dave spot the marksmen before they are spotted in turn, and hurry back down into our flat, breathless with laughter. They were lucky not to be shot, and I was quite mad with them, which would have been appropriate if they were twelve, but since Holland is thirty-two and Dave twenty-nine, it was a bit embarrassing.

Also rather embarrassing is the fact that when I am painting, and Frances is at home, she comes in and quizzes me about what is happening between her husband and my flatmate. I really have tried not to find out too much, although, as I have already admitted, I know rather a lot. And Frances is a good friend of mine. So should I tell her what I know, that her husband, while great fun to go down the pub with, is a total shit? Of course not. She knows that he's a total shit already. People are very strange. We fall in love with somebody, because of who they are, and then we expect them to change. This is a truism, I know, but that just makes it all the more true. It does not explain *why* it should be so. The odd thing is that I'm almost certain Frances herself is 'carrying on' with one of the post-grads in her department, an Antipodean like her. But she's still frantic about her husband's behaviour. There you have it: there's nowt queerer than folk.

One rather sad event has been the admission to hospital of our old friend Edgar, who lodges in one of the flats downstairs. He is eighty-three, and suffers from emphysema. Dolly, his landlady, thinks he's going to be OK because he's much too cussed to die, but it is very worrying hearing him wheezing. Frances or I pop in to see him most afternoons; the hospital is only up the road. I'm not very fond of hospitals, as it goes. He has a disciple, a good friend of ours called Prince Jeremiah (he really is a prince), who sits by his bedside noting down everything the old bugger says on the subjects of economics and international relations. In case I've drawn a picture of a saintly old guru, I should point out that he is an extreme free-marketeer, who advocates abolishing the Welfare State, and that the prince has to smuggle him in a bottle of Lebanese wine every day, which is not only disgusting stuff that tastes of dog turds and creosote but also incredibly strong. He is always, therefore, a bit tiddly, and he tries to goose the nurses, which is not easy when you're hitched up to a ventilator.

Sailor Dave, the flatmate who has just been off with the Stranglers, has also been going up to the hospital with alarming regularity, although his visits have been to the genito-urinary department. It's always the same when he comes back from tour; his NSU flares up, although he swears before each trip that this time it's going to be different. One of his old girlfriends, who called him Mr Floppy on account of his diseased knob, tells a rather amusing story of her first visit to the clinic. The nurse said, as she made out the poor girl's file for the first time, what are the names of your sexual contacts. David Ryan, said the girl, and before she could even give his address, the nurse brightened, and said, 'Oh, Sailor Dave!' She went off to get his file, which, so the girl claims, was so large that they had to use a fork-lift truck and bring it in on a pallet. I think she may have been exaggerating. Although it may sound unlikely, Sailor Dave is one of nature's gentlemen, and he really does try to abstain from sexual contact with women. This has a tendency to make him tense and broody, but he does try. On his return from tour this time, when I asked him how it went, he told me that he had been good right up until the last night of the tour in Stockholm, when a seventeen-year-old girl offered him and the tour manager a two-up. 'I couldn't say no to a two-up, could I?' he pleaded with me. 'It wouldn't have been right.' And so, of course, his trouble has flared up again. The sad thing is, I rather suspect him of being in love with Caroline, the girl who's knocking off Holland downstairs. I think she may have been tempted in her early days here, before the thing with Holland started, but as Dave didn't make a move, she assumed he wasn't interested, and so got herself into the thing with Holland. Of course, if Dave is interested in someone, being a gentleman, he treats them with respect, which precludes any kind of sexual relationship because of his condition. So he can't act. But Caroline thinks that he's a great listener, so every time he gets back from tour she latches on to him and tells him how crazy she is about Paul, and how he's going to leave his wife and all the rest of it. Which is rather sad, n'est-ce pas?

Highlight of the next few weeks is going to be our landlord's eightieth birthday party. He's a funny old stick who lives with his sister Jemima in the basement flat, but he's a great landlord and really gives us no bother. We all get on well, and we're all invited to his do, which is being held in the Old Ship, one of Brighton's posher hotels. There's no chance of him being admitted to hospital, as he is as fit as a butcher's dog; he goes swimming in the sea every day, never mind the weather, and he is as brown as a berry.

Well, I suppose I'd better get back to painting the Hollands' flat. It still needs a couple of weeks' work; less if Paul helped instead of

172

sitting about reading style magazines. Painting the flat means the arrival of spring; and spring means horses, so the book goes somewhat into abeyance until the autumn; but if you could give me an account of how it feels to be outside in winter, that would be great.

Good luck with the leopard seals' digestive system, and stay wrapped up!

Lots of love,
Bob Blossom

To the Lighthouse 2*

Robertson Blossom stared at the walls of the Hollands' flat in some satisfaction. It had taken almost a month, but he had managed it at last. The painting was finished. Frances stood beside him.

'It looks quite good,' she said.

'Quite good? Quite good? It's fucking brilliant, is what.'

'All right, it's fucking brilliant. Your time is your own again. Thank you. What are you going to do now? Back to the book? Or is it horsey time?'

'It's horsey time. But today, if you are free, I should like you to come with me to Newhaven on the train.'

Frances rolled her eyes to heaven. 'Oh Christ,' she said. 'It's not already is it?'

'It's today.'

'But the weather is so utterly shit.'

'That makes it even better. Please?'

'Oh Jesus. All right. Make yourself a coffee while I change.'

Blossom sat at the kitchen table idly turning the pages of Frances's *Spectator* until she came back wearing a long black sweater and a pair of chic black leggings.

*Any readers who are puzzled by this section are referred to Michael Holroyd's excellent biography of Lytton Strachey and *The Intellectuals and the Masses* by John Carey.

'Semen?' enquired Blossom, pointing to a stain on Frances's slim thighs.

Frances looked at her leg, and screamed in disgust. 'Ahh! Fucking Cats! I'll kill the little wanker this time, I really will!'

'Hey! He's only trying to express his sexuality. That's what you always say.'

Frances muttered under her breath and went to change into another, identical pair of leggings. Blossom and Frances put on their coats, and went out to wait for the bus to take them up to the station.

'I really don't know why we have to do this every fucking year.'

'Yes, you do, or you wouldn't keep coming.'

Frances sighed and turned up the collar on her coat. The bus came.

'Did you know that St Bartholomew's Church was built to the dimensions of the ark?' asked Blossom as the Newhaven train pulled out from the station and on to the great viaduct across the London Road.

'Yes. You tell me every time we get this train.'

'Sorry. Have you been out this way since last year?'

'Not on the train. I went to Newhaven by car with Paul to see his aunt a few weeks ago.'

Blossom looked out of the window as the train pulled out of London Road station. 'Is hate one of the Seven Deadly Sins?' he asked.

'I'm sorry, hon. My biblical scholarship is, at best, uncertain.'

'I hope not. I hate her so much.'

'I know.'

At Falmer, Frances saw her friend Brad getting on further down the train, so she went and sat with him till the train got to Lewes. She rejoined Blossom as the train left Lewes and entered the broad flat valley of the Ouse.

'How's Brad?' asked Blossom.

'Fine. Fine. Look. There it is.' Frances pointed from the window towards a small village on the opposite bank of the river.

'Rodmell,' said Blossom.

'You know they want to knock down Monks House?'

'Stupid cunts,' said Blossom.

'I thought that you would have approved?'

'Not at all. I think they should turn it into a museum. And put up signs all around here saying "Welcome to Bloomsbury Country". And take loads of Japanese tourists on coach trips to Monks House and Berwick Church and Charleston. She'd have hated that.'

Frances laughed. 'Ah,' she said, 'but then you are illiterate and ill-bred, a tedious, self-educated, working-class man. A callow board-school boy who doesn't know his place. A counter-jumper. Egotistic. Insistent. Raw. Ultimately nauseating.'

Blossom grinned. Frances pretended that this trip meant nothing to her, but if that was the case, how come she could quote huge chunks of Virginia's own words at him?

'I'm a white slug,' he said.

'Exactly.'

The train pulled into Newhaven Town station, and Blossom and Frances walked over the bridge and up into the town in the teeth of a howling gale. Bitter rain spat intermittently from the dull sky. In Safeways they bought a few essential supplies for their picnic, and walked back down to the riverside. Progress was slow in the face of the wind; they walked along the harbour wall, past the lifeboat station and the Marina, and along to the car park at the foot of the cliffs, from where they could see huge waves crashing over the breakwater.

'Do you think it's safe?' asked Frances.

'Probably. It's too late to turn back.'

It took them half an hour to walk the length of the Victorian breakwater. Although they had dodged into the arches which ran the half-mile length of the great grey structure every time they heard a wave smack against the wall, they were still soaking wet before they climbed the few steps to the platform around the lighthouse at the breakwater's end. A lone fisherman stood watching for waves which might knock him into the sea; in the bucket next to him, Blossom and Frances could see a few lugworms. He nodded at them, and Blossom held open the carrier bag for Frances.

'Pork pie?'

'Please. Did we get any pickled onions?'

'Of course.'

'Thank you.'

'Why do we do this every year?' asked Frances, her mouth full of pie.

'What, go to the lighthouse?'

'Yes.'

'A bit pointless really, isn't it?'

'Yes. And bloody cold.'

Blossom pulled two cans of Special Brew from the carrier bag. 'I propose a toast.' He lifted his tin.

'To Mrs Virginia Woolf. On the anniversary of her death.'

'Mrs Virginia Woolf.'

They drank from their cans.

'Fuck her, right?'

'Dead right.'

'And Jeanette Winterson,' said the fisherman, holding up the cup from his Thermos flask.

'What?' said Frances.

'I said, "And Jeanette Winterson." Fuck her too,' said the fisherman.

'Can you say that?' asked Frances.

'I just did.'

'Right. Well. Fuck Jeanette Winterson too, then,' said Blossom.

The friends finished their drinks, threw their tins into the sea, and watched as they disappeared under the waves.

They looked for the fisherman but he had gone; so had his tackle.

'Do you think a wave got him?' asked Frances.

'I doubt it. No, look, there he is, walking down the breakwater.'

They watched his retreating back for a minute. He walked with a pronounced limp.

'Who the fuck was he?' asked Blossom.

'How should I know?'

'I liked him though.'

'Yes. Well, come on,' said Frances. 'If we hurry we can just catch the five-to train.'

'What, is that the end?' said Blossom.

'Crap, wasn't it?'

'Not much happened really, did it?'

'No, I suppose not.'

Beating the Retreat

By anybody's standards, Geoffrey's eightieth birthday party had been a roaring success. As the hundred or so guests had arrived at eleven in the morning, their host and hostess, Geoffrey the landlord and his younger sister Jemima, had pressed glasses of Pimm's into eager hands. Then there had been a champagne breakfast, with overflowing glasses of the good stuff. Champagne had been drunk in Victorian quantities. And under silver platters there had been fat Sussex herb sausages, and good home-cured bacon, and black puddings, and great slabs of ham and a whole Severn salmon, poached, and eggs, scrambled and fried; and devilled kidneys, and young lamb chops, pink inside and tender on the tongue, and kedgeree, and mushrooms and tomatoes and seven different kinds of toast, and fried bread and marmalades and jams and honey and more and more champagne.

Then the North Laine Stompers had played a little trad jazz, while Geoffrey and his sister led the dancing, followed closely by the children, lots of them, and then, as their parents had their inhibitions stripped away by champagne, they joined in too, until the whole room was filled with a hundred drunken guests lurching about in at least approximate time to the music.

And then everyone had sat at the trestle tables, and there were speeches; one very funny one from the Eel, who had

179

been allowed out of the hospital for the occasion, and one rather touching one from Geoffrey himself. Neither had lasted longer than five minutes. And then there was nothing left to do except sit around and get quietly or even noisily drunk, and talk. Holland and Frances were between a marine biologist who introduced himself as Alan, Geoffrey's great-nephew from Plymouth who was sitting next to his wife Pip, and an opera singer who lived a little way further up Bloomsbury Place, who they already knew slightly, called Kenny, who was with his friend Mike. Blossom sat next to Kenny and Mike with Cats and Caroline and Sailor Dave. Caroline, in order to make Holland jealous, was flirting with Mike, but Mike, in order to make Kenny jealous, was flirting with Cats, who was giggling hysterically.

By four in the afternoon all the other guests had staggered off, including the Eel, whom Jeremiah had coaxed into a taxi and back to the Sussex County, and only this group remained in the elegant function room. Waitresses cleared the tables and the North Laine Stompers were packing up their instruments as Jemima and Geoffrey came tottering across to join the last of their guests, clearly the worse for drink. A ragged cheer went up, and still full glasses were raised as the old couple sat.

'Geoffrey!' said Holland.

'Happy birthday,' said Frances, a sentiment which was echoed around the table.

'Thank you very much,' said Geoffrey. 'I hope you've all enjoyed yourselves.'

They all agreed that they had very much. They were all steaming, especially Caroline, who was beginning to feel a little under the weather, and was over-compensating with an enforced heartiness.

'How does it feel, eh Geoffrey?' she said.

'How's that, my dear?'

'Being eighty. How does it feel?'

'Very little different from seventy-nine, to be honest.'

'Oh I don't believe you. You old rascal, I bet you feel all sagey and wise.'

'No, not really.'

'No, I bet you do. I think old people are wonderful, don't you? I bet you look back all that way, over that long long long life, and think – ha! Ha! I'm eighty!'

'Well, no, not really. I'm looking forward to my swim tomorrow.'

'Amazing,' said Caroline. 'That's, you know, amazing, and that. Looking forward. Amazing. But tell me, Geoffrey – do you have any regrets? I mean, eighty. You must have regrets.'

'A few,' said Geoffrey indulgently.

Holland opened his mouth to sing.

'Don't sing,' hissed Frances.

'No, but you must have. I have, and I'm only twenty. I mean, did you have any kids? Kids are a great worry, even when you're eighty. My mother says that you never stop worrying.'

Geoffrey laughed, and Jemima smiled into her drink. Frances kicked Caroline under the table.

'What?' said Caroline.

'No, I never had any children. Would have been a ruddy miracle if I had,' said Geoffrey.

'Why's that?' asked Caroline.

'Because, Caroline, I am what is known as a bumboy.'

Everyone started talking at once.

'Right,' said Caroline earnestly, a blush rising to her cheeks.

'Uncle!' said Alan, the marine biologist.

'I think you say gay now, don't you?' said Jemima.

'Caroline, you mustn't worry. The others hadn't told you.'

'There's no bloody reason why we should,' said Frances. 'This is Brighton, fer Chrissakes. No one gives a toss.'

'The lovely thing about Brighton,' said Geoffrey, 'is that there are plenty of people who are more than willing to give you a toss. Fifty years I've lived here, and I've lost count of the number of times I've met boys who'll give you a toss, or a suck, or a damned good rodgering. Brighton toilets.' He sighed nostalgically. 'So many happy hours of my life have been spent in Brighton toilets.'

'I've always wondered,' remarked Frances. 'For women, there is nothing less sexy than a public convenience. What *is* the attraction for gays?'

Geoffrey looked pained. 'Oh, don't use that horrible word. Call us uphill gardeners, call us kidney polishers, but please don't call us gay. It makes me sick. Gay. It's such a pretty word, so bloody feminine. Females are all right, but I've never seen anything sexy about 'em. All saggy and pappy. They suck up a man's strength. No, I'll tell you what's sexy. A lovely big hard cock, all purple and veiny, throbbing with desire, a clear drop of lovely juice peeping from its little eye. A nice big pair of hairy balls in your mouth. The tight pungency of a boy's arsehole. That's sexy. Wouldn't you agree, Mrs H? Kenny?'

'Well, to an extent,' said Frances. 'But what is it about bogs?'

'Oh, my dear, it's the stink and the excitement and the availability. It's the fact that you can go in and meet some-one, and give 'em a damn good seeing to, and then never have to see them again. None of this gooey emotional stuff. You just go in again the next day, and the next, and the next, and there's always a new bumhole, a new cock. Lovely!' Geoffrey rubbed his hands together and smiled at Kenny and Mike. 'Isn't that so, boys? Hmmm?'

Kenny and Mike shifted uneasily.

'The thing is, Geoff, things have changed a bit,' said Kenny. 'What with AIDS and all.'

'Damned shame,' said Geoffrey. 'Taken all the fun out of it. Worse thing to happen to the art of buggery since legalization.'

'Besides,' said Mike, 'we're in love. We wouldn't want to go cottaging even if we could, would we, Ken? Ken? I said, we wouldn't want to have casual sex even if it was safe, would we?'

'Hmm?' said Kenny, who had a faraway look in his eyes. 'What's that? Oh no, no, of course not. No. We're in love.'

'Aaah,' said Pip, the marine biologist's wife. 'How sweet. How nice to hear people say that.'

'I'm not sure that love really comes into it,' said Blossom. 'I think gay blokes just have loads of sex because they are . . . well, blokes. I mean, if a girl came up to me at the bus stop and offered to suck me off, I'd be up for it like a shot. And I wouldn't even have to fancy her or anything. It just doesn't happen, that's all. Women aren't like that. They like foreplay and all that. Conversation.'

'Well, actually,' said Holland, 'just that thing did happen to me at a bus stop. It was about four years ago . . .'

'Oh shut up,' said Caroline and Frances.

'Well, it's all a bit beyond me these days anyway. I have an Egyptian boy who comes and blows me off on Wednesday mornings, but it's not the same. Takes him all bloody morning these days. I haven't been up to the station for ten years or more,' said Geoffrey.

'Oh, but Geoffrey, were you never in love?' asked Caroline.

Geoffrey looked at her. If Caroline had never previously known what it meant when a moustache bristled, she did now.

'Love? Love? Love is something you feel for your mother,

or for your school or regiment. It is not something that you feel for a man.'

'What do you feel for men?' asked Frances.

'Admiration. Respect. Sexual desire.'

'Can't you feel that for women?'

'Some of it. Especially the last bit,' said Holland.

'Shut up!' said Frances and Caroline again.

'Yes, I can, apart from the sex,' said Geoffrey. 'I respect and admire my sister, and I love her too. But between men, I don't believe it's possible.'

'Well, Geoff, Kenny and I are living proof that you are wrong,' said Mike. 'Aren't we, Ken?'

'Yes,' said Kenny. 'Sort of.'

'What do you mean?'

'No. Nothing. We are in love. I love you.'

'Rubbish,' said Geoffrey. 'I don't believe it.'

'Come on, Geffers,' said Jemima. 'These people want to be getting home, and we've got to see the manager. Come on.'

The hosts rose from the table; and the company around the table rose with them, all except the marine biologist who seemed to be asleep. As the party were saying their goodbyes, he sat up and said, 'Do you know, Uncle Geoff, you got me going there. I quite fancy a bit of cock myself now.'

'Alan!' said his wife.

'It's the drink talking, hon,' said Frances. 'When they're like that, they'll fuck anything. It's nothing personal. It's their job.'

The next morning, Frances was surprised to receive a phone call from Geoffrey.

'I was wondering, Mrs H., if you weren't busy, if you and Blossom's hi-fi girl would care to come and have a cup of coffee with Jemima and me in half an hour or so.'

184

'Why, Geoffrey, thank you. I'd be delighted. I'll give Caroline a ring.'

'Would you? There is something I'd like to talk about.'

Caroline was always a little suspicious when Frances phoned her in the mornings, but she was fascinated by the invitation to visit the basement flat, which she had not seen in her six months or so of living in Bloomsbury Place. It was heavy with Benares brass, and ivory carvings, and framed representations of Shiva. Coffee was served black from a silver coffee-pot into tiny Turkish cups perched on a wooden table of ornate pierced design.

'I am so glad you could both come. Something has been troubling my conscience,' said Geoffrey.

'Oh?' said Frances and Caroline.

'Yesterday. I was drunk, you know.'

'Oh, Geoffrey, I'm so sorry,' said Caroline. 'I was very drunk myself. I really didn't mean to pry.'

'Oh, my dear. You mustn't worry. I've been "out" for seventy-three years. No, it's just that I wasn't quite straight with you both. You see, a very long time ago, and a very long way away, I was in love. Yes, I was. And I shouldn't have denied it. I shouldn't have denied Malcolm.'

Tears stood from his eyes. Frances took his hand.

'I'm sorry,' he said. 'It was all a very long time ago.'

'What happened?' whispered Caroline. 'Where's Malcolm now?'

'Oh, my dear, where do you think most of my friends are now? I'm eighty, you will remember.'

'Dead, you mean?'

'Of course, dead.'

'Well, not quite all, Geffers. A few of our old India friends are still alive. Some of them live in Cliftonville, and some in Frinton, and we have one friend who lives in Cheltenham,' said Jemima.

'Same thing,' said Frances.

'But Malcolm? Malcolm's dead?' asked Caroline, in fascinated horror.

'Malcolm's been dead for fifty years. No, more. More than fifty now.'

'How did you meet him?' asked Frances. 'If you don't mind . . . ?'

'No, of course not. No. In Burma. 1941. A place called Moulmein. I was twenty-four, he twenty-three. I was in the Burma Police, he was a subaltern with the Gurkhas. Very proud of his platoon, was Malcolm. His first command. And he had every right to be proud of them because they are the finest damn men in the world. I wouldn't be here now if it wasn't for them.'

'I didn't know you were in the Burma Police. Did you ever know Orwell?' said Frances.

'Years before my time. I never met him, though my sergeant had served under him. Remembered him as a fairly remote kind of fellow. Always liked the books myself, but the service tended to think of him as a bit of a pinko.'

'Tell us about Malcolm,' said Caroline.

'One of his men had been arrested on a charge of assault. Moulmein, which, as you may or may not know, is in the south of Burma, was my patch. It's a large port, one which was to assume strategic importance in what was to follow. Malcolm came to bail this fellow out. We hit it off straight away, especially when Malcolm saw that I wasn't going to come down hard on his man. He'd been in a fight with a lascar seaman, if I remember rightly. Anyhow, Malcolm and I started to see a bit of each other, going to the club and the races and so on. Moulmein wasn't Rangoon, but it was quite lively, and the war was a long way away. It seemed impossible that Burma would ever be in it at all, which was a bore for Malcolm and his chaps, because your Gurkha loves to be in the thick of it. Still. I told Malcolm about myself and he laughed, and said that it didn't worry him in the least. Said there were lots of chaps like that at his school, and that it was OK by him.'

'Oh. Wasn't Malcolm . . . ?'

'Oh no. Not at all. Besides, he wasn't my type, you know. He was very blond and pretty, very girlie. I like manly men. And he was married, to a girl in England. They'd got married just before he came out east. He used to show me her picture when he got blotto. She's the best little lady in the whole damned world, Geoff, he used to say in his cups. He was mad about her. And so we got to be great friends, Malcolm and I. Great friends. And then, one night in November 1941, we went for a drink to the Lower Burma Club as usual, and we sat at our usual table, and had our usual drinks, and Malcolm crossed his legs as he used to do, and I noticed that he was wearing red socks. Extraordinary thing. I'll never forget that night. Malcolm was wearing red socks. And that was it. A wave of realization swept over me. I was in love with Malcolm. Hopelessly, madly in love. That was all it took. A pair of red socks.'

'Oh, I know,' said Caroline. 'When Paul—' She stopped, and looked at Frances, who looked straight back at her.

'Well, I suppose the next part of the story is as predictable as possible. I couldn't eat. I couldn't sleep. I thought about Malcolm last thing at night and first thing in the morning. You know.'

Caroline nodded, and Frances yawned.

'I tried to fix it so that Malcolm and I could spend as much time together as possible. Lunches, walks, drinks in the club. I didn't hope for much; I didn't really expect him to love me in return. He had his wife. But I found that I had lost interest in sex. Couldn't be bothered. If I couldn't have it with Malcolm, and I knew that I never could, then I didn't want it at all. I was happy just to spend as much of our off-duty time together as could be arranged. And that was November, and the first week of December. And then, of course, the whole thing blew up.'

'Why?' said Caroline breathlessly.

Frances sighed. 'December 7th, 1941?' she said. 'No? Doesn't ring a bell?'

'No. Why should it?'

'Christ! What do they teach you at the uni?' asked Frances.

'Physics,' said Caroline.

'Don't worry, my dear,' said Jemima. 'It's probably more important to New Zealanders than to the English. The Japanese bombed Pearl Harbor.'

'Oh,' said Caroline.

'And the next day they attacked Hong Kong. And a few days after that, bombing raids started on Rangoon and Moulmein. Of course, both Malcolm and I had our worlds turned upside down. I was as busy as hell trying to keep order in the streets, and arrange evacuation for women and children, while Malcolm and his platoon were moved forward, preparing for a full-scale invasion. Moulmein was indefensible, and even I as a humble copper could see that; and so, of course, the Staff wallahs declared that it was to be held at all costs.

'You must understand that, in all of this, we were completely unprepared. No one had expected war in the East; no one. Malcolm was desperate to get back to North Africa, where he might see some action. Burma, regarded as a wonderful posting in peacetime, was a shameful backwater in wartime, especially for the Gurkhas. Now, in early January, the whole bloody Jap army started swarming into Burma, and we had nobody to stop them; nobody but a few companies of Gurkhas, a regiment of the line who'd been doing ceremonials in Rangoon, some Indian Army chaps, and the Burma Rifles, who were worse than useless. And all these poor bastards were supposed to hold Moulmein. It was hopeless, quite, quite hopeless. The night before he and his chaps were sent forward, I had a last quick drink with Malcolm.

' "Well, Geffers," he said, "that's probably the last drink we'll ever have together. Pray for us."

'And off he went. I cried myself to sleep.'

'Oh, how sad,' said Caroline.

'Wait. It was my job to guard the headquarters in Moulmein, and to co-ordinate the military and civilian authorities, so I was able to follow what was going on. Malcolm was with his company at a little village called Myawadi, some miles south of Moulmein, and they took the full force of the invasion. Malcolm's company commander radioed in to say that the Japs were on them, thousands of them, but that they were holding their position.

'And then they radioed in to say that they were completely surrounded. They were lost. The transmission broke down. And although, that early in the war, we didn't know as we did later what the Japs were like with prisoners, we all knew it was pretty hopeless. I knew that I had lost my Malcolm for ever.'

'Oh Geoff,' whispered Frances.

'I felt that my world had collapsed, that I had nothing to live for any longer. I don't know how I managed to get my work done, but I did. Had to. Had to. The Japs were coming closer and closer to the city; we all worked like blacks.'

Frances and Caroline winced.

'It was the work that kept me going, I suppose. I tried to focus on that. And then, bugger me blue if a week later Malcolm's company didn't come marching into the city, with grins all over their faces. They'd cut their way through the whole bloody Jap army, and made it back to Moulmein. I was in my office when Malcolm came in; I leaped to my feet and hugged him.

'"Steady on, old man," he said, but I could tell that he was pleased to see me. But there wasn't long to feel happy; the Japs were already on the outskirts of the city. Malcolm and his lads got a bath and a good meal – though the Gurkha can fight on an empty stomach if he has to – and the next day, all hell let loose as the Japs came flooding in. I was down at the river jetty, directing the final evacuation across the Salween. It was a mini Dunkirk, with all kinds of funny boats taking people off. A platoon of Madras sappers were working to blow the jetties, and I helped people on to the boats; still Malcolm and his lads hadn't turned up. It was like Myawadi all over, only this time I was sure he couldn't have escaped again. My superintendent ordered me on to the last but one boat, but I said I'd like to stay and help defend the jetty to give the sappers time to destroy it. So I stayed; a Staff major came huffing up, and the sapper captain asked for orders. "Keep the bloody Japs off this jetty," he said, and hopped on to the last boat out of Moulmein. I stayed behind, since I was probably the best shot left, sappers being much too clever to be any good at fighting.

'And now came the second of the three miraculous escapes Malcolm had in Burma: he and his platoon marched – marched, mark you – with the Japanese army literally yards behind them, up to the jetty and took over the final defence, while the sappers lashed together a raft. I stood next to Malcolm, having borrowed a rifle, and somehow we kept the buggers off just long enough for the sappers to finish the job. They blew the jetty, and we all leaped into the Salween, and held on to the bloody raft with Jap bullets hitting the water all around us, and got across to Martaban. About fifty of us, believe it or not.

190

'In Martaban makeshift defences were being thrown up all over the place . . .'

'Where's Martaban?' asked Caroline.

'Opposite bank of the Salween from Moulmein. Things were pretty anarchic. You must understand, it had all happened so incredibly quickly. Smyth, the commanding officer, had ridiculous orders to try and hold these forward positions, instead of falling back on Rangoon as he wanted to. So we did our best. There were probably jobs that I was better suited to doing than hanging around with Gurkhas, but I wasn't going to leave Malcolm; not to wait around to see if he got away with it again. Cats have nine lives; Gurkha officers are notoriously short-lived.

'So I became a kind of unofficial Gurkha – I am a tolerable shot, I knew the country, after all, and could speak Burmese, all of which was a help to Malcolm's platoon. And everyone was increasingly mixed up. So we held out in Martaban for a week, somehow, with thousands and thousands of Japs coming at us like lunatics. By this time we had had a few reinforcements. No bloody good though. Say what you like about the Japs, and I, I must admit, hate them still, but they are bloody fine fighting men. Nothing stops 'em. And they didn't have Staff, and the Pay Corps, and cooks, and fitters, and any of the stuff we were encumbered with. And they didn't wear shorts, which are the most useless article of clothing for jungle warfare ever devised by some daft old up-country brass hat. So we held on, and held on, until it became obvious that there was nothing to do but retreat. And retreat in disarray. I think we still felt that we might hold Rangoon, if only we could get there in time. So we set off, again very much at the rear. In front of us was a huge column of vehicles heading for Rangoon; right on our heels were the Japs; and ahead of us was the Sittang. The Sittang.

'Between Martaban and Rangoon lay the Sittang, one of

the great rivers of Indo-China; and the only viable crossing for this bloody great big army column was the Sittang bridge, a railway bridge. From Martaban to the Sittang bridge took us two weeks, fighting all the way. The Japs had accomplished a pincer movement, so that we were not just fighting those coming at us from behind, but on both sides. And we knew that if we were to make the Japs even pause before Rangoon, we had to get to the Sittang bridge before they did, cross it and blow it up behind us. And when I say we, I mean one of the strangest forces ever cobbled together by the British Army. The chain of command was collapsing all around us – and Gurkhas and Indian Army, and chaps from the Duke's and the KOYLI . . .'

'The what?' asked Frances.

'King's Own Yorkshire Light Infantry. KOYLI. We were all mixed up together, taking our orders, such as they were, from whatever officers were still alive. But somehow we just about kept a shape. And so we came to the banks of the Sittang. Christ, what a show. By the time we got there, and I should say that we were far from the last, the whole thing was a complete shambles. They had had no choice but to try to cross the bridge at night, and it was, you will remember, a railway bridge. All the trucks had to cross on were planks which were laid on the tracks, and, inevitably, some of the drivers were simply not up to it. Trucks kept getting stuck on the bridge, some of them field ambulances full of the wounded.

'Now I'm not saying that we should have learned a lesson from the Japs and left our wounded where they lay; what I am saying is that so few of those poor buggers were going to survive anyway that it might have been better to leave 'em behind with a few grenades to take as many Japs with 'em as they could. Anyway. So now soldiers were filing across the bridge on foot, trying to get past the trucks that were stuck;

some of 'em carrying the wounded. What's that bloody German painter you like called, Jem?'

'Hieronymus Bosch?'

'That's the feller. The Sittang called to mind nothing so much as one of his pictures. It became clear from where we were that there was a right side and a wrong side of the Sittang, and that we were on the wrong side. The Japs were quite literally ten minutes behind us, and there were still thousands of our chaps on the wrong side. And there was no cover; paddy fields come down to the Sittang on both sides. We had no choice but to turn and face the enemy; we charged up Pagoda Hill, and held it for the rest of that day, while as many of our people as possible got across. And then night fell. And still we held on while troops came out of the jungle, fighting as they came. We knew we couldn't hold on much longer. And then, that night, the British command took the decision to blow up the Sittang bridge. Had to. Had to, if there was to be any chance of stopping the advance on Rangoon. But the thing is, it left half a division on the wrong side of the river. Half a division.'

'How many people in a division?' asked Caroline.

'Men, my dear. Not people. Men. About ten thousand.'

'Oh, Jesus,' said Frances, who was sitting on the edge of her seat.

'So what did you do?' asked Caroline.

'What could we do? There was no bridge, and no boats. There were thousands of men milling about. We were being shelled from all directions. We could hold on no longer. So we swam. We swam the Sittang. A very wide and fast-flowing river, too, let me assure you. And your Gurkha is not necessarily the best swimmer in the whole British Army. See this?' Geoffrey rolled up his trouser leg to reveal a small white scar.

'Leeches. Leeches. Ugh. Still, most of Malcolm's platoon

made it across somehow. I think the crossing of the Sittang was the most remarkable of our close shaves with death. I swim every day here, as you know. I am a strong swimmer. But I still don't know how I managed that swim. But I did. I did, and I'm here telling you about it. And Malcolm made it too, and all of his men who had managed to get that far, except for an elderly soldier-servant who perhaps should have been on depot duties and not out fighting. But hundreds of others were less lucky. Hundreds of men drowned in the Sittang, hundreds more fought on to the last bullet on the wrong side of the Sittang. The Sittang.' Geoffrey wiped a tear from his eye.

'Oh Geoff, you don't have to tell us all this, you know,' said Frances.

'Oh well,' said Geoffrey. 'It serves me right for denying Malcolm yesterday. Besides, people should know. They called the men who fought in Burma the Forgotten Army, but when people do remember, they always talk about the Chindits. That seems glamorous. No one, but no one remembers the Retreat. I don't suppose you even knew it happened.'

'No,' said both Caroline and Frances.

'Even though it profoundly affected the lives of two of the people in this house?'

'Two?'

'Be patient. I shan't keep you much longer. Funny really. Between Moulmein and the Sittang is perhaps a hundred and fifty miles; in front of us . . . but then, I forget so much of what happened next. We came ashore on the right bank of the Sittang, and made our way to Waw, a tiny village with a railway station. Here the division regrouped and, by a miracle performed by the Ordnance Corps, we were re-equipped. I even managed to wangle a uniform; Lion and Unicorn, the General Service. I stayed with the Gurkhas, though I should have been in Rangoon; not that I could have achieved anything more there. It's just that the thought of leaving Malcolm was too painful to bear. Besides, I think I was thinking of my personal preservation. Malcolm had been so lucky so far, and his men were the best there were. They had crossed the Sittang after all; in Waw it became obvious that over half the division, some five thousand men, had been trapped on the other side or killed. But despite this, our spirits were still relatively high. We were a fighting force again, the 7th Gurkhas.'

Geoffrey sat to attention and saluted; Caroline started to laugh, but was warned off by something in Jemima's eye.

'We were sent to Pegu, a town a way north of Rangoon; again, there to defend the most forward position possible. Rangoon was being evacuated, not before our chaps had destroyed the docks and oil installations in an attempt to make it useless for the Japs. They had managed to get some trucks down to us, so at least we got to ride the twenty-five miles from Waw to Pegu, the first time we'd done anything except march since Moulmein. But Pegu was no good. There were so many Japs, and they moved so fast. I remember air raids, and a great deal of shelling. We held out for a week, but it was no good. No good. I got this one.' Geoffrey pulled down his shirt to reveal another whitened scar on his shoulder.

'It didn't seem too bad at the time; I got it patched up, and we fought on. But after a week, it became obvious that Pegu was lost, and we set off again, on foot this time, for Prome. From Pegu to Prome, is, I guess, about 150 miles. The road was blocked with vehicles, a huge convoy, mostly of ancillary staff, trying to get out of Rangoon. Thousands of vehicles, troops and civilians, exhausted, on foot, running before the Japs blocked our way. We were constantly strafed by Japanese aircraft; really, we had no air cover at all. It took us about a week, I think, but now I was beginning to lose my sense of time. My sense of everything.

'My shoulder was very bad, and I was in a great deal of pain. Only by focusing on the boots of the man in front could I keep going at all. And when we got to Prome, it was the same story; throwing up makeshift defences, keeping the Japs off just long enough so that our sappers could blow up oil installations, and then another ignominious retreat. By now it was obvious to all of us that we had lost Burma. The Chinese came in, fighting on our side, but it was too little and too late. It was bloody nearly too late for me. By the time we started our last chaotic retreat, I was delirious with fever. I should have been in a field ambulance, but the roads were so heavily blocked that it could not be done. I realized later that Malcolm would not give me up, and somehow he kept me going in the march northward. A week after leaving Prome, we came to Burma's dry belt. April is the hottest month in Burma, and we were crossing an area with no water.' Geoffrey licked his lips, poured himself another coffee and drank it in one gulp.

'Ever been without water? I doubt it. I was passing in and out of consciousness all this time, being half dragged, half carried by my Gurkha friends. I think they must have given me more than my fair share of the water ration, those brave men, or I don't think I'd be here now, telling you all of this. By the time we came out of the dry belt and down to the Irrawaddy, I was raving. I remember very little, though I do recall thinking that I was being carried by large yellow woodlice, oddly enough. Somewhere in there, a remarkable event occurred, an event at which I was present, apparently, propped up with my rifle against a tree, firing blindly in front of me. What happened was this.

'There was one major river crossing still to make before we could head into India, the Irrawaddy, and as with the Sittang

196

there was only one crossing point, the Ava bridge. What was left of our poor army had to cross this bridge safely, or it would have made the Sittang look like a picnic. So the Gurkhas, who were enjoying the retreat less than anyone else, were ordered to turn on the Japanese at a town called Kyaukse. There were seventeen hundred Gurkhas and four thousand Japs; we killed about five hundred of them. And do you know how many we lost? Three! Three men dead! It was a great victory, one which bought us enough time to get across the Irrawaddy. And do you think that was it?'

Caroline shrugged; Frances shook her head.

'Dear God, if only it had been. If only the Irrawaddy had formed the border. Do you know, from Moulmein to the Irrawaddy we had marched the best part of seven hundred miles. We were wounded, violently ill, our numbers vastly depleted. Only twelve men from Malcolm's platoon had made it thus far. Our kit was worse than useless; my boots had given up coming out of Prome, and thanks to our shorts, we had mosquito bites all over our legs; at least five of the men were showing signs of malaria, and almost all of us had dysentery to some extent. That meant you had to stop and shit every ten minutes or so.

'But not Malcolm. Malcolm was fine. He was so beautiful, and so brave. It was like he'd just been for a stroll on the Downs, though of course he was filthy and dog tired. And really we were only halfway. Once we got across, it became clear how bad things were. It was late April now and the monsoon was due to start in a week or two, and from here into India was nothing but jungle tracks; any motorized transport that we had managed to get thus far was clearly now useless. Malcolm managed to find his brigadier, and asked him for advice.

' "Walk, Malcolm," he was told. "Walk or die."

'From Mandalay to the Indian border is about four

hundred miles. Travelling on foot, at about a mile an hour, it took us a month, just over. I was lucky; we'd had a couple of days' rest on crossing the river; my wounded shoulder was seen to properly, and my dysentery cleared a little. So for the last part of the retreat I was a bit more use. There were Malcolm and me, two NCOs and ten men when we set out. When Gurkhas go on leave, they sometimes walk as much as a week from the railhead to their village, so they were used to walking long distances. And, by Christ, their faces! What's the word? You know, like the Chinese, so you can't tell what they're thinking?'

'Inscrutable?' suggested Frances.

'That's him! Inscrutable. Four of the lads died on the walk out of Burma, mostly from malaria. Did you know, for every soldier that was wounded in Burma, a hundred came down with tropical diseases?'

'I didn't know any of this stuff,' said Frances.

'Me neither,' said Caroline.

'Hardly anyone does. And they should. Yes. Four of us didn't make it. We had to walk through the Kalewa Valley, the Valley of Death, one of the most malarial spots on this earth. But did the Gurkhas complain? Did they show signs of weariness, even? Not they. Not they. Every morning, the Jemadar lined 'em up and we marched, in column. And you couldn't tell which of the lads would go next; one minute they'd be marching, the next – plop! down they went. It was remarkable. Quite remarkable.

'And then the monsoon broke, and the tracks, which were bad enough, turned into mud-slides. Horrible. There was no shelter from rain like that. You were soaked, and starving, and exhausted, and still you kept walking. What else was there to do? One of the men had dysentery so bad that blood and shit were running down his legs more or less permanently. He no longer bothered stopping for a shit. He died, of course. And everywhere, there were dead and dying people by the tracks. Hundreds of soldiers, and thousands of civilians. There was nothing you could do. All the chains of command were meaningless. You just walked through the jungle, and if you cared about anyone else, it was your mates, your men. And the stench! The smell of the jungle in the monsoon, and the stink of the rotting corpses, mostly unburied. My dears, you can't begin to imagine. You can't begin.'

Geoffrey sipped again at his coffee, his face distorted with long remembered disgust.

'I can't find it in myself to care when I hear people moaning about the desecration of the rain forest. Loathsome place. Loathsome. But it was wonderful too, you know. A wonderful time. Every night, we'd find such little shelter as we could, and try to fight off mosquitoes and parasites, and Malcolm and I would talk. We'd talk and talk, because we knew that each conversation might be our last. I shall always remember talking with Malcolm about anything and everything, and laughing. That last walk was a nightmare, but I'm not sure that I've ever been happier. Though Christ only knows we were bloody relieved one day when we met a platoon of Scottish soldiers coming the other way up the track. And they told us that we had crossed into India, into Nagaland to be specific. They were out cleaning up corpses from the track; we hugged them, and asked where we should head for.

'Now all this time, Malcolm had been the fittest of us all. It was his spirit that was the strongest and even the Gurkhas, who take some bloody stopping at the best of times, were lifted by his strength and courage. But it was as if he had directed everything into achieving India; and once we were there, he seemed to shrink away. The Scots told us we should get to Kohima, two days away, and it was as if those two days were two more months for Malcolm. By the time we came down into Kohima, his eyes were burning with malaria, and it was my turn to carry him. But I wasn't too worried; after all, we were safe now, and there would be hospitals, and Malcolm would be looked after.'

Frances noticed that the tone of Geoffrey's voice was changing; where it had been flat, matter of fact, it was now rising in pitch and becoming increasingly angry.

'But the thing was, they just weren't ready for us. India Movement Control, so called, had done nothing to prepare for the Burcorps, even though they knew we were coming, and thousands of us. In Kohima, the hospitals were full to bursting, and more poor sods coming in every day. They stuck us in tented barracks, and I nursed Malcolm as best I could, which wasn't much. For four nights he raved in his fever; on the fifth morning we were shepherded on to a train. And do you know what they had sent for the heroes of Burma? Cattle trucks, that's what. They were hell trains. Hell trains. Like the Jews. Except we were on the same bloody side. We wound our way over Northern India, with hardly any water, and bugger all food; and no medical equipment. Two days into this nightmare, Malcolm died in my arms.

'"I love you, Malcolm," I said, as I had said many times before; it was a last rite. At the next stop we buried him, Jemadar Nguyen and I. And that was it. My only love.'

'Bloody hell,' said Frances.

Geoffrey sniffed. 'I'm sorry if it all seems a bit Little Nellish, but there you are. Commonplace, trite little stories like mine happen all the time in war.'

'It's not commonplace, or trite,' said Frances.

'Not now,' said Geoffrey. 'But it was then. Cervantes said that even a bad story is redeemed by being true. My little story is at least true.'

'What happened to you?'

'Oh, the same again, really, only going in the other direction. I was gazetted into the Gurkhas as an officer, and we took Burma back.'

'You make it sound very simple.'

'It wasn't. It wasn't. But we did it, you know.'

'Can I ask you something, Geoffrey?' said Caroline.

'Of course.'

'Earlier you said that the retreat changed the lives of two of the people in the house. Who is the other one?'

Geoffrey smiled. 'When the war was over, they built a memorial to the men who died in Burma at Kohima. I was still working out there, so I was invited to the service of dedication. Nagaland is a bloody funny place; Westerners are still not encouraged to travel there, you know. Very strange people indeed. Anyway. You maybe know what it says on the Kohima Memorial?'

Both women shook their heads.

'When you go home,
Tell them of us and say,
For your tomorrow,
We gave our today.

'Not much, is it? I cried like a baby. Like a bloody baby. And there was a woman in the congregation I recognized. From the photo in Malcolm's wallet. His wife, you know. So after the service I introduced myself. We stayed in touch, and when I came back to England I became great friends with her. And her second husband. It's Dolly upstairs, of course.'

'Really?' said Frances.

'Yes, really. When Bill retired, I let them the flat. So Dolly would never have married Bill, or lived here, if it wasn't for the retreat.'

'Does she know how you felt about Malcolm?'

'Of course. That's what brought us so close. We had shared something very special.'

As they walked back upstairs, Caroline said to Frances, 'Who's Little Nell?'

'Just because you do physics doesn't stop you from reading, does it?' snapped Frances.

'Just because people read doesn't stop them from trying to understand physics,' Caroline retorted.

Frances smiled. 'I like you, Caroline. Maybe it's because we share something.'

Caroline blushed.

Frances said, 'A taste in men. We're not lucky like old Geoffrey, falling for the Flower of Empire. We like scumbags.'

They stood outside the door of the Hollands' flat.

'We shouldn't have been out there, should we, Frances? In Burma and India and places, I mean,' said Caroline.

Frances gave her a hug. 'I don't know, hon. Maybe not. But we let go of our empire, however reluctantly. I don't think the Japs would have done, do you?'

'No.'

'Letting go is never easy, Caro.'

'No. Thanks, Frances.'

'That's OK, hon. That's OK.'

Caroline climbed the stairs, sat down in the front room and clicked on the lunchtime news: '*These pictures just in show the devastation wrought by the Allied attacks. It is hoped that civilian casualties can be kept to a minimum.*'

'Doesn't anything ever get better?' she shouted impotently at the screen.

The Moulescoomb Free Festival

'It is said that high in the mountain fastness of Tibet, in a certain lamasery inaccessible to all but the most intrepid of high-country travellers, there is a spliff that never goes out. It is guarded by a caste of warrior monks, dedicated to keeping the spliff going. They use only the finest Nepalese Temple Balls, cropped by virgins, rolled into shape between their thighs, and carried over the mountains by mule train. The tobacco is grown by the monks and cured in the sparse Himalayan sun; the skins are of diaphanous rice paper from China, and the roach material consists of old BR tickets, flown out from the UK and trekked up to the lamasery by fortunate initiates, who are rewarded for their efforts by a couple of tokes on the Eternal Number. And if you ask me,' said Holland, looking around him with approval at the packed crowd in front of the stage erected in the Wild Park, 'these fuckers would get through that spliff in ten minutes flat.'

It would have been difficult to argue with Holland's logic. Brighton Council's desire to see that no one was excluded by some of the more straightforwardly highbrow events of the Brighton Festival had led to a decree that every May Moulescoomb's Wild Park should play host to a free festival, which attracted the wild and hairy from all across the South of England. The quality of the music could best be described as shameful, the food obtained from any number of stalls around the park as indigestible, and the ideas represented by the single-issue campaigners who thrust recycled pamphlets at the hirsute punters as half-baked, but no one seemed to mind too much. It was, after all, free.

By Caroline's reckoning, about five thousand people were crammed into the park. The glorious late spring sunshine had brought them out in larger than ever numbers. And there was so much to see and do. There were demonstrations of circle dancing and t'ai chi and Tibetan spinal massage, several practitioners each of psycho-regeneration, rebirthing and personal spiritual growth advocating their anodyne philosophies to anyone who would listen, and even a girl showing the best way to attach a rope around a dog's neck. There were enough crystal therapists to cure . . . well, there were lots of crystal therapists, anyway. There were countless crusties sitting around witlessly smacking at poorly tuned acoustic guitars, while others beat on African drums in a rough approximation of four/four, the white man's rhythm. Up on the stage a duo from Horsham, H-Block, were going into their most famous number: 'Just because I Killed Loads of People by Leaving Bombs in Litter Bins for No Purpose that Any Sane Person Gives a Toss About, the Fascist Police Put Me in Prison and It's Not Fair.'

For Holland and Caroline, it was very heaven. Porky was clearly enjoying himself too, emptying cans of Special Brew into his bottomless gut; to Caroline's unending horror he had removed his T-shirt, and was looking for all the world like Moby Dick working on his tan. Mad Rikki had tiptoed in from Newhaven and was now circling round the group, whistling 'Crazy Horses', obviously as happy as the day was long. Blossom and Sailor Dave, however, were much less convinced of the merits of all this free expression. Both still had some musical taste, and this was proving a handicap to their enjoyment of the spectacle. Both of them had managed to cling on to their critical intelligence, which is possible (though not easy) when your best friend is Paul Holland, who smokes cannabis like it's going out of fashion. Which it isn't. And normally, both of them would rather have eaten dog shit than been within a hundred miles of the Moulescoomb Free Festival. But today was special, and both of them had felt it their duty to attend.

Because Cats's band Wurmsbreth were second on the bill, second only to the legendary doyens of Brighton Oi-Rock, Peter and the Test-Tube Babies, and Cats was their good friend, attendance was mandatory. Even Frances and Jeremiah had promised to come along, though they were timing their arrival to coincide with Wurmsbreth taking the stage. This was probably a wise move. Two years ago, Frances had called the police when she found two eight-year-old girls, their faces painted to make them look like squirrels, locked in a cage and bleating, 'Please let us out! They drop cosmetics in our eyes!' only to discover that the girls wanted to be there as a demonstration against animal testing. Last year Jeremiah had been attacked and beaten up by members of the Kemptown Anti-Racist Group for calling them liberal scumbags. Besides, Jeremiah only ever wore suits, and he always looked somewhat out of place among the affluent unwashed. But no one wanted to miss Cats's moment of glory.

Cats had been in a fever of excitement all week. He had somehow convinced himself that several A&R men were coming down from London to see Wurmsbreth, despite Dave's insistence that A&R men never but never went south of the river except to score in Stockwell or to visit their white-haired mothers in Godalming. But what did Dave know? He had merely worked in the music business for the whole of his adult life, and all he had to support his argument were facts; Cats had dreams, which are far more potent, at least before the event. And so the Wurmsbreth camp had laid their plans. Harry, the singer, had fashioned himself a huge dragon mask from papier-mâché; Rodney, the guitarist, had had a really cool skeleton riding a well happening chopper bike air-brushed on to his axe; and Cats and Spakker the drummer had spent a great deal of time checking that their exploding drumkit was in full working condition. Blossom even thought that they might have rehearsed, but Dave said he was talking out of his arse. Blossom conceded that it did seem unlikely, but swore that Cats had told him so. Dave remained sceptical; Blossom said that time would show who was right.

As the afternoon turned into evening, Cats was becoming increasingly unbearable. He kept hovering around and asking if he looked OK. Since he was dressed in a large green lizard costume, rather than his customary golfing trousers and filthy T-shirt, and since his thinning ginger hair was hidden under his lizard head, the company assured him that he looked very smart, but he was not convinced, and kept pulling nervously at the crotch of his green tights in a manner which turned Caroline's stomach.

'Sit down, Cats, for fuck's sake,' said Holland.

'Oh, I can't sit with you guys. It isn't cool for one of the artistes to sit with the punters.'

'Well, Cats,' said Blossom, 'why don't you go into the backstage area and lig with the other performers?'

Cats seemed to think this a good idea, and the Bloomsbury Group watched his green head bob through the crowd and into the marquee behind the stage.

'Thank fuck for that,' growled Sailor Dave.

'Except . . .' said Caroline, 'I rather think he's coming back.' They looked up, and watched the five-foot-five lizard make its way back towards them.

'Either it's Cats or someone's slipped some very bad acid in my Merrydown,' said Holland.

It was Cats, and with him was no less a figure than Trapper, bass player with bill-topping act Peter and the Test-Tube Babies, gripping a bottle of Jack Daniel's.

Now, Trapper is a real person. I haven't just sat here and dreamed him up. You can read about him in old copies of the sadly defunct *Sounds*, in Issue 207 of *Record Collector* magazine and, if memory serves me right, even in the *Guinness Book of Hit Singles*; an entry the Testies have earned by virtue of the fact that one of their singles (either 'Banned from the Pubs' or 'Up Your Bum') got to number seventy-five for one week. What is more, you could order their CD, *Loud Blaring Punk Rock*, from your specialist record store. If you felt really inclined, you could try telephoning the Green Dragon, Sydney Street, Brighton, and asking if Trapper has been in. As often as not, he will be there, and you could have a chat with him. He won't mind; there is no side about Trapper. In fact, the chances are you already know him.

Because Trapper knows everybody, has had a drink with everybody. There is a quite well-known joke, whose punchline involves Trapper appearing on the balcony of St Peter's in Rome with the Pope. 'Who's that cunt up there with Trapper?' says one of the Swiss Guards. It's not that he's particularly famous with a wider public, but put any two professional British rock musicians in a room and, eventually, the talk will get round to Trapper: 'Trapper nicked my pint', 'Trapper shagged my bird', and so on. Once, in a hotel bedroom in Manchester, a well-known drummer, who has asked not to be named, told me that there have been many occasions when he has seen Trapper very close to getting a spanking off some irate punter – but that Trapper always gets away with it because of his wit.

It is a weasel word, is wit. There is a kind of classical wit, something which sophisticated urbanites in Soho studio flats are reckoned to have in abundance, as are the Irish. Terry

Wogan is widely regarded as a wit, for example. This is the kind of wit that we are expected to display at dinner parties. White working-class boys were not, at one time, supposed to be witty but, since the advent of mod in the early sixties, it has been possible, if not easy, and Trapper has definitely taken advantage of this opening. It is not, of course, the done thing to describe a character as 'witty'; as writers we are very much expected to *show* that a character has wit. But then Trapper is *not* a character; he is, as I have said, real, and I feel quite within my rights to describe him as 'witty'. Also 'fun-loving', 'vivacious' and 'one of nature's gents'. His visit is a fleeting if puzzling one, from another world, problematic for me and serving little to help your understanding of these stories. But it must be faced: he is here, and must be dealt with.

It is always an awkward moment when a 'real' person appears in a work of fiction. Are we ever fully convinced if a character in a novel gets analysed by Freud, or sleeps with Marilyn Monroe? I'm not sure that it ever quite comes off, and in some ways I wish that Cats had left Trapper backstage in the hospitality area at the Moulescoomb Free Festival. But once Trapper heard that Sailor Dave was in the crowd, he insisted that Cats take him across to say hi.

'Hi,' said Trapper.

'All right, Traps?' said Porky, Caroline, Blossom and Holland.

Sailor Dave, however, merely grunted. Sailor Dave does not much like Trapper. Sailor Dave is not a hail-fellow-well-met kinda guy; he is, it is fair to say, a little wound up, a little tense, a bit up his own arse sometimes. And he is taciturn. Name, number and rank, little more is lightly to be got out of the One-Eyed Sailor. Funny Trapper stories are not in his line. He is not always a fun guy to be with. While Trapper is a relentlessly fun guy. Which Sailor Dave finds difficult. Besides, it was Trapper who lost Dave's eye for him, fifteen years ago in Munich. Dave has hardly even attempted to forgive Trapper for this, and who can argue with him?

The Test-Tube Babies had been playing at the Bavarian Punk-Fest, third on the bill behind the UK Subs and the Exploited. It was Dave's first real job as a drum roadie. A reasonably accomplished tub-thumper himself, he had found it easier to get paid work as a roadie than as a drummer. Besides, he'd gone to school in Bexhill with Hoggins, the Testies' skinsman. So there he was, lurking behind the kit during the set, when Trapper went into his big solo. For this, Trapper removed all his clothes, stood on the bass amp, and waved his long, thin, disease-raddled penis at the crowd, at which point the crowd would all throw beer glasses at his head. It was a tour de force, really. Dave had often stood behind the kit during Trapper's solo; but in Munich, one of the glasses bounced from the side of Trapper's amp and into Dave's left eye, pretty much ending its effectiveness. Of course, everyone said that it wasn't really Trapper's fault, and in a way it was true. But it was Trapper's solo; just at that moment, he was the Star, and the buck stopped with him.

That was how Sailor Dave saw it, at least; and, I have long suspected, that's how it is for Trapper too. Traps will always go out of his way to buy Sailor Dave a pint. That must stand for something.

So Trapper sat with the friends for a while, sharing his bourbon with Dave, while Cats fretted around.

'Don't you get nervous, Traps?' asked Holland.

'Sometimes, before a big show I do. But not somewhere like this.'

'This *is* a big show!' shrieked Cats. 'It is! It's a very big show!'

'Oh yeah,' said Trapper. 'Sorry, Cats.'

'Island and Arista said they'd come and see us.'

Dave and Trapper looked at each other.

'Oh, right, good one,' said Traps. 'Yeah. Good luck.'

'Thanks, Trapper. We've really worked hard for this one. Wait till you see the dragon that Harry's made.'

'Did you rehearse?' asked Blossom.

Cats smiled. 'Nearly,' he said. 'Only Harry had to score, and Cheryl said that Spakker had to stay in with her. But me and Rodney ran through a few things. We'll be well tight!'

'Yeah, right. Good one,' said Trapper.

He and Dave finished the Jack Daniel's, by which time Cats was frantic.

'Take him back to the tent, wilya, Trapper?' said Dave; and as Trapper could never say no to the One-Eyed Sailor, and as Cats's showtime was coming closer, Trapper obliged, and said he would hand him over to Lenny, Wurmsbreth's manager.

Cats turned to Caroline and whispered, 'I'm wearing a pair of your panties under my tights. For luck. I hope you don't mind?'

'It's a bit late if I did, isn't it?'

Cats smiled, nodded and walked away.

I breathed a sigh of relief as Trapper disappeared from my narrative in search of a drink. Whether he has served any purpose other than to make me break cover, just to say hi, I'm still not sure. But he has gone now, this one person I wished to look after on his little trip across my screen; and I must go with him, and beg your indulgence for my presumption. It must have been the festival atmosphere.

As Trapper and Cats left for the tent, Caroline turned to Sailor Dave and started questioning him about his eye. Was it true, she asked, that Dave had lost it on tour with the Test-Tube Babies; and Dave, who was now quite openly treating Caroline as the only person in the world with whom he could talk, admitted that it was. And so Caroline and Dave put their heads together while he told her the whole story. Blossom had wandered off to try to buy something, anything, with meat in it, and Holland had fallen asleep with his head on the soft pillow of Porky's gut. Mad Rikki tiptoed around. Black Barney strolled across. He had been profoundly influenced by the visit of King Martin, and had picked up a smattering of jargon from the Marxist monarch.

'This is fucking great,' he said. 'All Our People, gathered together, to celebrate the Alternative Society! To show that there is something other than capitalist materialism in the world!'

'Yeah,' said Porky. 'And loads of fucking students you can sell underweight deals to.'

Barney smiled, sat down, and started to skin one up.

And this was the scene when Frances and Jeremiah arrived, a little before nine. Frances was relieved to find Caroline and Dave deep in conversation. She was worried that the thing with Paul had gone on for too long, and she believed in Blossom's theory that Sailor Dave was in love with Caroline. Little tête-à-têtes like this were all to the good. Frances kicked Holland in the balls to wake him up and Caroline didn't even notice, where a week ago she would have stormed off, tight-lipped and ashen-faced at such presumption on the part of her lover's wife. Frances sat down, and Jeremiah with her. Blossom wandered back with a kebab that he had managed to unearth from somewhere. Caroline and Dave were still engaged, with what Frances could not hear, not that she minded.

Classically, men can only open up to a woman, and if they do this too often to any one woman in particular, they will fall in love with her. This is Frances's Law. Lately she had begun to worry about Paul. He had stopped telling her about how difficult it was to get a job because his father once made

211

a disparaging remark about the size of his penis, or about how his low metabolism dictated that he must take a little nap every afternoon. She was concerned that Caroline had become the recipient of his little confidences, and that, finally, Holland might really be contemplating leaving her and the kids. If Caroline and Sailor Dave could be brought together, disaster might yet be averted. Sailor Dave, after all, was very good-looking; he had money; he was kind and reasonably intelligent. In fact, as Frances considered his merits, she found herself wondering if the Sailor might make a suitable replacement for Holland in her own affections. Brad, for that matter, had proved himself an amusing companion. And the flirtation with Blossom had simmered away for years. But Holland was part of her life, like a mouldering old pair of trainers; rank and disgusting, yes, but well worn and comfortable. All husbands are as shit as one another, and Frances had no great desire to break in a new one.

These reflections were interrupted by an announcement from the DJ that it was time for Wurmsbreth to take the stage. Everyone rose to their feet to see Cats's bid for greatness. The stage lights were dimmed, as Emerson Lake and Palmer's version of 'Jerusalem' blasted out over the Wild Park. A jet of flame shot out from the back of the stage; this was Harry, fire-breathing through his new dragon mask. The crowd cheered as the lads came on, dressed as dragons and lizards, and steamed into their legendary first number, 'Dismember Me'. For this Harry wore a false arm, which he ripped off in a shower of blood at the appropriate moment. It was a huge success with the non-meat-eating, peace-loving crowd, as were 'Jeffrey Dahmer's Dead' and a new song, 'Fred West's Bicycle'.

Blossom thought that 'Zombie Fuck Meat' was quite well played, and he offered this to Sailor Dave as evidence in

212

support of his argument that the lads had got together at some point to run through a few things; Sailor Dave felt that it was like a monkey attempting to type Shakespeare, and that Wurmsbreth had hit a groove by accident rather than design. No matter. People do not go to a Wurmsbreth gig for the great music; they go to see Harry tear off his arm and breathe fire, and most of all for the triumphant 'Bomb Scare Baby', a song whose climactic moment is the blowing-up of the drumkit. In the early days Wurmsbreth had finished their set with this number, only to realize that they could not then perform an encore because their kit was now a smouldering ruin, so nowadays they kept it back till the last possible moment; and the crowd, knowing this, had to keep bringing them back for encore after encore, which they didn't really want, in order to secure the fireworks, which they most definitely did. At last, when Blossom thought he could take no more, he recognized the opening riff for 'Bomb Scare Baby', as did the crowd, who exploded in ecstatic frenzy. Two minutes and fifty seconds later, so did the drumkit, and the show was over.

Throughout the set Frances had stood with Blossom and Jeremiah, but her mind was not really on the rockist antics on stage, but rather on the Caroline and Paul situation. When the band had come on, Caroline had moved away from Sailor Dave to stand slightly nearer to Paul; during the first number, she dipped her hand into his jacket pocket, took out his tobacco and skins and rolled herself a cigarette, without asking or even speaking to Paul at all. By the third number she was on his shoulders, waving her arms in time to the cacophony. By the time it came round to 'Bomb Scare Baby', Caroline was dancing close and slow with Paul, her blue head against his skinny chest; and as the kit went up, Holland, forgetful of the fact that his wife was standing three feet behind him, bent down and kissed his lover on the lips;

she, perfectly well aware of Frances's presence, responded enthusiastically. They were still kissing as roadies came on to the stage to remove the remnants of Spakker's kit and to prepare for the Test-Tube Babies. Only Blossom noticed that Frances had slipped away.

After he had changed out of his lizard costume and back into his Punk Golfer from Hell ensemble, Cats came bounding across the park, his lank hair smarmed over his narrow head with sweat.

'Whaddya think? Whaddya think?' he gasped.

'It was great, Cats,' said Caroline, nestling in Holland's arms.

'It was better than the one where Harry broke his leg,' said Holland.

'Really? Was it really?'

'Really.'

'Bob! Dave! Whaddya think? Whaddya think?'

'It was . . . energetic,' said Blossom.

'Did the A&R guys turn up?' asked Dave.

'No. I don't think so. It's strange. I spoke to their receptionists on the phone, and they told me they'd try and make it.'

'Perhaps they broke down on the way,' suggested Blossom.

Dave snorted, and Cats looked hurt.

'Well, it's their loss, Cats,' said Caroline consolingly.

Cats smiled.

'Thanks for the panties, Caro,' he said. 'I've got them in my pocket if you'd like them back.'

'Er . . . perhaps after you've washed them?'

'It will be an honour.'

Feeling that you can have too much of a good thing, Blossom, Sailor Dave and Jeremiah turned and headed for home, leaving Cats and Porky, Holland and Caroline to enjoy the Test-Tube Babies.

Jeremiah gave the others a lift in his new car.

'New car, Jerry?' asked Blossom.

'Yes. My parents bought it for me as a thank-you for helping them when they were over. Which is amazing really. The Old Man used to be dead against private transportation.'

'How are they doing now?'

'Fine. Dad just grows skunk, and Ma is teaching brother Martin how to eat sea slugs and sheep's eyes, and stuff like that. And my sister-in-law is pregnant, so everyone's very excited.'

'And how's the changeover from Marxism to the free market going?'

Jeremiah sighed. 'I know that you are European, and like to convince yourselves that you live in free market economies. You don't, you live in ratty little social democracies. My brother is turning Farafan into a parody of a European democratic state, not a free market. Edgar says . . .'

'He's out of hospital next week, isn't he?' said Blossom, keen to forestall the rant that Jeremiah was clearly in the mood for after having to spend even a part of his day in the company of a bunch of crazed hedge sparrows.

'Yes, all being well. He's looking much better, don't you think?'

'Much. I went to see him on Thursday. He seemed right back on form.'

'I think so. It's nice that I've got the car now. I can take him out for runs, get a bit of fresh air.'

'He'll like that. Coming in for coffee?'

They were back in Bloomsbury Place.

'Thanks.'

As Blossom, Jeremiah and Sailor Dave walked up the stairs, they heard a great deal of banging from the Hollands' flat.

'Paul sounds as though he's getting a thick ear off Mum,' said Sailor Dave.

'We left Paul at the Wild Park, if you remember,' said Blossom.

'With Caroline,' said Dave.

'I'll give Frances a bell, see if she's all right. Stick the stinger on David.'

Frances sounded breathless as she picked up the phone.

'Are you OK, honey?' asked Blossom.

'Sure,' she said.

'Only we heard a lot of banging as we came up the stairs.'

'I . . . I'm just moving a few things about.'

'So you're OK?'

'I'm fine. Fine. I'll ring in the morning.'

'You're sure? Paul wasn't on his very best behaviour tonight, was he?'

'Not his very best, no.'

'And you're OK?'

'I'm fine. I'll speak to you in the morning.'

Dave had made coffee, and the three friends sat talking. Jeremiah put on one of those coffee-table albums which people play quietly in the background when friends come back from the pub for coffee and spliff, but at no other time. Then Blossom made some coffee, and they talked some more. It was two in the morning before they heard Cats, Caroline and Holland coming up the stairs. Then they heard some more banging. They heard a great deal of knocking, and Holland's voice rose plaintively up the stairwell. Cats came into the flat, looking worried.

'Frances has locked Paul out of the flat,' he said.

Blossom, Dave and Jeremiah, sensitive to the fact that Paul and Frances might like privacy at this pivotal moment in their relationship, charged out on to the landing and hung over the banisters, all the better to hear. Cats followed, his look of worry replaced by a grin.

'Aw come on, sweet pea. Let me in,' said Holland through the door.

The chums could just hear Frances's replies through the door.

'Fuck off. Fuck off and live with her.'

'Come on, Paul. She doesn't want you. Come upstairs,' said Caroline.

'Please, sweet pea. Let me in. We can talk.'

'No! Fuck off!'

'Come on, Paul. She means it. Come away.'

'Shut up a minute, can't you? Please, sweet pea. Let me in.'

'It's very late and I'm going to bed. Now, will you please just fuck off?'

'Paul, leave it. Come and sleep with me.'

'You heard her, lover boy.'

'Paul. Come on!'

'Please! Sweet pea! I love you!'

From the top of the banisters, the eavesdroppers heard Caroline's choke, and they darted back into the flat and assumed positions of unconcern in the front room as she ran crying up the spiral staircase. Sailor Dave blushed, and followed her. He knocked at her door, and was admitted to her bedroom. Lesser men than Blossom, Jeremiah and Cats would simply have rushed back to the top of the stairs at this point; but they are caring types, who did not wish Caroline to think they were taking the piss, so they carefully tiptoed back to their previous positions so as not to alert her to the fact that they had been listening throughout.

They were just in time to hear the closing moments of the little drama. Holland was hammering on his front door, shouting.

'Please, sweet pea! Let me in! She's gone.'

They heard the sounds of the bolts being thrown back, of the door opening; they heard Holland say, 'Sweet pea'; they heard a heavy thump, and a low groan from Holland. They heard the door slam shut.

They heard more groaning. They looked at one another and, despite their best intentions, they began to laugh quietly. Blossom was red-faced with the attempt to keep his hilarity silent.

Holland's voice came up from the landing below.

'Who's there? You cunts! You fucking cunts! Who's there?'

The three of them filed down the stairs, still choking back their hysteria, to find Holland lying on the floor, clutching at his groin, a large holdall by his side.

'The bitch hit me in the balls with my bag.'

Only death is funnier than domestic tragedies of this kind; and, seeing Holland lying in pain; thinking of Frances's unhappiness, locked in her flat; and the misery of Caroline, inconsolable upstairs, and the unrequited and courageous devotion of Sailor Dave, the three friends lost it altogether. Holland tried not to, but found himself joining in.

'Shut up,' he was saying through his hysterics. 'Shut up! She'll hear us.'

This sobered them up a little, and they lifted the injured Holland to his feet. Blossom and Jeremiah helped him up to the flat; Cats brought the holdall.

They sat Holland down on the sofa; Blossom skinned up while Cats made some sweet tea. He took two cups upstairs. Holland said, 'Is Dave up there with her?'

'Yes,' said Blossom.

Holland sighed. 'I suppose I'll have to go up in a bit.'

'I suppose,' said Blossom.

Holland sighed again and, accepting his tea from Cats, looked around him at the flat where once he had lived himself. He smiled.

'Well, guys,' he said. 'I'm back.'

The Commissioners

The atmosphere in the house had been a little strained for a week or so. Holland was sharing Caroline's room; every time one of them wanted to come in or out of the house, they had to persuade Cats or Blossom to phone Frances, to make sure there were no meetings on the stair. Rather than be in the flat during the first couple of weeks in June, Sailor Dave had decided to go out on the road with a shit old Goth band for very bad money, instead of just waiting for the Rod Stewart tour he was due to join in late July.

Blossom's morning coffee over the newspapers with Frances (she the *Herald Trib* and the *Telegraph*, he the *Guardian* and the *Racing Post*, with both fighting for a turn at the *Sun*) had moved from his kitchen to her front room; everybody in the top flat knew that he was her main confidant, and everybody wanted to know what she was thinking, which Blossom wasn't saying. Frances had been very good about letting Paul see the children; each Sunday morning she had left them outside the flat, from where Holland had been forced to take them down the beach, or to McDonald's. No one appeared at all happy; least of all Caroline, which was strange, considering that she seemed to have achieved her heart's desire.

But a fortnight after the fateful night when Holland was ejected from the family home, things lightened up a little.

James Atkinson came down from Wales to stay for the weekend, and although he was supposed to be Holland's best mate from school, he stayed with Frances, and it cheered her up no end. In fact, since his arrival on Thursday evening, he had so far refused to see Paul at all. Frances urged their mutual friends not to take sides, but she was relieved to find that most of them ignored this directive, and sided with her anyway.

And the Eel, released at last from his hospital bed and free once again to terrorize *Guardian* readers at lunchtimes in the Eastern Star, had invited Atkinson, Blossom and Frances to dine with him and Jeremiah at the Blue Popadom on Saturday night, a treat which the Bloomsbury Group seldom indulged in. Additional excitement was generated by the announcement that Jeremiah would be bringing his new girlfriend to meet his friends. The Eel already knew her, of course, and even went so far as to claim to Frances that he had introduced them.

'She's Ghanaian,' he announced. 'She's twenty-four, and a nurse. They met when I was in hospital.'

'What's her name then?' asked Frances, who was visiting him with Atkinson in the ground floor flat.

'Zorena.'

'Nice,' said Atkinson.

'What's she like?' asked Frances.

The Eel looked at Atkinson, and back to Frances. 'Very intelligent. Quite quiet and shy, but with a very dry wit. Mordant even. No very clearly defined political position. Her father is a government official of some kind. Pretty. Nice hair.'

'What's she really like?' asked Atkinson.

'Petite. Good legs. Smashing little tits. Plump arse. Goes like a train, I should say.'

'How old are you, Edgar?' said Frances, annoyed.

'Eighty-three, and old enough to know the difference when a man or a woman asks me what someone is like.'

The party gathered in the restaurant at eight, the Eel wearing his DJ, resplendent with ribbons. Everyone else had dressed down, but the sight of even one solitary dinner jacket elicited a quite remarkable standard of service from the normally terminally lethargic staff.

'Works every time,' said the Eel. 'In fact, I suspect a direct relationship between the decline in the practice of dressing for dinner and falling standards of service in restaurants.'

'Which came first?' asked Zorena.

'I'm sorry, my dear?'

'Which came first? Did people stop wearing dinner jackets, thus causing standards of service to fall; or did standards fall so that no one bothered to wear DJs any more?'

The Eel looked at her over his spectacles and smiled, his dentures shining like phosphorescent bones in the table candlelight. 'She's sharp, this one, your highness. You must try and hang on to her.'

'I think so too, Edgar,' said Jeremiah. Zorena smiled into her curry.

Atkinson and Jeremiah had never previously met, and found that they had a great deal in common; the legalization of drugs, the removal of limits to consenting sexual behaviour, the dismantling of immigration laws and so on. Economically they were less close but, as anarchists will, they had found sufficient common ground that they felt like allies in the struggle against statism. Frances and Zorena, meanwhile, were discussing their lives.

'I mean, it's just typical, isn't it, hon? They've never met before – we've never met before. They talk about anything but themselves – we talk about little else. And they think that we are trivial because on a first meeting we like to talk about what's real, rather than about idealistic theoretical non-sense,' said Frances.

Blossom, overhearing, said, 'That sounds like theory. What you just said.'

'Fuck off,' said Frances.

'No, but really. You're always theorizing about relation-ships. And as for "idealistic"! You all want a "nice man", a "kind man", a "man with a sense of humour". But when he comes along, this homely type, do you shag with him? No, you do not. You shag the plumber, and moan 'cos he turns out to be a cunt.'

'Who rattled your cage, honey?' asked Frances.

'Sorry. Sorry. It's just that . . .'

'What?' asked Frances. Blossom had gone red.

'Oh, it's just that I don't know what it is that women want. Not really.'

'Power, money and fun, honey, same as anyone else. You've got it, we want it,' said Frances.

'But what do we get in return?'

Frances and Zorena laughed.

'Nothing, you useless twat. Why should we fucking care? You had all the power, money and fun; now we're taking our share,' said Frances.

'You get to spend more time with your family,' said Zorena.

'Great. Thirty thousand years of male domination on this planet, and I miss it by this much!' said Blossom. He held his thumb and index fingers a skin's thickness apart.

'Poor babies,' said Frances.

'Of course, it all started in the war,' said the Eel.

'What did?' asked Atkinson.

'All this stuff with the women. Never had any trouble with 'em before the war; after it, there was no stopping the buggers.'

'And how do you feel about that, Mr Luff?' asked Zorena.

'Not my place to feel anything. It's evolution. The environment changes, and we change with it or die. The war changed everything. Good thing too, probably. Why, I worked with lots of women in the war, served with 'em as equals. Good soldiers, some of 'em.'

'Soldiers?' said Zorena.

'Edgar was in the French Resistance,' said Jeremiah proudly, pointing at the Légion d'honneur pinned to the Eel's jacket.

'Were you? Really?' said Atkinson.

'Among other things, dear boy. Among other things.'

'Gosh,' said Atkinson.

'Story, story, story,' chanted Blossom.

'Oh no no no. You don't want to hear about any of that.'

'We do,' said Frances. 'What have we done? We've been to shit universities, we've got shit 2:1s . . .'

'You've got a shit First,' said Blossom.

'So have I, actually,' said Atkinson.

'But you take my point,' said Frances. 'We go out to shit jobs or try to write shit books or play in shit bands and in the evenings we sit about in shit pubs or smoke shit dope and worry about who's going out with who. You, and Bill, and Geoffrey . . .'

'You've lived. You've been there. You fought for something. All we do is fight the new bypass,' said Blossom.

'Nonsense,' said the Eel, smiling happily.

'Story, story, story,' said Blossom again.

'I'd love to know about what you did,' said Zorena, a little too politely, perhaps, Jeremiah thought.

'Come on, Mr Luff,' said Atkinson. 'I've never met anyone who was in the Resistance.'

'One with women in,' said Frances. 'Women in the war.'

'Women in the war? Yes.' The Eel drained his glass. 'Yes. It always struck me as offensive when I heard feminists claim that the world would be a morally sounder place if it was run by women,' he continued. 'Margaret put paid to that notion! No, either men and women are equal, or they are not. If they are equal, then they have similar capacities for good and evil. No one sex is morally superior to another. The worst atrocity I witnessed in the war was committed by a woman.'

'A German woman?' said Zorena.

'My dear young lady, of course not. Do you imagine that atrocities are perpetrated only by the losers in war? Or is it more likely that the winners write the books? We did some appalling things, sickening, sickening things. We won, so we got away with it, that's all. No, she was on our side.'

'Oh, please tell us,' said Jeremiah.

'Hmm. Shall we have another couple of bottles, then. Yes? Good. Let's freshen our glasses and I'll tell you about her. The first woman I fought alongside. Silya. Not her real name of course. Waiter!'

The waiters swarmed around the Eel's dinner jacket and served the wine.

'August 1940,' said the Eel, settling back into his chair. 'August 1940, and I'm in on the ground floor at SOE, looking after the Netherlands. No one really knows what is happening in the first weeks, but what we do know is that we'd better get some kind of operation going, or else—'

'Edgar, I'm sorry,' said Frances, 'but SOE?'

'Special Operations Executive. Terrorism, guerrilla warfare, spies, that kind of thing.'

'I should have guessed.'

'So what we decide on is to see if we can't get some agents into occupied territory for a few weeks, find out something of what's happening, see what the resistance situation is, come back and report. Then we should have some idea of what we might be able to achieve.

224

'Of course, after we've requested personnel, what we get are all the stinkers and mavericks unwanted by their regiments, every odd bod and loony hanging around London looking for a job, and a bunch of ragtag and bobtail foreign nationals deemed useful for our purposes. Among this latter group was Silya. She was about twenty-four when I met her . . . no, hang on, come to think of it she was twenty-six, because I got an invitation to her eightieth birthday earlier this year. Or was it eighty-five? Getting worse at adding up than ever. Anyhow, old Silya. She was a tiny woman, no more than five one, with a sweet, innocent, almost childlike face; that's what made me think of her as younger than she is, I suppose. My brief was to try to get some operatives into Holland, scout around a bit, come up with some sitreps, perhaps a few good ideas for our next move, and then get 'em out again. Nothing too spectacular at first. So they sent me Silya. She was a Dutch communist who'd come over here just before the war broke out, mostly because she was opposed to the Hitler/Stalin pact. Communists were supposed to see this as a good thing, but old Silya's brother had been killed in Spain and she hated the Fascists, and saw Uncle Joe's rapprochement as the worst kind of stab in the back. She never was one for toeing the party line, was Silya.

'What Silya and I came up with was this: we were going to put a small group ashore on one of the Frisian Islands, led by Silya herself, and they were to make their way across to the mainland as best they could at low tide. Ever read *The Riddle of the Sands*?'

Nobody had.

'You should. A little dated perhaps. I haven't looked into it for fifty years, come to think of it. Anyway, the thing is, some of the channels between the islands and the mainland are as good as empty at low tide, and Silya was sure they'd be able to get across. She was a Frisian herself. Frisian is supposed to be the language that sounds most like English, but if you ask me, Xhosa is a better bet. I never understood a ruddy word. Still.

'We'd managed to persuade the Navy to let us have a submarine for the night, to put our people ashore, and then to pick 'em up a fortnight later. We'd also managed to pick a couple of likely lads to go with Silya who were slightly better than the average run of SOE stinkers. A chap called Digby Gray who'd been seconded from one of the Highland regiments, can't remember which, who had been on holiday in Holland before the war and was rather a whiz with the wireless, and a big bugger of a sailor called Walter Oertling whose father was Belgian, and who we thought should be able to fight his way out of anything. Now all we had to do was train 'em up a bit.'

The Eel paused to drain his glass; Jeremiah refilled it.

'Now, as section head, I was, of course, not to go on the trip itself, but for the training it was decided that I should go with the others. Well, I decided myself. You see, we felt that it was necessary to get Gray and Oertling used to operating in flat country. We needed them to be able to use mudshoes; these are very similar to snowshoes, Mr Blossom, but are used, as you might expect, for walking on mud. Also, we wanted them to be able to handle rubber dinghies in tidal creeks; Oertling, as the sailor, was to be in charge here. So we had decided to send them up to the Fens for a couple of weeks, and I wasn't going to miss that. D'ye know the Fens at all?'

Nobody did.

'I thought you might, Mrs Holland. Holland is a very old Fenland name. No matter. I knew the Fens very well. I used to go shooting up that way before the war. Ah, those were happy days. I had a friend who rented the shooting on one of the last undrained Fens. We never used to set out for record bags, you know; a couple of dozen snipe and a few pair of wild duck, that we would see as a successful day. The idea was just to enjoy being out in the fen with dog and gun, or perhaps out in a punt. The boom of the punt gun o'er the plashy fen; I can hear it still.

'Of course, in wartime it was decreed that all the remaining Fens should be drained for agriculture; very good land, you know, the best. But it seemed a shame to me that the wild fen was tamed, and the old Fen Tigers caged. Still, that's progress, I suppose. Anyway, be that as it may, at this early stage of the war the draining was unfinished, and so there were still wetlands and river washes that suited our purposes well.

'We filled my old car with all our equipment, and set off for a pub where I had arranged for us to stay for a fortnight in the village of . . .'

The Eel paused, and looked thoughtfully into his wine glass.

'No,' he continued. 'No, I'd best not say the name. It's possible that some of the villagers may still be alive. I am, after all, and Silya. No. Suffice to say that it was in Cambridgeshire.'

'It's like a Victorian novel, isn't it?' said Atkinson. 'You know: "I was born of humble parentage in the village of B dash, in the year 18 dash dash." '

The Eel coughed reproachfully and continued.

'It was rather a sweet old inn. Reed-thatched roofs, like the rest of the village. I don't think I'm giving too much away if I tell you that.' He looked at Atkinson. 'I shall call it the Kicking Donkey. The landlady had done quite a trade in shooting parties before the war, but they had been pretty thin on the ground since. Shooting was our cover story, of course. We told Mrs W. that . . .'

Zorena giggled, and Jeremiah poked her in the ribs.

'Mrs W. that we should require an early breakfast and a

packed lunch, and we set out each day with our splatchers and our rubber dinghy and some shotguns . . .'

'What the F are splatchers?' asked Atkinson.

'Mudshoes. That's what they call them. A good word for them, I always thought. We set out each morning and headed deep into the fen, where I put them through their paces all day. They practised inflating the dinghy, and walking in the shoes, and hiding in drains, and wading through the fen with all their equipment; and each day I took care to bag a dozen or so wildfowl, so that our cover should be maintained. And in the evenings Mrs W. would have hot baths waiting for us and serve us a rather excellent dinner, in view of the restrictions under which she was forced to operate. On several occasions we set out at night, since those were the conditions they would be operating under in the field. This time we had to pretend to be fishing. But most evenings we sat in the bar and chatted with the locals. Silya got quite expert at shove ha'penny. They were fascinated to find a Dutch woman in their village; the story was that she was my wife, and that Digby and Walter and I were on leave from our regiment.'

'Edgar, you old sauce-pot,' said Frances. 'Did you and Silya sleep together?'

'Yes, we did. It was the war. Everybody slept with everybody else. It's just that we didn't write books about it, or hop about to silly songs in San Francisco about it. Sex was not our religion, like it is now. It was fun, not politics.'

'It's still quite good fun, too,' said Zorena.

'And I have always enjoyed sleeping with communist women, strangely enough. That's politics, I suppose,' said the Eel.

'Kinky too,' said Atkinson.

'Anyway. So, after a week,' the Eel continued, 'I was taken aside by the village bobby and the vicar, who had come to

228

have a quiet word; ostensibly to see how the shooting had been going but really to try to ferret out the truth of what we were up to. I suppose it did look a bit odd. I swore them to secrecy, and told them that we were training for a secret mission, and gave them a number in Whitehall to ring which would confirm this. Had to tell them. All England was obsessed with the idea of the Fifth Column. They were only doing their job, and whether or not they told anyone in the village I don't know, but for the next few nights we didn't have to buy a drink in the bar. The locals couldn't have been more friendly. The bobby used to come in for a drink at eleven, and we had some smashing lock-ins. And the vicar had us to dinner. Bad security, I suppose, but it was rather nice. And there was no Fifth Column, of course.

'Now, even if you don't know the fen country, you must know that much of it lies below sea level, and it is only by constant pumping that the Fens are kept drained. The sewers and drains and lodes and cutwaters and rivers run behind high dykes; the land is shrinking as it dries out, and the dykes have to get a little higher and the pumps work a little harder year after year. Although the fen around the village had not yet been completely drained, its fields were protected from the lode by a high dyke, which ran perhaps half a mile from the centre of the village.

'And just in case your history is as poor as your geography, I must remind you that late August 1940 saw the Battle of Britain at its height. In Cambridgeshire we were a way off the action, and almost all of the fighter squadrons were being flung at the German bombers; almost, but not all. At an airfield some twenty miles from us, a squadron of Hurricanes were kept in reserve. They would fly down each day as far as London, or they would patrol the east coast ports; I'm sure the poor pilots wanted to be based in Kent, but we had to have something back. But the Germans did not ignore this small force, and in an audacious attempt to wipe out almost the sole remaining British reserves, they launched an attack on the airfield, using Stukas, with some 109s as cover. Fighters, dear,' said the Eel to Frances as she opened her mouth to speak.

'109s were fighters, and Stukas were nifty little dive-bombers. The idea was obviously to slip in behind the main action in the south and bomb the Cambridgeshire squadron into the ground. But it didn't really work out as planned. It was Thursday morning; our last full day, as we were planning to drive back down to London on the Friday evening. The Hurricane pilots, desperate for action, were all airborne before the Nazis arrived (we had radar, of course); and even from where we were, standing outside the pub, we could watch the dog-fights high up. And we watched one aircraft, obviously a Stuka from its wing shape, start to trail smoke from its starboard engine, and peel off towards us, a Hurricane in earnest pursuit. And we watched as the two came closer, and lower, until we saw the German pilot and his gunner bail out, perhaps a mile away; and, with increasing horror, we watched as the Stuka came screaming down, on fire now, and exploded, its bomb still underneath, into the dyke which protected the village from drowning. And the Hurricane roared past to inspect his handiwork, dipped his wing in salute and went back after the rest of the retreating Nazis.

'Most of the villagers were out in the street watching, and as the Stuka hit the dyke there came a great shout; and then people started to run as it became obvious that the dyke was breached, and that the water from the lode was starting to spread across the fields towards the village. Every man started to run for the breach; every woman hurried indoors to lug heavy sandbags across the doorways. The vicar was in the forefront of operations, and my men and I prepared to follow him towards the wrecked aircraft.

'"Shall I get the dinghy, sir?" Oertling asked me, and it seemed like a good idea, so he and Gray and I grabbed it from where it lay beside the car and set off over the fields. And Silya just said, "Give me the keys," and jumped into the car and roared off, where I knew not. I think I just thought that she was taking the car out of the reach of the flood waters.

'Well, we were lucky. The lode was low, and the area was already wetter than many other parts of the Fens, as I have said. The Stuka helped to some extent as well; although its bomb had breached the dyke, its wreckage was obviously slowing down the flow of water. Someone had clearly telephoned to the sluice keepers, who had closed off the flow into the lode. But still, perhaps a foot or more of water was flooding through the breach, and it soon became impossible to run. We gave the vicar a lift in the dinghy to inspect the damage, while other men from the village began to organize a chain of sandbags, which were kept stored in the village and at various points in the lee of the dyke.

'All morning and into the afternoon we worked, passing sandbags from hand to hand. They were thrown into position by some of the bigger village lads, according to the vicar's directions, and by about three everyone seemed fairly satisfied that we had averted the worst of it, and that the repair would hold until the morning. By then some clay could be obtained, and perhaps some bog oak, and the breach made good more permanently. A roster was drawn up, again by the vicar, so that watchers were always on hand to raise the alarm if anything went wrong. And so we set off back to the village.

'Say it though I shouldn't, the fields did look rather lovely, much as the old Meres must have looked before the drainage programme really got under way. We paddled the vicar back to see what had happened in the village. Things were not too bad; several of the cottages nearest to the breach had got a bit wet, but other than that, there seemed to be no serious damage. A tractor was pulling an emergency pump out into the field. They were very well prepared for this contingency. It was not, you must understand, a terribly serious breach.'

The Eel stopped and gulped at his wine. He lit a cigarette and continued.

'No. Not serious at all. And when we got back to the pub, bugger me, but there was my car outside again; and in the parlour was Silya, grinning all over her face, with her revolver pointing at two rather shaken Luftwaffe airmen. She'd watched where the parachutes had come down and gone after them and caught them, single-handed. They were wandering about near to the raised road in a remote part of the fen, wet and cold and unhappy. They both had Lugers, but they were dazed and confused, and the sight of this tiny hate-filled Dutch woman waving a British Army issue revolver at them must have broken their nerve, and they surrendered to her. Do you know, she'd driven them back into the village with one hand on the wheel, and one on her revolver to cover them? Extraordinary thing. And here they were, tied to two chairs in the parlour of the Kicking Donkey, and Silya looking happier than I'd yet seen her.

'Well, as senior officer, I felt that it was my duty to contact the local military police, and see that they were handed over to the appropriate authorities. Here they were; we'd seen their plane go down, they were in Luftwaffe uniform, and there was no question but that they were prisoners of war, and entitled to the protection of the Geneva Convention. D'ye know, it's many and many a night I've wished that I'd just made that phone call? But when I put it to Silya, she said, "No, Ed. There must be a meeting of the Commissioners first. It's the law. I've spoken to" (and here she mentioned the bobby's name) "about it. He says that it is the custom, and that the Commissioners have total jurisdiction over this matter."

'I didn't understand. What matter? And who were the Commissioners? When the bobby came by a few minutes later, to take the prisoners in charge, I asked him what it was all about.

'"They breached the dyke, sir," he said. "Nothing can be done with 'em until they've come before a meeting of the Commissioners of Sewers and Drains."

'I could have laughed. There is something about the idea of Commissioners of Sewers and Drains which strikes the outsider as ludicrous, isn't there?

'"All right, Constable," I said. "If that's the way of it. When is the next meeting to be?"

'"Well, sir, vicar's called an extraordinary meeting tonight, here in the Donkey. They'll be dealt with then."

'"And we'll be able to give them up to the appropriate authorities in the morning?"

'"Oh yes, sir. We will that." And he looked at Silya, and smiled. And she raised her pistol in salute. So.'

The Eel lifted his fingers like a child playing at guns.

'The bobby took the Germans away to keep them in the lock-up until the meeting of the Commissioners. I said to Silya, "Well done, old girl. I think you may expect a decoration for that." And she smiled at me again, very coldly, and said, "I don't want a medal. I just want dead fascists."

'"Well, I don't think you'll be getting your wish just yet. These men are for a prison camp."

'"If you say so. Sir." I thought she was being a little formal. Nothing like as formal as the meeting later that evening of the Commissioners of Sewers and Drains for the Parish of . . .'

'B dash,' said Atkinson.

'If you like. The vicar was in the chair, wearing a horsehair wig, and to his left was Mrs W., the landlady of the pub, looking very formidable in her best frock. To his right was a ruddy-faced old buffer who I took to be the squire. They sat at a table at the end of the room; at a smaller side-table sat a bewigged clerk, who I recognized as the schoolmaster. And practically the whole village was crammed into the pub parlour.

'"The Special Court of the Commissioners is now in session," said the clerk. "Will the Beadle please bring forward the accused?"

'Up stepped the bobby, looking rather splendid in a navy-blue frock coat with gold buttons, pushing in front of him the two airmen.

'"Are you . . . ?" and here he confirmed the prisoners' identities, to which they nodded assent. "Prisoners at the bar," he continued, "you are charged with wilfully breaching the dyke in this parish, causing damage to crops and stock, and with endangering the life of the village. How do you plead?" I think they must have been prompted by the Beadle, or perhaps Silya herself, who spoke a little German, because they both said, "Guilty." I must say, they looked quite relaxed. They knew their rights as prisoners, after all, and at least they would be safe for the rest of the war.

'The vicar turned and whispered to the red-faced old gentleman and Mrs W., who both nodded at him.

'"Prisoners at the bar," he said. "You have been found guilty of breaching the dyke. The Court of the Commissioners of Sewers and Drains therefore exercises its prerogative to sentence you according to the customs and procedures as established by precedent from time immemorial. The sentence of the Court is that you shall be taken from this place to the site of the breach, where you shall be buried alive. And may Almighty God have mercy on your souls."'

'Jesus,' said Blossom.

'The airmen were nodding and smiling. Clearly they had no idea what was happening. The room exploded into cheers; I stood up, and prepared to unholster my pistol.

' "You can't do this!" I shouted above the din, but before I could get out my gun, I felt Silya's pistol in my ribs.

' "Sit down, sir," she said. "Sit down or I will kill you."

' "You can't do this. You'll be court-martialled for this, you stupid bitch."

' "Will I, sir? We shall see."

'The villagers had grabbed hold of the prisoners, and were dragging them out into the fields, already nearly drained by the emergency pumps. Completely contrary to any sane blackout regulations, some arc lamps had been set up to light the breach; a trailer load of clay had been hauled out to the site. Oertling and Gray were, I think, unaware of the fact that Silya had a gun in my ribs as we walked out to the site. I don't know. They may just have approved of the whole thing. I don't know. Silya poked me to keep me moving.

' "I shouldn't say anything if I was you, sir," she said. So I didn't. What could I do? She had the gun. And so we all splashed through the field. And as we walked, the airmen began to realize that something was not right. Thank Christ neither of them spoke English; gave 'em less time to think about what was happening. But it must have been obvious that this was not allowed for under the Geneva Convention. By the time we came to the site itself, they were clearly agitated – and when the Beadle and his men bound their feet, they started to shout.

' "You can't want this, Silya," I said.

' "But I do. I want it very much. These are the first fascists I have killed."

' "But the law! If we don't have the rule of law, then we are no better than they."

' "But sir, it is the law. Didn't you hear? The Commissioners are legally entitled to do this. Really, they are. The Beadle told me this afternoon."

'So there we were. Several pieces of bog oak had been pushed into the wall of the dyke to hold the wreckage of the Stuka and the sandbags in place; all that remained was to cover the whole thing with clay. The village men stood ready with spades; the airmen, shouting and struggling, were lowered on to the sandbags, and the men started to pile clay on to them. I shall never forget their shouts, their screams; never forget their faces as I saw them for the last time, grey and bubbling, or the way that the clay seemed to move for a while after they had disappeared. And then was still. People were leaving the site, talking and laughing. Silya put her gun away, and I was sick.'

Frances noticed that the Eel was becoming distressed and that his breathing was growing shorter.

'Are you OK, Edgar?' she said.

'Yes. Yes, my dear. Perhaps Jeremiah could find my inhaler. I . . . I've always had a horror of being buried alive.'

'Christ, it's not surprising, is it?' said Atkinson.

Waiters hovered around anxiously as Jeremiah helped the Eel with his Ventolin; Blossom and Atkinson looked at each other, embarrassed and impotent.

The Eel leaned back in his chair and panted for breath. 'I'm sorry. I'm sorry. I shouldn't have told you.'

'No wonder you didn't want to tell us the name of the village,' said Zorena.

The Eel smiled. 'Thought I was just being a stupid old fart, didn't you, being circumspect after all these years? Well, the thing was, I looked it up when we got back to London, and it was true. Commissioners of Sewers did have the power to punish people who breached the dykes by burying them alive. But of course it hadn't happened since the seventeenth century, and there was no way that any real court would have allowed the sentence to stand. But . . . it was the war, and terrible things were done. We drove back to London in the morning. Silya sang the whole way.'

'She was hard,' said Blossom.

'She needed to be. She had some awful experiences later on. Needed to be hard. But she survived.'

'Did the thing with the sub and the Frisian landing go ahead?' asked Atkinson.

'Of course. Of course. Went very well. Silya and the others made some good contacts with the new Dutch Resistance. Very successful.'

'But we weren't any better than them, were we, Edgar?' said Frances. 'I mean Dresden and Hiroshima and all that. It wasn't necessary, was it?'

'Well, I don't know, my dear. What Silya, what the commissioners did, that was a war crime, no question, which went unpunished, wrongly in my opinion. We should have made a point of rooting out our war criminals after the thing was over. We should have gone out of our way to do that. I filed my reports. There is no question that my superiors knew. But we were defending the bad against the worse, that's all. We did it, and asked questions afterwards. The Nazis were evil; we were just confused, and stupid, and with our backs to the wall. But people like Silya, they thought they knew what had to be done, morality aside, and they did it. And we won.'

'Did we though?' said Atkinson. 'I mean, look at Germany and Japan now.'

'I've heard that for years, young man. Oh yes, we won. Evil must always be vanquished, don't you think, no matter the cost? Or what is the point? And my German friends are glad that Hitler was defeated. Us moaning about Japanese and German economic success is just sour grapes. They are industrious, ingenious nations who were bound to do well anyway.'

'I don't know that I believe in good and evil,' said Frances.

'You should come to Africa,' said Zorena.

'And I should pay the bill,' said the Eel. 'Thank you all for coming.'

'And thank you for telling us about . . .' began Blossom.

'You shouldn't envy us for the war, you know,' said the Eel. 'It was vivid, but it was a nightmare. We fought it precisely so that you lot could be feckless and idle.'

'That is a relief,' said Frances.

'Which reminds me,' said Atkinson. 'I suppose I'd better go see your husband tomorrow.'

Frances looked at him and said, 'Send him my love.'

'Did you just say that?' said Blossom.

'What?'

'Oh, never mind. Do you know what my grandfather used to say about women?' said Blossom.

'No?' said Frances.

'They're funny cattle, boy.'

'Sexist old bastard.'

'He was right though, wasn't he?' said Blossom.

'Yes,' said Jeremiah and the Eel.

'No,' said Frances and Zorena.

'Sometimes,' said Atkinson. 'Everyone is. From time to time.'

'Liberal scumbag,' said Jeremiah scornfully.

Bacon Sandwiches

On an idyllic morning in early June, Blossom lay abed concentrating on a certain horse race which was to be run that afternoon on Epsom Downs. It was the first day of the Derby meeting. Blossom never bet on the Derby as the odds were seldom attractive enough, but this particular race looked perfect for his purposes. A pot of tea sat on a tray beside the bed and the *Racing Post* lay open on the counterpane. The sun streamed through the windows, and if Blossom hadn't known better, he would have suspected himself of being happy. Of course, he realized that it was simply a manic phase he was going through, but it was none the less welcome for all that.

There came a tapping at his door, and Holland's voice whispering, 'Bob, Bob!' through the panel. He ignored it and the knocking became more insistent, and Holland's voice louder. 'BOB. BOB!' He turned the page of his *Post*, and ran his eye over the list of declared runners for tomorrow's meeting at Lingfield. The knocking turned into a hammering, and Holland's voice into a shriek.

'BOB! BOB, YOU DEAF CUNT! WAKE UP!'

'No. Fuck off, Paul.'

'Please, Bob. Let me in. I must talk to you.'

Blossom groaned, climbed out of his nest, wrapped his mackintosh around his ruined body, and opened the bedroom door. Holland, wild-eyed, charged in, sat down on the edge of the bed, and poured himself a cup of tea, his hands trembling.

'Still no drugs, then?' said Blossom, as he climbed back under the covers.

'No. None. Even Barney is down to personal. It's the longest drought since 'eighty-seven.'

'I was trying to work actually, Paul. I don't know that I can help, really.'

'Oh, it's not that,' said Holland. 'The drought's not helping, but it's not that. It's Caroline.'

'Poor old Caro.'

'Do you know what she wants me to do now?'

'I neither know nor care.'

'She wants me to go to Glastonbury with her.'

'What's wrong with that?'

'Well, nothing, I suppose, usually. But you know she works in that shit macrobiotic place?'

'Lentils for Mentals?'

'Or whatever. Well, they've got the concession to sell vegan soya curd yoghurt, in the Green Field, and she wants me to help her run the stall.'

Blossom whistled sympathetically.

'She says that if I'm really committed to animal liberation—'

'Oh my Christ! Not you too?'

'Oh, not really. You'll say anything if they'll get their kit off, won't you? No, but she thinks I am though. She thinks I'm a veggie too.'

'For fuck's sake. How have you kept that up all this time?'

'Well, it didn't matter till I moved in. I could fake it. But I haven't half eaten some shit these last few weeks.' Holland scratched at his crotch thoughtfully.

'You poor old thing. Where is she now?'

'On campus. And then she's going to work.'

'Would you like me to make you a nice bacon sandwich?'

'Oh God, would you?'

'Sure. Hang on a mo.'

Blossom got out of bed, pulled his mackintosh around him again, picked up the tea things, and said, 'Come on.' They went into the kitchen, and Blossom put six slices of smoked streaky under the grill, and spread butter on four slices of white bread. Holland was grinning like a lunatic.

'I mean, I'd quite like to go to Glastonbury this year,' he said. 'The main stage is a bit ordinary, but there's some great stuff on the other stages. Anyway, Glastonbury is always a laugh. At least you can score there.' He licked his lips. 'But I really don't think I can eat vegan soya curd yoghurt for three fucking days.'

'Mustard?'

'Yes please. I mean, she's all right, is Caroline. Good legs. But . . .'

'What?'

'Oh, I don't know.'

'Rocking horse?'

'Please. Thanks.'

Holland gratefully accepted his sandwich, oozing red and yellow over the not quite clean plate.

'So what can I tell her, Bob?' he said, between mouthfuls.

'Tell her to stop avoiding the meaty side of her nature and take her out for a steak,' said Blossom before taking a large bite of his own sandwich.

'But really?'

'Tell her it's unprincipled to be a vegetarian. Ask her where her mung beans come from. They're cash crops, that's what, grown halfway round the fucking world by slave labour. A nice bit of Southdown lamb only has to come from Lewes. Tell her it's ecologically sound to eat meat.'

'She's not going to have that, is she? She thinks she's helping bring about the revolution by being finicky about what she eats.'

'Look out, Western Imperialism.'

'Look out, Capitalist Materialism. Here come the middle-class veggies.'

The two friends laughed.

'Sometimes I think she sees eating bird food as striking a blow against her father, as well,' said Blossom.

'She doesn't seem to get on with him, does she? I don't know that she likes men much.'

'I wonder why,' said Blossom.

'I've been a good bloke. I even wear a johnny . . .'

'Condoms, I believe they're called now.'

'Whatever. I do the washing up and everything. I don't mind. There's never much to do anyway.' Holland sighed, swallowed the last mouthful of his sandwich, and licked his fingers.

'Is vegan soya curd yoghurt as bad as one might imagine?' asked Blossom.

'It's not unlike spunk in consistency, but it tastes much worse, even with organic kiwi fruit mashed up in it,' said Holland.

'I admit that Caroline does have good legs . . .'

'I wish she'd shave them though.'

'What's her bacon sandwich like?'

Holland choked with laughter.

'Too much hair. Not enough mustard,' he replied.

'You are a wicked man.'

'I just wish she wouldn't crap on at me about this Glaston-bury thing.'

'I wish she wouldn't crap on about saving the whale.'

'She's going to crystal therapy. And a friend of hers is supposed to be drawing up our horoscopes.'

Holland fell silent, and stared from the kitchen window towards the sea.

'Thing is, Bob, I really miss Frances. And the kids. I want to go home,' he said.

'I thought so.'

'What do you think, Bobbers? She talks to you. Do you think she might have me back?'

'Ask her.'

'Shall I? How?'

'Take her out for dinner.'

'Good idea. Great idea. I'll take her to the London Unity. Yes. No.'

'No?'

'No. No money.'

'Borrow some.'

'Cheers, Bob, you're a real pal. I'll pay you—'

'No. Not from me. From someone else.'

'Oh. Or, I tell you what, I could catch Caroline at work.'

'You're not going to eat in Cabbages for Cretins?'

'No. I thought I might borrow some money off her.'

'And are you going to break the news about the Glaston-bury trip then, or will you wait a bit?'

Holland rolled a cigarette, lit it and rubbed his chin.

'No,' he said. 'On balance, I think I'll wait.'

'On balance, that sounds like a wise decision.'

'At least until after I've spoken to Frances.'

On an idyllic morning in early June, Blossom lay abed concentrating on a certain horse race which was to be run that afternoon on Epsom Downs. It was the second day of the Derby meeting. Blossom never bet on the Derby as the odds were seldom attractive enough, but this particular race looked perfect for his purposes. A pot of tea sat on a tray beside the bed and the *Racing Post* lay open on the counterpane.

From the front room he could hear the insistent bleat of the telephone. He decided not to worry. After all, who could it be? Everybody but himself was out. It was hardly going to be Madonna offering him a shag, or Lester Piggott with a sure thing for that afternoon. It would probably be a market researcher, and he was comfortable and happy, and not about to interrupt his study of form just to answer questions about jam or double glazing.

Nyeep-nyeep! Nyeep-nyeep! Nyeep-nyeep!

They were persistent, whoever they were; Blossom was determined not to give in. He turned the page of his *Post*, to cast his eyes over the list of declared runners for tomorrow's meeting at Chester.

Nyeep-nyeep! Nyeep-nyeep! Nyeep-nyeep!

'Oh for fuck's sake!'

Blossom climbed from his bed, wrapped his mackintosh around his ruined body, and answered the phone.

'Hello?'

'Bob. Bob, I knew you'd be home. Can I come up?'

'Hello, Frances. Well, actually, I was trying to work.'

'Good. I'll be up in a tick. Put the kettle on.'

When Frances burst in Blossom was waiting in the kitchen, coffee ready for her on the table. She was smoking a Silk Cut; Blossom watched as she took another out of the packet and started to light it before realizing she already had one in her other hand.

'Jesus, hon, I'm hungry,' she said. 'You haven't got any scram, have you?'

'Well, I could do you a bacon sandwich, I suppose.'

'Good on yer.'

Blossom put six slices of smoked streaky under the grill and spread butter on four slices of white bread, while Frances paced about the kitchen, smoking for New Zealand.

'Bob.'

'What?'

'You'll never guess what.'

'Mustard?'

'Yes. The Slimy Cunt phoned me last night, and you'll never guess what?'

'Rocking horse?'

'Yes. You'll never guess what.'

'What?'

Blossom passed Frances her sandwich.

'Thanks, hon. Fuck me, I see the hedge sparrow's got Paul doing the washing up.'

'I'm afraid so.'

'She should get a dishwasher and a Filipino to load it, like me.' Frances took a huge bite from her sandwich.

'Bob,' she said with a full mouth.

'Frances,' said Blossom before taking a large bite of his own sandwich.

'You'll never guess what?'

'Keep me in suspense no longer.'

'He phoned me last night, the slimy little cunt, and asked me out to dinner! Tonight! Can you believe it?'

'Is it so strange?'

'Oh, come off it, Bob. You know he only ever takes me out to dinner when he wants to come home.'

'Are you going?'

'Are you kidding? You have to be kidding! After what he's done? Little fucker. "Oh sweet pea," he says, "let's go to the London Unity." Little cunt. Where did he get the money from, I'd like to know.'

Blossom, perhaps wisely, stayed silent.

'Did you lend him money?'

'No.'

'Little shithead. Does he really think I'm falling for it again? How many times has he done this?'

'What?'

'Run off with some stupid little tart, and then come crawling back after a couple of weeks with his schlong between his legs?'

'I don't—'

'Four! Fucking Jesus! This is the fourth time he's tried this. What does he think I am?'

'His wife.'

'His fucking wife! Little fucking wifey! Thanks.' She handed Blossom her empty plate, wiped her mouth with the back of her hand, and lit a Silk Cut. 'And now he thinks he can do it again! It's incredible, isn't it?'

'Y . . .'

'So whaddya think?'

'About what?'

'I mean . . . should I go?'

'I'm sorry?'

'Do you think I should go to the Unity with him?'

'Didn't you just say that it was incredible?'

'What?'

'That the little cunt had the nerve to try it on again.'

'You've got to hand it to him though, haven't you? He's got a fucking nerve, hasn't he?'

'I suppose so.'

'You have though, haven't you?'

'Er . . .'

'I mean, does he think I've missed him? Does he? Listen, hon, my inner thighs are rubbed raw from the shagging I've been getting off Brad. Raw! I've got blisters on my labs!'

'Well, there you are.'

'Oh but Brad is so boring. And he never comes. I mean, you dream about a bloke who can keep it up, but I could smoke twenty fags while I'm waiting for him. Fucking Aussie retro-ejaculator!'

'Yes, but . . .'

'You're right. The kids have missed him, fuck only knows why. Er keeps crying at bedtime. I say to her, listen, kid, no man is worth crying about, specially that wanker, but she's not having it.'

'She is only eight.'

Frances stood up, lit another fag and resumed her pacing about the room.

'What did you tell him?' asked Blossom.

'Who?'

'Paul. What did you tell him?'

'When?'

'When he asked you out to the Unity.'

'Can you believe it? The little bastard.'

'So what did you tell him?'

'I said he should pick me up at eight.'

'I don't believe it!'

'I'm not going! Not after what he's put us all through again! He'll call for me, and I'll slam the fucking door in the little cunt's face.'

'Probably a wise move.'

'Do you think so?'

'Yes.'

'I think I should go.'

'Really?'

'I mean, I should hear what he's got to say, shouldn't I?'

'Well . . .'

'Just to hear him beg. Just for the pleasure of hearing him beg.'

'Revenge.'

'So whaddya think?'

'About hearing him beg?'

'No. Should I go?'

'No.'

'You're right. I'll go.' Frances exhaled sharply, stubbed out her dog end, lit another Silk Cut and said, 'Thanks, Bob.'

'For what?'

'For the advice, man. I don't know what I'd do without you.'

'Oh, I'm sure you'd manage.'

'Right. I'd better go and start getting ready.'

'But it's only eleven o'clock.'

'Lots to do, Bobbers. Hair to wash, sheets to change!' Her eyes were bright, and she licked her lips.

'Wish me luck!' she said as she left the flat.

'Oh, right. Good luck.'

As Blossom collected his *Post* from the bedroom and prepared to go to William Hill's, he reflected that, as a gambler, he was nothing. Nothing against the mindless optimism of a woman preparing to believe the lies of her husband. Again.

On an idyllic morning in early June, Blossom lay abed concentrating on a certain horse race which was to be run that afternoon on Epsom Downs. It was the third day of the Derby meeting. Blossom never bet on the Derby as the odds were seldom attractive enough, but this particular race looked perfect for his purposes. A pot of tea sat on a tray beside the bed and the *Racing Post* lay open on the counterpane.

A strong feeling of déjà vu overcame him, and he braced himself for a further assault on his tranquillity. But there was nothing. Blossom smiled, relaxed back into his pillows, and cast his eye over the list of declared runners for tomorrow's meeting at Doncaster. Again, some primeval instinct for trouble made Blossom sit up and sniff the air. An ambulance sounded close by in the street; that was not it. A helicopter clattered overhead; it was not this that concerned Blossom. He settled back uneasily.

Now he heard raised voices from the kitchen, those of Holland and Caroline. This did worry him. He was, of course, concerned for his friends, but mostly he was concerned that nothing should happen which might shatter his repose. Blossom was a great believer in atmosphere, and the atmosphere in the flat had not been right for weeks. From the sound of the increasingly heated dispute in the kitchen, it was not about to get dramatically better.

Blossom heard the front door slam, and from the kitchen the keening wail of a woman in great distress. He tried, and failed, to concentrate on marking his card as Caroline's ululating cry filled the flat. Blossom blew air through his teeth and, wrapping his old mackintosh around his skinny body, went into the kitchen.

Caroline sat at the table, her head in her hands. The noise she was making reminded Blossom of nothing so much as televised scenes of the funeral of the Ayatollah Khomeini.

'Hello, honey,' said Blossom gently.

Caroline lifted her head from the table, looked at Blossom and redoubled her wailing.

'Can I help?'

Caroline looked up again, her nose running, her eyes red, her blue hair tangled, and shook her head. Huge sobs racked her slender frame.

'What's the matter?'

'Huh, huh-huh-hit's Paul . . .' Caroline started to keen again.

'Oh dear. What's he done now?' said Blossom.

'Huh-huh-he's . . . he's gone back to Frances!'

'No!'

'Ye-e-e-es! He h-h-h-has!'

'I . . . I, er, expect the kids are pleased to see him back.'

This thought did not seem to console Caroline, who cried even harder.

'Would you like a cup of tea?'

'No! I don't want anything!'

'I'm making some anyway.'

'No!'

Blossom made the tea, and took care to spoon extra sugar into Caroline's. By the time he put it down in front of her, she had regained some of her composure.

'Thanks,' she said. 'Sorry.'

'For what? You're bound to be upset.'

'It's just that he must have lied to me all along. He said that Frances meant nothing to him, except as a friend. And now he's gone back to her! And she told me, you know, when I moved in, that this might happen. Pig! Pig! Pigpigpigpigpig-pigpigpigpigpig!'

'I . . . er . . . the kids. I expect he missed the kids.'

'I thought . . . I thought we might have some. Paul and I.'

'Oh, darling, you're a bit young for that, aren't you? You're only twenty. And you've got your degree to get.'

'I meant one day. In a few years.'

What was it in human nature, Blossom wondered, that could allow somebody like Caroline, ostensibly intelligent and sensitive, to believe that someone like Holland was going to stick around long enough for her to finish her degree, and live a bit, and then have some kids? He remembered something he had read about Jung – something about projection? You project on to your loved one all the qualities you wish to see in them, even though they're total sods? Something like that. Blossom promised himself that even when the cannabis drought was over, he was never touching the stuff again. His memory and concentration were shot, no question. Only last week, in a pub quiz, he had been unable to remember the name of Sheffield United's ground. Wednesday, yes, that was easy, but United? He must . . . Blossom realized that Caroline was talking again.

'Do you know what he said?'

'Who?'

'Paul. Do you know what he said?'

'No. When?'

'When he told me he was going back to Frances. Do you know what he said?'

'No.'

'He said . . . he said . . . it could never work between us because I don't eat meat . . . and . . . and . . . because I don't shave my le-e-e-egs!' She was off again.

'That wasn't very kind.'

Caroline stood up.

'I'll show him, the pig. I can eat meat with the best of them. Don't worry about how it gets to the supermarket, all the suffering and horror, oh no, why should I care about that? I'm just a stupid hippy. No more.' She opened the fridge door and began pulling things out on to the floor. 'Cheese. No. You only have to rip out the lining of cows' stomachs for that. Eggs. No. You lock the poor fucking chickens in tiny cages, but you don't have to kill them, do you? We want something dead. Ah ha! What have we here? Piggy-wiggy! Dead piggy! I'll have that!'

'Er, that's my bacon actually, Caroline.'

'OK. OK. Well, can I eat it?'

'Oh come on, Caro. You don't really want to eat bacon.'

'I do. I bloody do. I want it now.' She stood holding three limp rashers of bacon, salting them with her tears. 'But . . . I . . . hi . . . hi don't know what-hot-hot to doooOOO!'

'Oh Caro, please stop crying. Give me the bacon, sit down, and I'll make you a sandwich.'

'Re-he-he-he-heally?'

'Really.'

Blossom put the three slices of smoked streaky under the grill and spread butter on two slices of white bread.

'Oh, Bob, what am I to do?'

'Calm down. Please. Just calm down. Mustard?'

'I don't know. What do you think?'

'I think it's what mustard was invented for.'

'Mustard then.'

'Rocking horse?'

'What?'

'Tomato sauce.'

'What would you recommend?'

'You might as well.'

'All right.'

Blossom passed Caroline her sandwich, which she accepted doubtfully, her lip curling as she watched the thing oozing red and yellow over the not quite clean plate.

'You don't have to eat it.'

Caroline looked defiantly at Blossom, and took a huge bite.

'How is it?'

'Very good, actually,' said Caroline with a full mouth.

'Welcome back,' said Blossom.

Despite herself, Caroline giggled, spitting bread and bacon bolus on to the table.

'Bob?'

'Yes?'

'Does it put you off if a woman doesn't shave her legs?'

'Well . . . a bit. Not armpits, though. I like hairy armpits on a woman.'

'But not legs?'

'Not really.'

'Bob?'

'Yes, honey?'

'Can I borrow your razor too? As well as your bacon?'

'Of course.'

Caroline giggled again.

'And you know Dave fancies you anyway, shaven raven or not,' said Blossom.

Caroline looked up again, some of the dullness gone from her eyes.

'No!'

'Really. What's that?' Blossom had heard something.

'But he never tried anything. Up on the roof, my first night here—'

'It's the door. Hang on,' said Blossom.

He hurried to answer; it was Frances, who swept past him into the kitchen, tears streaming down her face. She yanked open the cupboard where the drinks were kept and necked at the vodka. Caroline sat with her sandwich halfway to her open mouth, staring at her triumphant rival. What the fuck did *she* have to cry about?

'What is it now, darling?' said Blossom.

'Didn't you hear the ambulance?'

'No. Yes. Yes, I did. What is it? What's up?'

'It's Edgar, Bob. It's the Eel. He's dead.'

Necropolitan

Paul Holland was struggling to suppress a smirk right from the moment he entered the crematorium and saw the coffin sitting on the catafalque, and his hilarity mounted dangerously throughout the service. Fortunately, his place in the pecking order of the Eel's friends and family was such that he and Frances and Blossom and Sailor Dave and Cats were right at the back, so his disgraceful behaviour was mostly hidden from the large congregation. Man that is born of a woman hath but a short time to live, and is full of misery; but there is no question that a funeral is one of the occasions when the gloom lifts to be replaced by near-hysterical mirth. From the moment the service began, Holland was red-faced with the effort to keep back the explosion of laughter which threatened to go off at any time. He kept his head down, bit his thumb as hard as he could and trembled with exertion. Tears rolled from his eyes, his shoulders shook, and beads of sweat stood out from his temples. Frances was little better, and had to turn away as seeing him would only start her off. The proximity of his shaking body was almost too much for her; she could feel the vibrations in the pew. As an atheist, she did not live in sure and certain hope of the Resurrection, but as an optimist, she accepted that she could be wrong, and hoped that her current desire to laugh out loud did not blot her copybook irrevocably.

At last the coffin began its stately glide through the little curtains and towards the incinerator, and Holland prepared to run out into the air. He turned, watched the undertaker's men open the bronze crematorium doors and dashed into the brilliant sunlight. Frances followed as quickly as decency would allow, and hurried him around the corner, where he would be hidden from the eyes of grieving relatives. They clung to each other and wept with relief.

It is perhaps a matter of taste, but there are those who prefer their funerals in the rain; the sun is too dumb, too optimistic. Blossom was among their number, and as he emerged with Sailor Dave into the sun, he felt that it was wrong somehow, indecent almost, that he felt nothing at the loss of his old friend. He, Sailor Dave and Cats waited for Jeremiah (who had been one of the coffin bearers) and Zorena to come out. They both lit cigarettes, as a tribute to those brave men like Nat King Cole, Yul Brynner, Kenneth Tynan or, indeed, the Eel himself who continued to enjoy a smoke in the face of adversity. They walked around the small arbour by the entrance to the Garden of Remembrance, where floral tributes from acquaintances around the world were on display. There was a particularly nice wreath from Jeremiah's parents, in the shape of the star of the Farafan Order of the Garter. The Hollands, still grinning and holding hands, joined their friends.

'I lost it,' said Paul.

'You never had it, hon,' said Frances.

'Do you want a fag?' said Blossom.

'Go on then,' said Frances.

'Cheers,' said Holland.

'Poor old Edgar,' said Frances. 'Still . . . eighty-three.'

'A good innings,' said Blossom.

'I wonder what people used to say before cricket?' said Holland.

'Who are all these people?' said Frances.

'I've no idea. Here's Bill and Dolly. They might know,' said Blossom.

The Ashbrooks walked over.

'Hello, my dear,' said Dolly to Frances. 'A very sad day. Still . . . eighty-three.'

'A good innings,' said Bill.

'I don't really know any of these people,' said Frances. 'Do you?'

'Some of them. Do you see that rather handsome couple over there with the teenage children?' said Dolly.

Holland did because he'd been looking at the eldest of these 'teenage children', a rather glamorous blond in a little black dress, who he calculated was about twenty-three.

'Yes,' he said.

'That's Edgar's son and his family.'

'I didn't know he had any children,' said Frances.

'Oh yes. He's in the Foreign Office too.'

'And that fat old dear talking to them is his mother. Edgar's wife,' said Bill.

'No!' said Frances.

'Yes,' said Dolly. 'Milly, she's called.'

'His ex-wife, surely,' said Blossom.

'Well, she is now,' said Dolly. 'But they never divorced.'

'Is that so?' said Frances.

'Yes. She lives in Gloucestershire, in a big old house in the Cotswolds. Didn't you know?'

'I had no idea.'

'That's why Edgar was so poor,' said Dolly.

'That's why he lodged with us. He had to pay all the bills on that bloody great big place,' said Bill.

'Why didn't they live together?' asked Frances.

'Couldn't stand one another,' said Bill.

'I don't think that's fair, Bill,' said Dolly. 'I think they always loved one another very much, from the way he talked; it's just that . . .'

'They couldn't stand one another,' said Bill. Frances and Holland laughed.

'Ah, here's Geoffrey and Jemima,' said Dolly. 'Oo-oo! Over here.'

The brother and sister came across to join the Bloomsbury Group, Geoffrey looking very vigorous and cheerful. Few things make old men happier than outliving their contemporaries.

'Hello!' he said.

'Wasn't it a nice service?' said Jemima.

'Yes,' said Dolly.

'Poor old Edgar,' said Jemima. 'Still . . . eighty-three.'

'A reasonable innings,' said Geoffrey, contemptuously. 'The trouble was, the old fool wouldn't look after himself. Smoking like a trooper till the day he died. I used to try to get him to come for a swim with me. Silly old fool.'

'Geoffrey! You shouldn't speak ill of the dead,' said Jemima.

'Nonsense. Best time to speak ill of 'em, when they can't hear you.'

'Who's that rather dishy bloke who looks like Robert Kilroy Silk?' asked Frances. 'I'm sure I recognize him from somewhere.'

'I expect you do, m'dear. That's the Dutch Foreign Minister,'* said Geoffrey.

'And that tiny little old lady with him is his mother. She served with Edgar in the war. They were lovers at one time, I believe,' said Dolly. 'Certainly he used to have her picture in a frame in his room.'

*Clearly not the real Dutch Foreign Minister or any previous, possibly litigious ones, but an entirely fictional creation.

'Silya!' said Blossom and Frances.

'No, I don't think that was the name,' said Dolly uncertainly.

At last Jeremiah emerged from the crematorium chapel, Zorena looking like a princess-in-waiting in a white dress by his side. He spoke to Edgar's son, shook hands with the Dutch Foreign Minister and his mother, and walked across to look at the floral tributes.

'Jerry!' said Frances. 'That's Silya. The woman you just shook hands with.'

Jeremiah smiled sadly, and said, 'Not her real name. But the same woman, yes.'

'Poor Mr Luff. Still . . . eighty-three,' said Zorena.

'A good innings,' said Jeremiah, 'from a great man.'

'Right,' said Frances. 'Who's coming in what car?' The party was to move on to tea, and perhaps a sherry or two, at one of the swisher hotels. Blossom declined the invitation.

'Sorry,' he said. 'I just don't feel up to it.'

'Shall we see you back at the flat then, honey?' asked Frances.

'Later.'

As the main party walked towards the cars, Frances said to Holland, 'Poor Bob.'

Blossom didn't feel poor, as he walked in the other direction from the cars, on the path which wound down the hill away from the crematorium, through the Garden of Remembrance and into the Victorian Necropolis. He felt empty. He found his spot in the Garden of Remembrance: a small melamine plaque stuck on a spike beside a yellow rose bush.

In Memory of Katherine Alice Blossom

7-8-56 – 28-4-85

'Hi, Katie.'

'Hi, Bob. How's things?'

'Not so bright, girl. The old Eel is dead.'

'I know.'

'Do you know everything now, Katie?'

'Of course not. I know less and less. I'm fading, Bob.'

'I think . . . I think I'm glad. That you're fading away at last.'

'So am I. Glad for you.'

'I'll still come up here. Sometimes.'

'You always liked to walk in the cemetery anyway.'

'Paul and Frances got back together again.'

'That's nice. Nice for the kids, anyway.'

'I wish we'd had kids.'

'Do you?'

'Yes. Then I would have had something of you. Other than a bloody rose bush.'

'How would you have coped on your own?'

'Somehow. I'd have managed.'

'You'd have been a good father.'

'Would I? Maybe they'd have stuck me with the loons in Haywards Heath.'

'Maybe they will anyway. You're talking to yourself again.'

Blossom shook his head and rubbed his eyes, and walked on into the oldest part of the Necropolis. Broken columns, angels on pedestals, tombs sunk into the hillside; it was all here, all the paraphernalia of continuance, of life after death, of the sure and certain hope which Blossom was unable to feel. He had walked here many times, with Kate, on his own or with other girlfriends, and it still got to him. It wasn't the death, it was the romance. He longed for a romantic encounter of some kind, something that would take him out of himself. He'd always felt that he might meet her in here, this theoretical Significant Other, someone he could love, and who might hold a mirror to his own increasingly pallid existence. He could see her: small and dark and younger than he; funny and clever too – another writer perhaps, or a musician. He'd always had a thing about cellists. But not today.

Today he walked through the gates of the Necropolis and on to the shabby life of the Lewes Road. A No. 49 bus rocked past. Along the road, past the junk shops and insurance brokers, past the kebab joints and video stores, and up on to Elm Grove. He smoked too much, much too much; Elm Grove was steep, but it was always worth the increasingly breathless climb.

At the top was Brighton Racecourse, a place where he always felt relaxed. He lit a fag to celebrate achieving the summit, and sat on the rail by the furlong marker. You could see everything from up here. It was a clear day, a day of perfect vision. A long way beneath him the Marina squatted in the sea, clinging to the cliff; away on his left he could see the pitch 'n' putt, and Roedean and St Dunstan's, and in the sea he could just make out the end of Newhaven breakwater, under the shadow of Seaford Head. To his right, the whole of disreputable Brighton still stretched away into Hove; he looked at the tower of the hospital and remembered Kate's last days up there on the top floor; tied to a machine which the doctors refused to turn off until they had taken out her heart and her kidneys and her eyes. Someone was looking out through her eyes, but he wished that he'd never given his consent for that; she had such beautiful eyes, fading now in his memory. He walked on, down the hill, past Queen's Park and on to St James's Street. A beggar asked him for change, and he searched in his pocket and unearthed fifty pence, for all the good it would do.

Back in Bloomsbury Place, Blossom found Caroline by the front door, her suitcase, rucksack, boxes of books, rubber plant and hi-fi all packed and ready to go. She had dyed her hair black, and wore a tight silk chintz mini-dress. Her newly razored legs like gooseflesh ended in a pair of unwise plat-form trainers. She'll be embarrassed by those in old photos, thought Blossom. In twenty years, her kids will laugh.

'I'm glad I caught you. I like your makeover,' he said.

She smiled. 'Thank you. I'm glad too. Mum's just bringing the car round. How was the funeral?'

'Oh, you know. Much like any other. There was quite a good turnout.'

'Poor old Edgar,' said Caroline. 'Still . . . eighty-three. He seemed so . . . irresponsible. I saw his cock, the day I moved in.'

'Ah,' said Blossom.

'Will you miss me?' asked Caroline.

'You know we will. It's not like you're going to the ends of the earth, anyway.'

'Sometimes Haywards Heath feels like the ends of the earth.'

'It's only for the summer though, isn't it?'

'Yes. I'm getting a flat with some friends from my course for next year.'

'Will you let us know your new address?'

'Of course. Tell the One-Eyed Sailor I'll give him a call later in the week.'

'Be kind to him. Don't aggravate his NSU.'

Caroline punched Blossom in the chest, and then hugged him.

Her mother pulled up with the Volvo, and Blossom helped them load Caroline's things into the back. She waved at Blossom from the front seat as he watched the car move away down Bloomsbury Place and turn out on to the seafront.

Climbing the stairs, he paused to sit in one of Edgar's armchairs. At least he wouldn't get moaned at for it now. In the gloom of the landing, out of the brilliant sunshine, at last he could feel something for the old bugger. Tears ran down his cheeks. When we grieve, he wondered, is it for the dead or for those of us who have to keep going somehow, for those of us who are left behind to cope? He wiped his eyes with the sleeve of his suit and felt better.

In the flat, Robertson Blossom stared despairingly at the space where Caroline's hi-fi had sat. Perhaps the time had come to get one for himself? But then again, a reasonable one would cost five hundred nicker or so, and that represented a large chunk of Blossom's stake money. On sober reflection, he felt it would be better to wait until *In Southern Waters* was published. He'd be able to afford a fuck-off stereo from his world-record-breaking advance. He made himself a coffee, found a notepad and pen, and sat down to compose.

Wanted. Female to Share Large Flat. Must be Hi-Fi Enthusiast, Smoker, Non-Vegetarian.

He thought for a moment, and then crossed out 'non-vegetarian'. Caroline was all right. It was a shame she felt she had to go. Perfectly understandable, but a shame.

That should do it.

That flat was too quiet without music.

Almost inevitably, it was the sound of Holland's laughter on the stairs which alerted Blossom to the return of his friends.